Hitchcock's People, Places, and Things

Hitchcock's People, Places, and Things

✦

John Bruns

NORTHWESTERN UNIVERSITY PRESS
EVANSTON, ILLINOIS

Northwestern University Press
www.nupress.northwestern.edu

Printed in the United States of America

10 9 8 7 6 5 4 3 2 1

Library of Congress Cataloging-in-Publication Data

Names: Bruns, John, author.
Title: Hitchcock's people, places, and things / John Bruns.
Description: Evanston : Northwestern University Press, 2019. | Includes bibliographical references and index.
Identifiers: LCCN 2018056990 | ISBN 9780810139954 (paper text : alk. paper) | ISBN 9780810139961 (cloth text : alk. paper) | ISBN 9780810139978 (e-book)
Subjects: LCSH: Hitchcock, Alfred, 1899–1980—Criticism and interpretation. | Hitchcock, Alfred, 1899–1980—Themes, motives. | Motion pictures—Setting and scenery.
Classification: LCC PN1998.3.H58 B78 2019 | DDC 791.430233092—dc23
LC record available at https://lccn.loc.gov/2018056990

For my parents

CONTENTS

ACKNOWLEDGMENTS

I'd like to thank the following people for their thoughtful observations and comments. Without their support I would not have been able to see this book to its completion. My editors at Northwestern University Press, in particular Michael Levine, Nathan MacBrien, and Trevor Perri, deserve thanks for their guidance and confidence in me. I also wish to thank my colleagues at the College of Charleston who read all or portions of this book or engaged with me in lengthy conversations about Hitchcock: Colleen Glenn, Tim Carens, and Terry Bowers. I also benefited from the generous support of my dean, whose discretionary funding allowed me to visit on several occasions the Academy of Motion Picture Arts and Sciences' Margaret Herrick Library, as well as the USC Warner Bros. Archive.

Other friends and associates have made invaluable contributions to this book, including Richard Allen, Leo Braudy, Timothy Corrigan, Sidney Gottlieb, Jim Kincaid, Tania Modleski, Mark Osteen, and Pamela Wojcik. Ned Schantz, too, has been a searching critic of these pages. Not only is he a dear friend, he is the beacon for my thoughts. I also want to thank my father, Gerald Bruns, for his input and words of encouragement. I am grateful to my students, whose enthusiasm, curiosity, and questioning have, over the years, deepened my understanding of Hitchcock. Finally, I wish to thank my loving companion, Alicia, for her boundless support.

Parts of this book have been published previously and are republished here with permission. Chapter 2 appeared in *Hitchcock Annual* 18 (2013) as "Hitchcock's Newspaper: A Thing in the Crowd." A portion of chapter 4 appeared as "'The Proper Geography': Hitchcock's Adaptation of Daphne du Maurier's 'The Birds'" in *Clues: A Journal of Detection* 31, no. 1 (Winter 2013) and was then reprinted, in slightly different form, in *Hitchcock and Adaptation: On the Page and Screen*, edited by Mark Osteen (New York: Rowman and Littlefield, 2014).

Hitchcock's People, Places, and Things

Introduction

✦

Navigating the Hitchcock Landscape

> When we speak of men, of societies, culture, and objects, there are everywhere crowds of other agents that act, pursue aims unknown to us, and use us to prosper.
>
> —Bruno Latour, *The Pasteurization of France* (1993)

Perhaps more widely known than his definition of suspense is Hitchcock's definition of the MacGuffin. Coined by screenwriter Angus MacPhail but repeated countless times by Hitchcock, most famously in an exchange with François Truffaut, the MacGuffin is, as everyone knows, a plot device. It is the thing that everyone in a Hitchcock film cares very deeply about. Whether it takes the form of uranium-enriched sand (in 1946's *Notorious*) or a statuette (in 1959's *North by Northwest*), the MacGuffin is a thing of vital importance. And yet it is also a thing of absolutely no importance. This is the great lesson of the MacGuffin: Hitchcock's films are not about things but about people. "So the 'MacGuffin' is the term we use to cover that sort of thing," Hitchcock told Truffaut, "To steal plans or documents, or discover a secret, it doesn't matter what it is. And the logicians are wrong in trying to figure out the truth of a MacGuffin, since it's beside the point. The only thing that really matters is that in the picture the plans, documents, or secrets must seem to be of vital importance to the characters. To me, the narrator, they're of no importance whatever."[1]

The logicians are wrong if, indeed, they are trying to figure out the "truth" of a MacGuffin. The bottles in *Notorious* could be filled instead with diamonds and nothing would change in the film. A tweak or two to the plot is all that is required. To a sociologist like Bruno Latour, however, the "truth" of the MacGuffin is not what makes it important. What makes it important is its agency, in the sense of making people go places and do things. This agency finally becomes visible as the MacGuffin's sole observable property, since it's been emptied of any other distracting features (which, one might say, is what Hitchcock means when he says the MacGuffin is of no importance whatever). The MacGuffin, then, has a very different lesson to teach us: places and things as well as people participate in the action of a Hitchcock film. Imagine, then, an approach to studying Hitchcock's films that thinks of the MacGuffin as a real player. Imagine an approach that treats any person, place, or thing—even those that seem to be "of no importance whatever"—as being of the utmost importance.

Those who are familiar with Bruno Latour's *The Pasteurization of France* know that the "crowds of other agents" referenced above are microbes. But people familiar with Latour's work in general know that microbes are what Latour calls, in this text and elsewhere, "actants"—participants in social connections that are invisible to us (and therefore "pursue aims unknown to us"). They are invisible not because they are too small to see with the naked eye (although some are) but because we omit them from our understanding of what constitutes the social (who in his right mind would claim that microbes are members of society?). But for Latour, what we call the social—whether it is an urban neighborhood, Little League, a cross-stitching club, or a city bicycle coalition—is not a material space filled with the people who are its functioning members, "but a *type of connection* between things that are not themselves social."[2]

Should we decide to find a social explanation for, say, Little League baseball, we might allow ourselves the time to trace the history of bubblegum. This, in turn, might lead us to look at the ways the bubblegum wrapper depicts, usually in cartoon or comic strip form, the game of baseball as it is played by children, or to look at how sales of bubblegum compare to that of sunflower seeds in towns that historically have supported Little League, and so on. To choose to exclude the bubblegum wrapper from our explanation of Little League is to posit a preconceived idea of what this particular society, Little League, is. But if we already assume we know what does and does not belong in "Little League," what is the purpose of our investigation? The idea, argues Latour, is to reverse the process by which sociologists study the social. In other words, we should allow people, places, and things to tell *us* what a social aggregate is. Of course, this slows down the process of explanation considerably, but that's the idea; it's why actor-network-theory is also known as ANT. Reassembling the social, Latour tells us, means moving at an ant's pace.[3] What follows is an attempt to trace the associations that socialize the Hitchcock landscape, to attend particularly to crowds of other agents that have remained invisible to us. In doing so, I will "inhabit" the Hitchcock landscape and follow traces wherever they take me, never in haste and, if necessary, at an ant's pace.

Once inside a Hitchcock film, however, one should remember to keep the landscape flat, to resist the temptation to add volume or scale to people, places, and things. Which is to say, perhaps, that to inhabit the Hitchcock landscape is to follow traces wherever they may lead, remembering that one is inside a two-dimensional world. An example Latour offers is company managerial structure: "2-D analysts will ask about you about the office space in which one manager sits, then the bookkeeping procedure she uses, then the chart on which she has labeled the names of her collaborators, then the chain of command that allows her to call meetings, then the pie chart which she has received from marketing and that describes consumer response to her latest campaign."[4] In literary and film studies, this sounds a lot like close reading—or, to use D. A. Miller's term, "too-close reading."[5] The *supplement* to close reading that actor-network-theory brings is the emphasis on tracing associations not just of people, but equally of places and things.

To my mind, few if any scholars have attempted to apply Latour's actor-network-theory to film and media—and to be honest, I am unsure what a broad application of actor-network-theory to film and media would look like, or if it is even possible. Yet I do feel actor-network-theory has a few fertile concepts that apply to film and media, and specifically to the work of Alfred Hitchcock. Navigating the Hitchcock landscape means following the actors—not only in the most obvious, filmic sense (the way we follow James Stewart following Kim Novak in *Vertigo*)—but in the sociological sense as described by Latour, when he invokes the etymology of the word *social*: "The root is *seq-*, *sequi* and the first meaning is 'to follow.' "[6] And here it might be of use to remind Hitchcock fans and critics alike that a very interesting account of *Strangers on a Train* results from careful attention given to a cigarette lighter—where it goes, who uses it, how is it used, etc.[7] Indeed, many nonhuman agents have been given critical attention in Hitchcock's films (wedding rings, keys, purses, windmills, eyeglasses, and so on), though more often they are treated symbolically rather than socially. Yet there are many nonhuman agents we would consider full-fledged members of the Hitchcock society, not least the MacGuffin, even if Hitchcock disavows it as a real player.

Hitchcock's People, Places, and Things attempts a sociology of associations in Hitchcock by tracing the complex relays of both human and nonhuman agents throughout his films. In a word, Hitchcock's films are *relational*. This is what Gilles Deleuze identifies as the most crucial insight of Claude Chabrol and Eric Rohmer's *Hitchcock: The First Forty-Four Films*. The critics concentrate on relations in Hitchcock ("the exchange, the gift, the rendering"), and for Deleuze, it is the chain of relations that elevates Hitchcock's films to the status of what he calls "the mental image." For Deleuze, what makes up the fabric of a Hitchcock film is not simply the pair—innocent and guilty, detective and killer—but the addition of a third element, which is the relation itself.[8] It is not enough to say that *Shadow of a Doubt* is about doubling. The film is constituted by a *tripling*—of Charlie (Teresa Wright), her uncle (Joseph Cotten), and their relation. "This perpetual tripling," writes Deleuze, "also takes over objects, perceptions, affections."[9] The relation itself disturbs the Hitchcock landscape, disrupts and unsettles it. In all the films, continues Deleuze, "the relation introduces an essential instability between the characters, the roles, the actions, the set [*décor*]."[10] That is to say, the Hitchcock landscape is both relational and unstable.

While Deleuze argues that Hitchcock's films tilt from this relational disequilibrium toward final equilibrium, he concedes that this equilibrium is often "devastated, desperate or even monstrous."[11] Thus we have the devastated ending of *Vertigo*, the desperate ending of *The Birds*, the monstrous endings of *Rebecca* and *Psycho*. Yet to me, and perhaps to many a Hitchcock fan, such endings hardly suggest equilibrium. The ending of a Hitchcock film is like the ending of an earthquake—chaos gives way to calm but not without a lot of collateral damage and a serious threat of aftershocks. To inhabit the Hitchcock landscape, then, is to encounter noise, interference, and especially danger (even a navigator as skilled as Melanie Daniels is sure to confront the unexpected). But it is a move we willfully, and rightly, take when we watch a Hitchcock film. The guiding assumption of *Hitchcock's People, Places, and Things* is that by underestimating important agents both human (anonymous crowds) and nonhuman (horses, newspapers, telephones), and the places they navigate and determine (Bodega Bay, Quebec City, a Manhattan apartment), we fail to appreciate the scope and density of the Hitchcock landscape.

The title of the book is not meant to suggest that people, places, and things occupy discrete categories in Hitchcock's films. Indeed, quite the opposite is true. Take, for example, the scenes from the 1956 remake of *The Man Who Knew Too Much* in which Ben McKenna (James Stewart) and his wife Jo (Doris Day) try to find the location of their kidnapped boy, Hank (Christopher Olsen). The only clue given to them is Ambrose Chappell, a name whispered into Ben's ear by a dying Frenchman. Ben finds that there is, in London, a taxidermist by the name of Ambrose Chappell and sets out to find his son there. Jo, however, rightly deduces that Ambrose Chappell is not a person but a place, Ambrose Chapel. Consider too that Mount Rushmore, featured in *North by Northwest*, is a place (a national park in South Dakota), a thing (a monument or large-scale sculpture), and a group of people (four American presidents). Bearing this in mind, and perhaps true to the Hitchcock spirit, this book anticipates that people will stumble into the wrong places at the wrong times; places will be made most uncanny by things; and things exchanged between people will act as (not so) secret agents that help map the landscape of Hitchcock's films.

This project engages most directly with classic and contemporary works in the field of Hitchcock studies, although my work comes closer to that of Murray Pomerance (*An Eye for Hitchcock* and *Alfred Hitchcock's America*), Tom Cohen (*Hitchcock's Cryptonomies*, vols. 1 and 2), and D. A. Miller (*Hidden Hitchcock*) than others. What differentiates my work from others is that I am also concerned with the larger implications of the kinds of analysis these scholars undertake. By using Hitchcock's films, I show that our visual engagement with cinematic screen space is far more complex than previously understood. To "experience" a Hitchcock film is to experience radical disorientation or dislocation. This is by no means a new insight. But what is missing from Hitchcock scholarship—particularly those works that have tried to account for the uncanniness of his films (Neil Badmington's *Hitchcock's Magic* being one recent effort)—is a sustained exploration of his films. By this I do not mean there is a want of thorough critical examination of

Hitchcock—quite the opposite. Hitchcock studies is an industry unto itself. By "explore" I mean to combine critical examination with the idea of navigation and discovery. In this way, *Hitchcock's People, Places, and Things* is more critical field book than monograph.[12] My work is an attempt to inhabit the Hitchcock landscape in search of new passages through a sometimes strange and unforgiving environment.

In this regard, one might see this book as being part of the "spatial turn" in film studies—or what Barney Warf and Santa Arias put simply as "the reinsertion of space in the humanities and social sciences."[13] But my understanding of the social in Hitchcock is not limited to spatiality; it also includes the things that interact with space. The idea is to allow not just places but *things* in Hitchcock to express themselves. A necessary step into a critical navigation of the crowded Hitchcock landscape—a step I am gambling is one the Hitchcock scholar is willing to take—is to assume that objects (lighters, keys, bottles of wine, glasses of milk, windmills, wedding rings, and so on) function as nonhuman agents. I am encouraged to take this next step, not simply because of the growing scholarly interest in "thing theory" in general, but because there is a long-standing interest in Hitchcock's "things." Although much overstated, Jean-Luc Godard's point, made in Toronto during a 1996 interview with Jonathan Rosenbaum, is clear:

> And something which is very astonishing with Hitchcock is that you don't remember what the story of *Notorious* is, or why Janet Leigh is going to the Bates Motel. You remember one pair of spectacles or a windmill—that's what millions and millions of people remember. If you remember *Notorious*, what do you remember? Wine bottles. You don't remember Ingrid Bergman. When you remember Griffith or Welles or Eisenstein or me, you don't remember ordinary objects. He is the only one.[14]

One could use Godard's comments as a way of thinking about how to *engage* with Hitchcock's films: by considering not just their plots (which, for Godard, are inessential, or at any rate forgettable), but the various interactions between human and nonhuman agents as they move through the Hitchcock landscape. To trace these movements of associations, it is necessary to apply a more peripatetic mode of analysis. More slow and curious than swift and systematic, my approach will be threefold: demographic, cartographic, and forensic.

X Demarks the Spot

While Godard's claim that after having watched *Notorious* one will not remember Ingrid Bergman very likely strikes the reader as truly bizarre, it may also strike the reader as (perhaps only slightly) less bizarre that one would remember the wine bottles. This book argues not only that one can and should remember both Bergman *and* the wine bottles but that one can and should trace the relation of the two. In doing so we can map the Hitchcock landscape cognitively, affectively, and politically. Yet this book does not promise that such a map can or will cohere. As chapter 4 will show, the master director was just as adept at *mis*direction as he was at direction. Navigating the Hitchcock landscape means recognizing the director's equal penchant for "the proper geography" (Hitchcock's own phrase) and "creative derangement"—a phrase I borrow from Murray Smith.[15] That the people, places, and things in Hitchcock will never entirely cohere should not dissuade us from tracing their relations. On the contrary, the thrill of watching a Hitchcock film is knowing you will lose your bearings even as you try to gather them.[16] As the director himself once said, "I am out to give the public good, healthy, mental shake-ups."[17]

The organization of this book resembles a guided tour with several stops along the way. What will solicit our attention is not only character and plot but what Deleuze calls the *demark*—the image or sign that leaps out of the context it would otherwise attenuate.[18] The *demark* can be a person (Tracy from *Blackmail*), a place (the taxidermy in the 1956 version of *The Man Who Knew Too Much*), or a thing (the luminous glass of milk in *Suspicion*), but it is always a bearer of some relation. The Hitchcock landscape is full of *demarks*, and they are sometimes (although not always) hidden, like landmines. Readers of this book may find similarities between my critical approach and that of D. A. Miller, who assembles in his book *Hidden Hitchcock* three impressive essays devoted to showing, while not exactly sharing, what he calls "the hidden picture": "A strongly narrativized image [which] has been fashioned to conceal something that—if ever seen—would not enhance its coherence, but explode it."[19] I hope to be a bit more giving and, as a tour guide, mindful of the fact that Hitchcock is shared by everyone.

Indeed, this book is an invitation to join me in my efforts to inhabit Hitchcock, to take Deleuze as literally as possible when he claims that Hitchcock "brings the cinema to completion" by including the spectator in the film.[20] While inside this two-dimensional world, I will lead us to various points of interest in Hitchcock. The point may be an unusual shot, a spoken line that baffles, or an unexpected cut that throws us off our tracks. It may be a moment in the film when the viewer senses a Benjaminian constellatory flash, a moment of recognition and resonance. Perhaps it is a real flash of light at an unexpected moment, such as the one visible in the opening moments of *Rear Window*. As the camera passes the complex across from Jeff's apartment in the film's first pan, we see on the floor above the sleeping couple's apartment a darkened room lit for an instant by what appears to be a photographer's flashbulb. This apartment is not featured in the film—we never learn who lives here, and even if it were in frame more frequently, it is just high enough to make it difficult to see inside the windows.[21] We will never know whence and why the flash comes. But we could say with some certainty that this flash is no error, no mistake. It is timed perfectly. Given that this fourth-floor apartment remains unknown to us, we are encouraged to meditate on just what that flash is meant to signal. Does a photographer live there? Perhaps Jeff's double? And that flash we see—does it signal that the occupant is at work, or that he or she is, like Jeff at the end of the film, in danger? Is this a preview of the attraction we are watching?

This literal flash—and its numerous figurative siblings in Hitchcock's films—induces what Peter Wollen describes in his "Alphabet of Cinema" (*D* is for dance, *E* is for Eisenstein, *F* is for festival, etc.) as a "strange fascination." Having reached the third-to-last letter in the alphabet, he is for a moment stymied as to what it stands for. After a couple of tries, he makes up his mind: "X stands for an unknown quantity—for the strange fascination that makes us remember a particular shot or a particular camera movement. . . . It is an interruption of narrative by a moment when time freezes and we are fascinated by the image in front of us. Barthes tried to find a name for it—the symbolic, the third meaning, the punctum. Let's call it X."[22] If *X* marks the spot, it succeeds in doing so because it is among the simplest of signs. As a single line never could, two lines crossed indicate intention. In cinema, to encounter *X* is to feel the presence of intention and therefore meaning, however cryptic.

Consider, for example, Eugenie Brinkema's reading of the arresting image of Marion's tear as she lies lifeless on the bathroom floor in her room in the Bates Motel. Brinkema traces a trajectory of this tear, beginning with Norman's "passionate appeal" about the cruelties of the "someplace" where Marion, sharing a moment with Norman in the parlor behind his office, suggests he put his mother.[23] In this appeal, Norman speaks of "the laughing and the tears, and the cruel eyes studying you." This "someplace," where laughter bellows, wild tears flow, and probing eyes watch, reflexively evokes another place: the movie theater. "The institution at stake in Norman's horrified description slides," argues Brinkema, "from madhouse to art house, from mental institution to cinematic institution."[24]

And while Brinkema is determined to preserve the tear's "insistent exteriority," its obliqueness, and its singularity—her aim is to "delink" the tear, to attend to its form, to question whether, even, it *is* a tear. Her close reading points to a host of possible associations.[25] The aim of this book, one might say, is the opposite of Brinkema's: to link people, places, and things that make up the Hitchcock landscape. What follows is an illustration of the approach this book takes, by way of a short but close reading not of *Psycho* but of its theatrical trailer, starring the fabulous Mr. Alfred Hitchcock.

"The Fabulous Mr. Hitchcock Is About to Escort You"

"The fabulous Mr. Hitchcock is about to escort you." These are the words that welcome us in the theatrical trailer for *Psycho*, a remarkable piece of publicity, not just in terms of its length (it is six and a half minutes long) or what it reveals about the film (how and where the murders take place). What is also remarkable about the trailer is that it so perfectly dramatizes the impulse to navigate the Hitchcock landscape that motivates me throughout this book. The trailer is not at all a preview in the conventional sense (the trailer shows us no scenes from the film). Instead, we are escorted "on a tour of the location of the new motion picture, 'Psycho.'"[26] The trailer opens, appropriately enough, with a crane shot. We are high above, looking down on Hitchcock, who stands in front of the set of the Bates Motel at the Universal International Studios. The shot is an example of the Hitchcockian shot that Murray Pomerance names "the topographic shot," a shot that "centers on the arrangement or design of space as an explicit, self-avowed feature."[27] Some examples of the topographic shot are "the lengthy panning commencement of *Rear Window* (1954)" and "the establishing shot of Mount Rushmore in *North by Northwest* as a map of potential action."[28] The theatrical trailer for *Psycho*, one might say, is an elaboration of the Hitchcockian topographical shot's cinematic proposition.

Accompanied by a dramatic musical stinger, Hitchcock says the Bates Motel set is "the scene of a crime." But one gets a sense that this place is not just a "scene" but an *agent* of the crime as well. "Rather than using settings casually or arbitrarily," writes Pomerance, "Hitchcock gives them full consideration as active agents in the recounting, and shows them openly in their agency."[29] Once inside, Hitchcock incriminates the Bates mansion by telling us, "You see, even in daylight this place still looks a bit sinister." The camera follows Hitchcock to the bottom of the staircase, where he stands and then describes, in gruesome detail and with near perfect accuracy, the murder of Detective Milton Arbogast (Martin Balsam). Hitchcock invites us upstairs and, in a close-up, begins to describe to us "the woman," Mrs. Bates: "She was the weirdest and the mo—well, well, let's go into her bedroom." What is curious about this split-second shift from description ("She was the weirdest") to direction ("Let's go into her bedroom") is that it is less an interruption of a line of thought than a concatenation of natural causality, from person to place.

No doubt James Allardice, who scripted the theatrical trailer for *Psycho* and many of Hitchcock's other trailers from this period (as well as the intros and outros for *Alfred Hitchcock Presents*), is having a bit of fun by making Hitchcock fumble with contrary impulses: to divulge important narrative information and to withhold it. But the pattern repeats. Every time Hitchcock veers away from exposition, he veers into exploration. The theatrical trailer for *Psycho* enacts a desire to inhabit a Hitchcock film, to chart its territory, to trace the contours of the objects that occupy it, to study the composition and behavior of its population. More important, the theatrical trailer for *Psycho* reveals that we often find our line of thought or course of action first by observing a person who might lead us to a place and, in turn, to a thing. Consider when, now inside Mrs. Bates's bedroom, Hitchcock says,

"Here's the woman's room, still beautifully preserved." Now, anyone familiar with the film (and the many double entendres screenwriter Joseph Stefano gives Anthony Perkins's Norman) cannot but hear that Hitchcock is talking both about Mrs. Bates's bedroom and Mrs. Bates herself, the latter being still preserved (if not as beautifully as her room). He then steps close to the bed and with a gesture of his outstretched arm traces the outline of the imprint of her figure. In doing so Hitchcock traces the way people and things can be fused, can dissolve, swap places, and overlap with one another.

After a few comic diversions (Hitchcock opens Mrs. Bates's wardrobe, and we watch him shudder at what he sees inside it; then, we watch him stroll down the hallway and open a door: "The bathroom," he says, as if he has come upon this door only now), we are led to Norman's "favorite spot, the little parlor behind his office in the motel." Again perilously close to a spoiler, and again in close-up, Hitchcock interrupts himself and says, "Well, let's go in." Pointing at a picture on the wall, the one that hides the peephole through which Norman gazes upon Marion as she undresses, Hitchcock says it has "great significance." There is a pause. "Because . . ." Another pause. "Uh, let's go along to cabin number one." This painting, which astute observers of the film have noted depicts the biblical story of Susannah and the Elders, indeed has great significance. This thing, no mere prop, plays an active part in an extended series of relays between person, place, and thing in *Psycho*. The painting collaborates with Norman in his stealthy act of perversion; it covers the peephole through which he watches people, which in turn gives Norman cover in this darkened parlor as he visually invades the place on the other side of its wall, cabin number one.[30]

There is one final stop on the Hitchcock-guided tour: the bathroom in which Marion is murdered. And here, Hitchcock stages the ultimate authorial gesture: setting foot in his own film.[31] When he enters the bathroom from the right, a bright light behind the camera and to our right casts a shadow of the director's profile on the wall behind him. The popular anthology series *Alfred Hitchcock Presents* was nearing the end of its fifth season when *Psycho* premiered, and no doubt audiences were closely familiar with the opening sequence, in which Hitchcock's silhouette steps into his profile sketch. Here, at the end of our tour of *Psycho*, we have a curious "doubling *en abyme*" at play: the director himself casts his own shadow and, as he turns toward the shower and reaches for the curtain, steps into his silhouette.[32] The two figures, director and signature, merge precisely as they become Norman Bates, who has become his mother, and reveal behind the shower curtain a screaming Lila, who has become her sister Marion.

What is so fascinating about the theatrical trailer for *Psycho* is the way it performs the experience of inhabiting a Hitchcock film, of taking a tour (guided or no) of the Hitchcock landscape. But as the trailer reaches its climax, we experience a fundamental instability. As Hitchcock steps into the bathroom, he enters the heart of his own film, its most pivotal scene (and one of the most memorable in cinematic history). But it just gets confused from there. Is Hitchcock guiding or enacting? Is he showing or narrating? And what do we make of Lila being in the shower instead of Marion? Of course, one could argue that Hitchcock *can't* put Marion in the shower, as it would give too much away. But hasn't Hitchcock already given too much away at this point? Isn't the theatrical trailer of *Psycho* one long series of spoilers?[33]

The point may be that, by inhabiting the Hitchcock film, we suspend our need to accumulate narrative information, as well as our obligation to conventional causality. What happens, I will show, is that tracing in a slow, deliberate way the complex relations between people, places, and things in the Hitchcock landscape means being open to the incoherent, being able to confront the strange without feeling estranged. One might argue that this is what happens when criticism chooses not to follow the path of plot, of narrative, but to trace in Hitchcock's images the complex figuration of people, places, and things. This is, I think, what Pomerance, in many of his recent writings on Hitchcock, is proposing. "Scholars and fans discuss Hitchcock's plots more often than his images for a number of reasons, but the most salient of these is that it is far easier to speak of stories, causations, and events than of composed images."[34]

While I do wish to consider plot—particularly at moments of odd deviation—the following book is devoted primarily to close analysis of Hitchcock images. Like other critics of the medium today, I benefit from new technologies of playback and scrutiny. And I take D. A. Miller's point that such new technologies do not necessarily guarantee we won't, in the end, use our close readings to double down on our allegiance to "narrative-driven" viewing habits as Hitchcock's "Pavlovianly trained mass audience."[35] If I am, at times, guilty of turning to the work of Hitchcock scholars loyal to the mass-audience experience of cinema, it is because I believe they are barking up the right trees. Their mental states and sense pleasures—cued even when Hitchcock held no bone—have inspired this present work.

Preview of Coming Attractions

Writing in 1965 on the art of motion pictures, Hitchcock felt that a screenwriter had some resources a novelist or dramatist did not, "in particular the use of things. This is one of the ingredients of true cinema. To put things together visually; to tell the story visually; to embody the action in the juxtaposition of images that have their own specific language and emotional impact—that is cinema. Thus, it is possible to be cinematic in the confined space of a telephone booth."[36] Hitchcock then proceeds to describe a hypothetical scene in which a telephone operator listens in on a couple embracing in a telephone booth (evoking a similar scene from Hitchcock's 1928 film *Easy Virtue*): "A step forward in the unfolding of the drama has been taken. . . . Things, then, are as important as actors to the writer. They can richly illustrate character. The skilled writer will know how to make effective use of such things."[37] This book is an examination of the "specific language" that is Hitchcock's cinema. One might say that through Hitchcock, I will elaborate a cinematic grammar, with an emphasis on the familiar linguistic category of nouns: *people* (say, a couple embracing), *places* (an apartment in Rio), and *things* (a telephone). In studying cinematic grammar, I will concentrate on the ways in which Hitchcock not only "put things together visually" but people and places as well. And we should remember that these categories are under pressure in Hitchcock, and that the kinds of relations our sentences conventionally imply don't work. For to say that a grammatical subject (person) within a grammatical setting (place) does something with a grammatical object (thing) considerably distorts what's actually going on in the Hitchcock landscape. So as we explore, we will put this cinematic grammar to the test, observing the ways in which people, places, and things are both arranged and deranged.

In chapter 1, I examine what I call a Hitchcock propensity: the crowd. While many filmmakers populate their films with crowds, few use crowds as frequently as Hitchcock (who remained largely a filmmaker of modern urbanity). Simply put, there are lots of people in the Hitchcock landscape. And these people, as William Rothman has argued, are a people in and of the cinema—Hitchcock's cinema.[38] Taking a more general view, Lesley Brill argues that the cinema "shows its audiences reflections of themselves (however idealized or otherwise distorted), not just as individuals but also as groups."[39] These groups, whether they are large crowds or smaller packs, are particular to the films in which they appear. Sometimes, as in violent action films, crowds gather as a show of force. In other films, such as comedies, crowds enact other types of rituals—of restoration, integration, and consummation. Regardless of the type of film, an intimate bond is formed between the moviegoing crowd and the crowd on the screen. Thus, returning to his statement, Brill believes that "the exhibiting of movies, like their content, can be understood as designed to create and sustain crowds."[40] As useful as Brill's application of crowd theory is, it stops well short of its possibilities, particularly when it fails to consider how *cinema itself* is an extension of the crowd. Like Siegfried Kracauer, who points out the natural affinity of cinema and crowds, Brill considers the crowd as something both *in* a film and created *by* a film. Yet the affinity of crowds and cinema, I argue, is much closer and far more complex even than this. If they have an *affinity*, it is in that word's sense of shared characteristics and nature. By tracing their relation in Hitchcock, we will see that crowds and cinema are fluid, dynamic, and mutually transformative.

Chapter 2 traces the numerous, ubiquitous appearances of the newspaper, an emblem of the modern urban crowd, in Hitchcock's films. Much has been written about the Hitchcockian object (the lighter in *Strangers on a Train*, the ring in *Shadow of a Doubt*, the key in *Notorious*, etc.). But unlike most "things" Hitchcockian, the newspaper is not limited to a single film. Nor is it any one "thing." It is constantly being transformed and recontextualized (as a telescope in *Marnie*, then a toy barn in *Shadow of a Doubt*, then a portable safe in *Psycho*). Put another way, the newspaper is both itself and something else, or more than itself; it is an altered cinematic figuration. Like Hitchcock's camera, the newspaper—spying, scrutinizing, knowing, dissimulating and dissembling—is a harbinger of violence and death. For this reason, this chapter considers the many ways the newspaper functions at critical moments in Hitchcock's films, to attend to its conspicuous visibility, its shape-shifting materiality, and more importantly, to look at the trace it produces and see what visible effects it has on other agents. It is my argument that in this mode of engagement with the cinema, we register views of the Hitchcock landscape rarely seen.

Chapter 3 gets small; its focus is a modern, urban apartment and the people that reside in it. What occurs inside this place is Hitchcock's apartment plot, and the name given to this apartment plot is "The Case of Mr. Pelham," an episode of *Alfred Hitchcock Presents* directed by Hitchcock himself. In a career significantly defined by the theme of doubling, it is Hitchcock's only exploration of the literal double—that is, an actual lookalike, a living, breathing dead ringer—and the nightmare of his intrusion.[41] Informed by Pamela Wojcik's *The Apartment Plot: Urban Living in American Film and Culture, 1945 to 1975*, this chapter considers the Hitchcock apartment as porous, permeable, and subject to startling and unexpected visits. This is demonstrated to frightening effect at the climax of *Rear Window*, when Lars Thorwald pays a call to Jeff; or at a pivotal moment in *Dial M for Murder*, when Swann's dramatic appearance at Margot's apartment results not in her death but in his; and after Brandon and Phillip's grotesque dinner party has ended in *Rope*, when Rupert makes his sly return to further question the pair. As in other apartment plots, "The Case of Mr. Pelham" presents us with person and place set some distance from the normative ideals of the white, heterosexual middle class of the 1950s. Pelham, I argue, is the sort of "queer encoded character" that Wojcik shows to be typical of the apartment plot.[42] The episode enacts a cat-and-mouse game between Pelham and his double, with the apartment functioning as a sort of battleground for identity. Pelham's efforts to assert his identity are a matter of the placement of people and things—a matter that proves to be considerably complex and fraught with difficulties. In "The Case of Mr. Pelham," Hitchcock is attenuating what he calls a fear worse than death: having no alibi. Worse because Pelham spends most of his leisure time in the company of other men, thus raising the specter of homosexuality—and the need for an alibi, an alleged "elsewhere" of place.

The Hitchcockian theme of spatial dislocation—and the anxiety it induces—is the subject of chapter 4, "Lost and Found in Hitchcock." In it, we visit two peculiar locations in the Hitchcock landscape: Bodega Bay, California, and Quebec City, Quebec. I argue that *The Birds* and *I Confess* reveal a special obsession with dislocation and disorientation.[43] Indeed, both films have, to put it mildly, a funny way of mapping places. The question this chapter asks, then, is "What does it mean for a location to be engaged with the camera that records it, to play a role in the show, to codirect (and, since cinematic spaces are often dizzyingly difficult to navigate, co-*mis*direct)?" As we watch a typical narrative film, we expect the cinematic apparatus to keep the diegesis coherent, spatially and temporally. Yet fear of dislocation is, I argue, at the heart of *The Birds*. While much is changed from the film's source material, Daphne du Maurier's short story, Hitchcock retains what he called "the basic idea," which is death falling from the sky. *The Birds* goes further by compounding this fear with a sense of disorientation, a sense of having no direction—home or elsewhere. In my reading of the film, I reach the conclusion that evoking disorientation is an essential feature of Hitchcock's attitude toward the cinema, and it is precisely this notion that allows the viewer to see two seemingly disparate films, *The Birds* and *I Confess*—films separated by a decade and more than five thousand kilometers of terrain—as being in accord.

Many critics have made note of the peculiar opening to the latter film. The camera follows a number of signs reading, in French, DIRECTION, as it makes its way along the darkened cobblestone streets of Quebec City. I argue that DIRECTION is meant to refer to orientation—and, more interestingly, to the anxiety-inducing feeling of *mis*direction, of *dis*orientation. To further add to our sense that *I Confess* is indeed a film about DIRECTION, a city map makes several appearances—a curiously unnecessary reminder that this film takes place in Quebec City. But the common phrase "This film takes place in" does little justice to the importance of space in a motion picture, and Hitchcock's film gives us many reasons to rethink what the term *takes place* can possibly mean. I argue not simply that *I Confess* is as important a film about Quebec City as *Vertigo* is about San Francisco, as Pomerance has done (both films depict cities that mobilize their own histories and play with their respective pasts), but that *I Confess* helps us understand how Hitchcock's camera maps the city and how the city, in turn, relocates and redefines itself through Hitchcock.[44]

In the book's closing chapter, I concentrate on a motif in Hitchcock that betrays, once and for all, the permeable boundaries of people, places, and things: telepathy. It is, I argue, a motif as far reaching as any in Hitchcock, and it is my aim to demonstrate how this motif is bound up with Hitchcock's fascination with—and fundamental ambivalence about—the female. Crowding a vast telepathic network, the women in Hitchcock—Alicia from *Notorious*, Charlie from *Shadow of a Doubt*, Marion from *Psycho*, Marnie from *Marnie*, and Blanche from *Family Plot*, as well as numerous other sympathetic female listeners—frustrate the efforts of men who, like Hitchcock himself, seek access to private, female knowledge. Following Tania Modleski's feminist analyses of Hitchcock's films, my concern will be the people who risk the most as they traverse the Hitchcock landscape. In this chapter I trace the social networks not only of telepathy but of other forms of occult transmission that crisscross the Hitchcock landscape. This network of occult intimacy is hard won and—given that the Hitchcock landscape is, for women especially, fraught with danger—no sure solution to the central problem of female violence and victimization in Hitchcock. Yet it is the women in Hitchcock who, perhaps better than their male counterparts, appreciate how complex and entangled the Hitchcock landscape is and can therefore turn its anomalies and unknowns to their advantage when necessary.

This book's afterword returns to an idea I allude to above, of keeping the Hitchcock landscape flat. It is an idea I try to abide by throughout the course of this book: flatness is operational rather than literal or visual. For Latour, keeping the social flat means maintaining the symmetry between the human and the nonhuman. To hierarchize one over the other would be to add scale and dimensionality to our sense of the social. "How to Keep Hitchcock Flat" offers brief analyses of three creative interpretations of, and engagements with, the Hitchcock landscape: Jeff Desoms's digital short *Rear Window Timelapse*, Christoph Girardet and Matthias Müller's video installation piece *Phoenix Tapes*, and the online 1000 Frames of Hitchcock project, which is part of the *Alfred Hitchcock Wiki*, maintained by Dave Pattern. I argue that each of these projects can help Hitchcock scholars keep their explanations of his work flat.

Chapter 1

✦

Hitchcock's Crowds

> The reporter who would write the story of crowds must have two faculties wielded into one: first, a keen power of observation that records on the plate of memory a procession of vivid images instantly at his beck and call; and second, a masterly gift of expression.
>
> —Harry Franklin Harrington, *Typical Newspaper Stories* (1915)

> I want plenty of space.
>
> —Alfred Hitchcock, "If I Were Head of a Production Company" (1935)

The love of crowds is a Hitchcock propensity. As Hitchcock himself notes, he wants plenty of space. And Hitchcockian space is seldom empty; the director firmly believed that space is not to be wasted. It's odd, then, how little critical attention has been paid to the subject of crowds in Hitchcock, especially given how frequently Hitchcock makes use of them—and throughout his entire career. As the few attentive critics have rightly noted, Hitchcock's fascination with the crowd stemmed in part from the German influence on his filmmaking style.[1] One must stress, of course, that the fascination with crowds is not solely Hitchcock's (Griffith, Pabst, Vidor, Eisenstein, Riefenstahl, Lang, and Lubitsch, to name but a few, were all drawn to crowds). In fact, the alliance between cinema and crowd is forged in the very first publicly projected motion picture: *La sortie des usines Lumière à Lyon* in 1895—the year in which Gustave Le Bon's influential book on crowds first appeared. To be sure, the love of crowds, which helped shape the nineteenth-century aesthetic, also "helped create the conditions essential to the cinema's birth and growth."[2] It should come as no surprise, then, that one of the cinema's greatest filmmakers should be so attracted to cinema's greatest attraction of all: "the crowd and its eddies."[3]

One might think of the number of cameos in which Hitchcock places himself within a crowd.[4] In only a few instances do we find Hitchcock alone or in the company of only one or two people. Some examples: Hitchcock walks the streets alone in his cameo for *Mr. and Mrs. Smith* (1941); he posts a letter in a relatively empty village street in *Suspicion* (1941); his profile can be seen walking at the top of the steps in a terrifyingly vacant Quebec City in *I Confess* (1953); although his apartment is crowded with party guests, the composer in *Rear Window* (1954) hosts Hitchcock alone. He looks at Marnie in *Marnie* (1964), then at us, as he stands in the empty hallway of a boarding house. Virtually all of Hitchcock's other cameos can be said to appear in crowds, or in spaces in which we can only assume there are large numbers of people just offscreen—as in, for instance, his cameo for *Vertigo* (1958), where he is seen walking through the entrance to a shipyard. It's only natural that the man of the cinema is also a man of the crowd. Yet Hitchcock wants more than just plenty of space for himself (he anticipates, in the essay cited above, that his demand for more space will draw "derisive grins . . . from readers who know my corpulence"). He wants "more space than even that demands." One might say that the cameos only point to what is, in Hitchcock's films, a far more pervasive interest in crowds and street scenes.

Like many filmmakers, Hitchcock portrays crowds as mostly terrifying, unpredictable, and capable of sudden and unspeakable violence. But his street scenes reveal both a fear of and an attraction to crowds, which are at once a force of disruption and potential violence, as well as a mass of laughing, like-minded, and mostly harmless onlookers. This should come as no surprise to Hitchcock scholars familiar with the filmmaker's contradictory impulses. As Lesley Brill has recently noted, "Hitchcock was fascinated by and ambivalent about crowds."[5] It has been suggested that Hitchcock's fascination with and ambivalence about crowds stemmed from his socioeconomic background. Paula Marantz Cohen believes that, as the son "of lower-middle class Cockney-Catholics," he was very much a part of the crowd: "Physically ungainly and socially inept, he often sought to place himself in the background—to disappear into the anonymity of the crowd (a placement that is ironically transformed into the self-promoting gimmick of the cameo appearances he makes in the background of his films)."[6] Although it is likely that Hitchcock's ungainliness and social ineptitude drew him to the crowd, it seems just as likely that this was the source of his ambivalence about it. As one childhood friend recalls, Hitchcock would seldom join the other schoolboys at play, preferring instead to remain isolated, withdrawn from the crowd—even in contempt of it. Patrick McGilligan refers to an exchange between Truffaut and Hitchcock's childhood friend Hugh Gray: "Gray told François Truffaut that he would always remember Hitchcock standing up against a wall, watching the other boys contemptuously."[7] Whether or not Gray was, himself, equally removed from the crowd is left to speculation. There is little doubt, however, that Hitchcock mostly kept to himself, studying the nature of the crowd as an outsider.

But it is not only the nature of the crowd *as such* that interests Hitchcock, as Michael Walker rightly notes in *Hitchcock's Motifs*.[8] Hitchcock also crowds his films with people to fully explore different varieties of seeing, of looking, of being looked at, of reflecting, projecting, distorting and dissimulating. The very public (and very urban) spectacle is, Walker observes, Hitchcock's "most wide-ranging" motif. Further, it points to "a fundamental feature of his cinema. His dramatization of situations in which onlookers—the diegetic audience—jump at his bidding is a reflection of his general approach to cinema audiences."[9] I agree that Hitchcock's principal aim is to demonstrate his mastery of orchestrating emotional responses, but Hitchcock's crowd scenes do much more than this.

Of Crowds and Crowding in Hitchcock

Let us begin with an attempt to sketch a Hitchcock crowd typology. In figures 1.1 and 1.2, we see two types of crowds in Hitchcock. The first (figure 1.1) is of the more familiar sort: urban, anonymous, bustling, and harboring unforeseen danger. The image is taken from the famous sequence from *Sabotage* (1936) in which little Stevie attempts unsuccessfully to deliver a package (which contains, unbeknownst to him, a bomb set to detonate at precisely 1:45 p.m.) to Piccadilly Circus. The second image (figure 1.2) is taken from a sequence in *Champagne* (1928) in which the heroine (Betty Balfour) and the man (Theo Van Alten) hired by her father to follow her are seated at a table placed near the edge of a crowded dance floor. In the first image, we have the nominal form of the crowd (i.e., Stevie walks through the crowd). Here, the crowd appears as a common social phenomenon, an emblematic feature of the modern city. The latter image, however, presents us with a somewhat more complicated understanding of the crowd in Hitchcock. One might argue that the only distinguishing feature between the two examples is that the first is outdoors and the second indoors. And while the crowd appears in its nominal form in *Champagne* (a large number of people gathered together), its presence its felt particularly as a force, operating as much as a thing (the crowd) as an imposing threat (a crowding). In Hitchcock, the latter form of the word *crowd* (as verb) is as significant a motif as the former. The crowd, one might say, is a thing that *is* and a thing that *does*.

Indeed, it may make little sense to distinguish the two types (crowds and crowding), given that both are conditions of a physical and social density. As John Plotz argues in *The Crowd: British Literature and Public Politics*, a grayness hangs over all forms of the word. "It might be argued," continues Plotz,

> that all that really changes in the semantic fluctuations of "crowd" are metaphorical extensions of the word. Thus De Quincey's "crowd" of phantoms pressing within his brain during opium visions is simply analogy, and the Riot Act's proclamation that twelve makes a crowd,

Figure 1.1. *Sabotage*: Little Stevie enters the crowd

> like the common-law reduction of that number to three (as well as the subsequent idiomatic borrowing, "three's a crowd"), may seem nothing more than linguistic gerrymandering. Such elongations and condensations do not, one could argue, absolutely destroy what might be called the essential properties of the (noun substantive) crowd.[10]

But given the indeterminacy of reference, what exactly *are* the essential properties of a crowd? Plotz warns against the danger of falling back on some variation of "a large number of people" as an answer, given that the precise definition of *crowd* is, depending on the time and situation, in constant flux. Indeed, Plotz's key aim is to undermine ahistorical conceptions of the crowd that, following Gustave Le Bon, fix its essential properties and lose a sense of the peculiar ways, both legal and literary, in which the term is used throughout history—to highlight, rather than erase, the "gray space between crowd as thing and crowd as action."[11]

By attending to this "gray space" in Hitchcock's work, one discovers there are a significant number of instances in which the meanings of *crowd* and *crowding* seem unfixed and thus add an unnerving quality to a scene. Consider the scene from *Strangers on a Train* when Guy Haines (Farley Granger) meets with his estranged wife Miriam (Kasey Rogers) at Miller's Music Store,

Figure 1.2. *Champagne*: Crowding Betty

where she works. The discussion instantly becomes heated. Seeking some privacy, the two enter a listening booth. "Now this is cozy," remarks Miriam. Yet the two are hardly alone, as the booth is connected to a second by two large glass panes (which, in turn, is connected similarly to a third). In a single long take, lasting just over two minutes, we watch as Guy and Miriam's private spat becomes increasingly nasty, and their space increasingly crowded. In one particular moment in this shot, a young boy in the adjacent booth seems to squeeze himself in between Guy and Miriam just as the camera frames them most tightly. The shot is illustrative of the crowding motif that runs straight through *Strangers on a Train*—from Guy and Bruno (Robert Walker) bumping feet in a crowded train compartment at the beginning of the film, to Guy and Anne's abrupt departure from another crowded compartment at the end.

But as demonstrated just now, crowds and crowding do not always assume their most recognizable forms in Hitchcock.[12] A careful examination of crowds in Hitchcock requires a willingness to attend to the numerous forms in which they appear—the nominal, the verbal, and the "gray space" between those two. Further, we might consider how *cinema itself* is an extension of the crowd. Both William Rothman and, more recently, Leslie Abramson have noted the link between the cinema and crowds in Hitchcock—one need only think of how frequently Hitchcock depicts masses of people "drawn to visual attractions," as Abramson puts it. Rothman suggests we can even think of these audiences, lured by the spectacle of murder and sex crimes, as Hitchcock's own.[13] Yet the relation of the cinema to the crowd is more complex, as we shall see. What follows is a brief compendium of crowds and crowding in Hitchcock, culminating in a close examination of two crowd films from Hitchcock's early and late career, *Sabotage* and *North by Northwest* (1959). It would be difficult to do justice to the repeated examples of the crowd and of crowding effects, and perhaps a bit obvious to point them out even to the least informed Hitchcock viewer. Nevertheless, I wish to give an account (not at all exhaustive) of crowds and crowding in Hitchcock.

It should come as no surprise that the very first sequence in the very first Hitchcock film is of a crowd.[14] Just after the opening titles of *The Pleasure Garden*, we see dancing girls descend a spiral staircase, from the top of the frame down through the bottom of the frame. They fill the stage of the nightclub known as the Pleasure Garden, which is crowded with onlookers. Later in the film, a crowd gathers at the dock to watch the ship carrying Levett (Miles Mander) to the colonies. Lost in the crowd, Levett's wife, Jill (Carmelita Geraghty), waves goodbye to Levett, who doesn't bother to say goodbye. The crowd makes several appearances in Hitchcock's next film, *The Lodger* (1926), the first important Hitchcock film and the first to place the crowd front and center. The most memorable appearance of the crowd is in the form of what Elias Canetti calls the "baiting crowd"—a crowd out for blood.[15] In the climax of the film, we see this baiting crowd pursuing the innocent man (Ivor Novello) mistakenly believed to be the serial killer known as "the Avenger."[16] The extraordinary (and curiously neglected) *Downhill* (1927), made right after *The Lodger* and also starring Ivor Novello, features some of the most fascinating urban crowd scenes in early Hitchcock, as when the young Roddy (Novello) stumbles, in a daze, through the crowded London streets in search of his home. In what the director himself called "the next Hitchcock film," *The Ring* (1927), we see crowds of people at a carnival.[17] A montage sequence for which Hitchcock said he received a standing ovation shows us people hurled through the air on mechanical thrill rides, lured to the sideshows by big-mouthed barkers, and drawn into what is no doubt the carnival's biggest attraction, the boxing ring.[18] Filled to maximum density with people, Hitchcock could have titled this film *The Crowd*, and in doing so beat King Vidor to the punch by several months.[19]

The wealthy owner of a champagne business (Gordon Harker) finds himself headline news in the opening sequence of *Champagne* (1928). Furious, he hurls from his desk one newspaper after the next, sparing the *New York Daily News* just long enough for us to read its headline: "Wall Street Magnate Again Defied by Headstrong Heiress Daughter." In the ballroom of an ocean liner, excitement erupts when it is announced that the heiress is arriving by plane and will join the liner midocean. En masse, the passengers make a mad dash to the deck to witness the heiress's dramatic arrival, forming an ophidian-like beast that coils up the liner's grand, marble stairways. The opening shots of *The Manxman* (1929), Hitchcock's last silent film, are of a crowded wharf and, subsequently, of a crowd of "lowly fishermen" who gather to petition against the powerful fisheries on the Isle of Man. At the close of the film, a large group of villagers gathers to form a small baiting crowd that very publicly and very angrily shuns the couple, Phil and Kate (Malcolm Keen and Anny Ondra).

There are incidental crowd scenes in both *Easy Virtue* (1928) and *The Farmer's Wife* (1928). In the former, Larita Filton (Isabel Jeans) leaves a packed courtroom to find a crowd of newspapermen waiting to ambush her. As Marilyn Fabe has noted, Hitchcock will shoot a very similar scene for *Notorious* (1946) fifteen years later, in which Alicia Huberman (Ingrid Bergman) exits a courtroom after watching her father stand trial for espionage. She, too, is ambushed by a pack of hungry newspapermen.[20] In a slapstick scene from *The Farmer's Wife*, Postmistress Hearn (Olga Slade) bursts into hysterics when Sammy Sweetland (Jameson Thomas) proposes to her. A crowd, assembled in a nearby garden, comes racing into the room to find the postmistress laughing uncontrollably. The packed room erupts in chaos, something like the overcrowded cabin scene from the Marx Brothers' *A Night at the Opera* (1935). In *Blackmail* (1929), Alice White's long walk from Crewe's apartment to her bedroom takes her through a crowded Piccadilly Circus. At one point, she passes through a large group of people emerging from a theater, where "A New Comedy" has just been performed. This juxtaposition of collective high spirits and private dread is repeated, with similarly chilling effect, in Alan J. Pakula's *Klute* (1971), when an anxious Bree Daniels (Jane Fonda) makes her way across a crowded disco floor toward the table where her ex-pimp is seated.

A crowd scene was written especially for Hitchcock's next film, an adaptation of the Sean O'Casey play *Juno and the Paycock* (1929). According to Patrick McGilligan, O'Casey was persuaded to write the scene to "open up what had been a single-set play."[21] Surely this change served Hitchcock's desire for plenty of space. The film begins on the streets of Dublin, where we see a man, played by the great Irish actor Barry Fitzgerald, giving a speech about solidarity. In a signature move, Hitchcock's camera pulls back and up, revealing a large crowd gathered around the man. Gunfire suddenly erupts, and the crowd disperses. Most of the people, including two of the play's principal characters, Captain Boyle and Joxer Daly, spill into a nearby bar (where it is said Hitchcock was to have his cameo—as a bartender—before the idea was scrapped) and share a drink.[22]

In the opening sequence of *Rich and Strange* (1931), workers file out of their offices, cascade down staircases and, by twos, fold their umbrellas in unison as they make their descent into the London Underground.[23] A constable, standing in front of an overcrowded tube train, is unable to hold back the flood of people wanting to board. Once on the crammed and tumbling train, we watch as Fred Hill (Henry Kendall) grabs the feathers on an old woman's hat in an attempt to keep his balance. The sequence ends when Fred spots an ad in the newspaper he is reading that asks, "Are you happy with your present circumstances?" and, falling forward as the train brakes, tries to steady himself once more with the old woman's hat, this time knocking it clear off her head.

The crowd is just as ubiquitous in the films of Hitchcock's late British career, particularly in those Hitchcock shot back-to-back: *The Man Who Knew Too Much* (1934) and *The 39 Steps* (1935). The earlier film begins and ends with a crowd scene. The film opens on a crowd of spectators gasping as one when a downhill skier, the Frenchman Louis Bernard (Pierre Fresnay), takes a breathtaking fall to avoid hitting Betty Lawrence (Nova Pilbeam), who has dashed impulsively in his path. The Albert Hall sequence, which Hitchcock would revisit in his 1956 remake of the film, begins with a shot of a marquee poster, on which a crowd of shadows hurries to and fro. In a shot that suggests something like the ambulatory rhythms of the heart, we see audience members circulate throughout the lobby and into various chambers to their seats. Just outside the doors of the hall, Jill Lawrence (Edna Best) helplessly searches the crowd for Ropa, the dignitary who is the target of an assassination plot. Just as she spots Ropa, the sniper Ramon (Frank Vosper) appears, out of nowhere. He hands her a tiny figurine, a reminder that her husband and her daughter will die if she does anything to prevent the assassination. For the next several shots, we see Jill in her seat, nervously looking around the packed auditorium. As the concerto continues toward its climax, Jill, tears filling her eyes, stares blankly at the orchestra. An interesting point-of-view shot follows: Jill's view of the crowded pit slowly blurs into white effluvium. Then, from the right of the frame, the long barrel of a pistol emerges. It's a powerful effect, one that suggests that menace and violence is always lurking within the blind spots of the crowd. And what is a crowd (particularly a crowded theater) but an undulating hive of a thousand blind spots, a nightmare version of "Where's Waldo?"

After the Albert Hall sequence, the film shifts to yet another crowd scene. A large audience has gathered to watch the final gun battle between the police and the fleeing Ramon—and there is no reason to suggest that this is not the same audience that filled the Albert Hall. Thus Hitchcock shows us the fluidity of the crowd, its movements and transformations as it is baited from one visual spectacle to another. I take it this is what the crofter's wife (Peggy Ashcroft) means when she says to Hanny (Robert Donat) in *The 39 Steps*, "You should see Sauchiehall Street with all its fine shops, and Argyll Street on a Saturday night with the trams and the lights and the cinema palaces and their crowds" (running the length of Scotland's most popular shopping district, Sauchiehall is the Glaswegian version of Oxford Street). Her final emphasis on crowds and cinema is especially apt given the context: the scene is an explicit retelling of the old farmer's wife story Hitchcock was so fond of.[24]

As Ned Schantz notes, the scene hovers around what he calls the "appalling logic of hospitality," which "relentlessly pursued, entails sexual access to the master's women."[25] It's a logic borne out in a number of Hitchcock films, including *Shadow of a Doubt* and *Under Capricorn* (1949). But in *The 39 Steps*, what stands in for the promise of sex is a conversation about big cities and their crowds. After the crofter's wife describes Sauchiehall (with a palpable sense of longing), Hannay the handsome stranger says, "You certainly don't get those things out here." The crofter's wife looks down, sadly, and says, "No." Hannay then asks, "You miss them?" As the scene continues, the referents (for *those things* and *them*) slip effortlessly about, back and forth between crowded cinema palaces and sex. If this is not clear enough, the crofter's wife stops Hannay from telling her about "those things," saying her husband would not approve. Hannay then says, "Well, why not listen now before he comes back?" Thus Hitchcock demonstrates both the attraction and the danger of crowds and visual spectacle: similar to that of *The Man Who Knew Too Much*, the climactic ending of *The 39 Steps* takes place in the crowded London Palladium, where Mr. Memory (whose head is crowded with facts) is shot and killed.

Yet Hitchcock was also interested in crowds of far less physical density and force. While important crowd scenes bookend *The 39 Steps*, the film is also rife with allusions to crowding. When Hannay barters for a room, the Crofter asks him, "Can you sleep in a box bed?" to which Hannay responds gamely, "I'll try." The comic sequences with the handcuffed Hannay and Pamela, set in motion by a large flock of sheep blocking a squad car, suggest a kind of enforced crowding. To be sure, well before *Lifeboat* (1944) and *Rope* (1948), Hitchcock proved he was interested in the moments of social awkwardness and embarrassment that confined spaces allow. In *The Lady Vanishes* (1938), a large group of travelers crowds a small inn. When the innkeeper announces that a train bound for England has been delayed by an avalanche, the travelers crowd the registration desk.[26] Two cricket enthusiasts, Caldicott and Charters (brilliantly played by Naunton Wayne and Basil Radford), soon learn that the inn is completely booked and must spend the evening in the only room available: the maid's quarters. In a marvelous visual gag, Hitchcock shows us a very cozy situation: lying in bed holding a copy of the *Herald Tribune* in front of him, we hear Caldicott from behind the newspaper complaining that it has all the baseball scores but not a word about cricket. "The Americans got no sense of proportion," he complains. Indeed, as we'll see in the following chapter, the newspaper disturbs our sense of proportion and beguiles our most trusted perceptual systems. Even here, in a harmless sight gag, the newspaper conspires in an act of dissembling and dissimulation: the maid, who has come to retrieve a few of her personal items, knocks on the door; at that moment, the newspaper drops, revealing both Caldicott *and* Chalmers behind the newspaper, the latter with no nightshirt and the former with no bottoms. The two men bide their time with noticeable irritation as the maid busies about the room. "I can't stand this ridiculous lack of privacy!" decries Chalmers. In Hitchcock, three's a crowd.

The "three's a crowd" phenomenon is common in Hitchcock, as suggested with the family quarrel sequence in *Strangers on a Train* described earlier (and with the film's final sequence, cut from what is commonly referred to as the preview version). It's no surprise that it occurs in moments of blackmailing, the bullying logic of which is that someone is crowding in on a shared secret. In *Blackmail*, the shared secret belongs to Alice White (Anny Ondra) and her boyfriend from Scotland Yard, Frank Webber (John Longden): Alice, under the threat of rape, has stabbed to death a man named Crewe (Cyril Ritchard). While Frank tries to keep the true identity of Crewe's killer a secret, an interloper named Tracy (Donald Calthrop) has come into the possession of an incriminating piece of evidence: Alice's glove (whose mate Alice left behind at Crewe's apartment). Tracy makes himself an unwelcome guest in the shop belonging to Alice's father, and in several shots crowds both Frank and Alice. Hitchcock repeats this scenario in *Rebecca* (1940), when Jack Favell (George Sanders) avails himself of the picnic basket that Maxim (Laurence Olivier) and the second Mrs. De Winter (Joan Fontaine) have packed.

But the "three's a crowd" phenomenon in Hitchcock is not always governed by the logic of blackmail: one might think of Tom Doyle (nearly) overstaying his welcome in *Rear Window* (1953) after rudely dismissing Lisa's claims about Thorwald's guilt, or the unexpected return of Rupert (James Stewart) at the end of *Rope*. But properly generalized, the "three's a crowd" phenomenon can be a blanket term for *any* moment in Hitchcock when awkwardness and discomfort is created by multiple bodies in small or confined spaces. Think of Roger Thornhill (Cary Grant) trapped in a crowded elevator with his kidnappers and his less-than-sympathetic mother, or the hallway in the Tides restaurant in *The Birds*, just after the bird attack in the center of Bodega Bay.

Even more dominant in Hitchcock's late British and early American period, the crowd is portrayed in all its manifestations, in often less humorous (though no less inventive) ways. *Sabotage* (1936) is an important crowd film and will be given fuller treatment below. In *Secret Agent*, made that same year, we have a classic example of the panicked crowd when Richard Ashenden (John Gielgud) sets off the alarm in the chocolate factory, sending hundreds of female workers and their supervisors running from the factory floor toward the exit. Crowds erupt in chaos and violence on two occasions in *Young and Innocent* (1939). The first occurs inside a café, when Erica (Nova Pilbeam) manages to get a tramp to reveal that Old Will (Edward Rigby) has the raincoat that will exonerate Robert Tisdall (Derrick de Marney). Then in a crowded doss house, Robert avoids a good thumping when he grabs Old Will and runs to Erica, who waits in a car. Fittingly, Hitchcock's last British film, *Jamaica Inn* (1939), ends with a crowd scene. The dramatic death of Sir Humphrey Pengallan (Charles Laughton) is played out in front of a large group of onlookers. "What are you all waiting for?" Sir Humphrey shouts, with fitting final words, from atop a ship's mast: "A spectacle? You shall have it!" He then plunges to the deck of the ship to a chorus of shrieks.

In an early sequence in *Foreign Correspondent* (1940), an assassin emerges from a group of reporters on the steps of the Amsterdam Town Hall during a heavy rain and shoots a man who we are led to believe is the diplomat Van Meer. The assassin then takes flight into a small crowd of people, whose patchwork of black umbrellas provides a cloak that bulges and undulates as the assassin forces his way through. At the climax of *Saboteur* (1944), a massive crowd gathers at the Brooklyn Navy Yard for the christening of a warship, which is the target for fifth-column infiltrators. In the film's opening sequence, which bears a striking resemblance to that inceptive crowd film *La sortie de l'usine Lumière à Lyon*, a crowd of workers at a defense factory breaks for lunch ("Here come the wolves," says the cook). As the crowd hurries past us, we watch Barry (Robert Cummings) and his friend Kenneth having a brush with a man (Norman Lloyd) they take to be a happy fellow worker. As the man pushes his way past Barry and Kenneth, he drops some small personal items, including an envelope, which Barry hands to him after glancing casually at a name and address: Frank Fry, Tobin Ranch. The man hurries away, offering no apologies or thank-yous, but mistakenly leaves behind a hundred-dollar bill. Barry finds the man at a lunch table and returns the money, only to get for his trouble a scornful look. In less than four minutes of running time, the crowd has produced from within its belly all the necessary elements for the film: the hero, the villain, and the evidence that absolves the former and incriminates the latter.

In a Hitchcock film, people always seem to get in the way. Even the small town of Santa Rosa, in *Shadow of a Doubt* (1943), seems annoyingly overpopulated. Young Charlie (Teresa Wright) rushes past people—and nearly into oncoming traffic—in her flight to the library, which has just closed when she finally arrives to search for the incriminating story her uncle ripped out of the daily newspaper. This is the second of three times we follow Charlie through the crowded streets of Santa Rosa. The first time, she walks proudly arm in arm with her uncle as the two visit the bank where Mr. Newton (Henry Travers) works. Charlie rightly senses that, with her uncle in tow, she stands out in the crowd. "Oh, Uncle Charlie," she coos, "I love walking with you, I want everyone to see!" So it is: all eyes are on her and the inappropriate suitor. On her third flight, however, she is running from her uncle and the home she feels he has corrupted ("Can't we have a little peace and quiet here without dragging in poisons all the time?"). In the second of these three flights, Charlie is stopped by the traffic cop and chastened for being so reckless.

Even sparsely populated films, such as *Rope* and *Lifeboat*, rely on the tensions created by the physical proximity of individuals. D. A. Miller has suggested that Hitchcock's tight framing of men in the former film amounts to a kind of "visual teasing"—the image surrogate of that which can bear no image, the spectacle of gay male sex.[27] Indeed, Brandon (John Dall) and Philip

(Farley Granger) are much too close from the first moment we see them. Further, it is a closeness they share with others, including Kenneth (Douglas Dick) and Rupert. However, this sort of crowding is not limited to Brandon, Philip, Kenneth, and Rupert. In one particularly odd moment (in a film rich with oddness), Mrs. Atwater (Constance Collier), Rupert, and Janet (Joan Chandler) stand close together over the "buffet" Brandon has arranged, on top of the chest in which David's body is hidden. It is a tight shot—so tight that Brandon, who is just to the right of Mrs. Atwater, remains offscreen. It's not clear why Brandon is not in the shot, given that Mrs. Atwater directs several of her comments to him (when she says, "Definitely a Scorpio," and again when she says, "You know, it was sort of . . ."). It's as if the point is for Brandon to keep breaching the frame. Indeed, on three occasions Brandon leans his head into the shot, just below Mrs. Atwater.[28] Rupert, too, gets a little too close to Mrs. Atwater on a few occasions. When he says, "I once went to the movies, I saw Mary Pickford," he cranes his neck to the right and swoops in about four inches from her face. When Rupert gently mocks Mrs. Atwater with his own "something-something," and Brandon pokes his head into frame again, a fifth head sneaks in—that of Mrs. Wilson (Edith Evanson), who whispers in Janet's ear, "If I were you, I'd go easy on the pâté, dear. Calories."

All of this face crowding is no doubt the by-product of working without cuts and having to manipulate multiple crowded scenes simultaneously, as is common in *Lifeboat* as well. When John Kovac (John Hodiak) is alone (as much as one can be in this film), reading the boat's much-appreciated newspaper, Connie (Tallulah Bankhead) pokes her finger through it and pulls it away from him, as her head sweeps into frame. The shot is just to the left of John's point of view and tightly framed. But face crowding in Hitchcock is not limited to these two similarly unusual films. In a sense, any close-up or extreme close-up of a character's face could be considered a form of face crowding (the lodger's kiss over chess in *The Lodger*, or Uncle Charlie's diatribe against "fat wheezing pigs" in *Shadow of a Doubt*). Hitchcock knew that face crowding is more often felt to be a frightening invasion of personal space than an expression of intense desire. Thus *Marnie* and *Frenzy* (1972) both employ extreme close-ups at the moment of the most violent invasion of all. Upon reflection, one may find there are far more examples than needed to suggest that we cannot disassociate the extreme close-up from violence in Hitchcock (violence sometimes aimed at us, as when in *Strangers on a Train* and *North by Northwest* a character punches the camera). The most extreme close-up in *Lifeboat*—of Willy's sweaty brow—is a prelude to the violence of the baiting crowd: after hearing Willy (Walter Slezak) confess that he has thrown Gus (William Bendix) off the boat, the thirsty passengers notice that he is sweating, a sign of hydration; a few moments later, the passengers attack Willy and throw him overboard.

During this period in his career, from *Strangers on a Train* to *North by Northwest*, Hitchcock's interest in the double and the crowd was at a peak—as evident not only in his films but in his television anthology, *Alfred Hitchcock Presents*. As we shall see in a subsequent chapter, the episode "The Case of Mr. Pelham" (which aired December 4, 1955) demonstrates the terrifying, body-snatching logic of the double: that an impersonator could not only move into your office, your apartment, and your haunts, but into your very being, crowding you right out of it. Hitchcock combines the idea of the double with face crowding in the famous dissolve in *The Wrong Man* (1956), when the guilty man, Danny (Richard Robbins), walks into a close-up of Manny Balestrero (Henry Fonda). What's peculiar, of course, is that this instance of face crowding arrives quite late in the narrative, well after Manny has been accused of Danny's crime, well after the transference of guilt from the one to the other. It's as if Hitchcock's aim here is to show the transference of guilt *back* to Danny from Manny. After all, it is Danny who "walks into" Manny here, who steps into the identity of the accused. This frightening porosity of bodies facilitates the transference of guilt, which is why, perhaps, the crowd in Hitchcock is a dangerous place to find oneself.

The Wrong Man begins with Hitchcock's cameo appearance, as a small figure on a dark and empty soundstage, backlit and casting a long shadow before him.[29] Then as the credits appear, we find ourselves among a crowd at the famous Stork Club, where Manny plays double bass with Peter Rotunda and His Orchestra. Gradually, with a series of dissolves, the club empties. Manny then packs up his double bass for the night. With the first exterior shot we see him emerge from the entrance to the Stork Club and happen to walk between a pair of police officers who are passing by, giving the distinct impression that Manny is being escorted to jail. Thus from the outset, Hitchcock associates the crowd with criminality—and the double (figured not only with the M/Danny coupling but also with Manny's double bass, which links him to Hitchcock, who—in his cameo appearance in that other great film about doubles, *Strangers on a Train*—is himself seen carrying a double bass).

Although Hitchcock's interest in more conventional baiting crowds continues during this period—one might here consider the hissing and judging crowd that presses in on Father Logan after the trial in *I Confess* (1952)—what emerges is a conception of the modern, urban crowd that has echoes of Charles Baudelaire and Edgar Allan Poe.[30] In Hitchcock, the crowd provides opportunities for the fleeting chance encounter. While certainly the chance encounter figures in Hitchcock's films before this period (I'm thinking here of Barry Kane's chance encounter with Fry in *Saboteur*), it is given considerably more prominence beginning with *Strangers on a Train*. To be sure, the lesson one learns from Hitchcock's films is that you never know whom you will bump into in a crowd—a lesson Marion Crane (Janet Leigh) learns quite unexpectedly when she encounters her boss, George Lowery (Vaughn Taylor), at a crowded intersection in *Psycho* (1960). In one of the film's many brilliant little strokes, Marion and Lowery exchange pleasant smiles before being struck by the awkwardness of the encounter. Earlier, Marion told her boss that, due to a headache, she would be heading straight home after depositing the $40,000 in cash that Mr. Cassidy has given Lowery for safe deposit (later, Marion will hide the cash in a newspaper). It is at the precise moment of this unexpected encounter that we begin to fear Marion is not safe, and Bernard Herrmann's score stresses this sudden change with dramatic emphasis. Of course Marnie Edgar (Tippi Hedren), in the film that bears her first name, is a veteran of such unexpected encounters. She is spotted at Atlantic City Race Course by a man of the crowd, who then spies her through a rolled-up newspaper. While *The Man Who Knew Too Much* (1956) is best known for the climactic sequence in a crowded Royal Albert Hall ("A single crash of Cymbals and how it rocked the lives of an American family," reads the opening titles), it is important to note its other crowd scenes, particularly the one in which a disguised Louis Bernard (Daniel Gélin) is chased through the crowded markets of Morocco. The knife of the man chasing him catches up with Bernard, who then staggers his way to Dr. Ben McKenna (James Stewart), whom he singles out among others in the crowd.[31] Yet these two men are not strangers. Their chance encounter occurs in the film's opening sequence, aboard a crowded bus.

Key crowd sequences in Hitchcock can be traced beyond the period I've outlined here. One might think of *The Birds* as one of Hitchcock's great crowd films, with frightened mobs forming with each new attack. But it is also worth remembering that Melanie Daniels (Tippi Hedren)has had several encounters with the paparazzi, which we can imagine forming around her like a pack or baiting crowd. Melanie is the daughter of a wealthy newspaper magnate whose rival has orchestrated these encounters. By catching Melanie in compromising positions (one newspaper story has her frolicking naked in a public fountain in Rome, "with a pretty wild crowd," as Mitch Brenner puts it), the rival hopes to destroy the reputation of Melanie's father and, in doing so, drive her father's newspaper to financial ruin. By the time she reaches Bodega Bay, however, the paparazzi are the least of Melanie's worries, for a new crowd has found her: the birds.

Throughout the film, the birds are referred to as a mass. Mitch (Rod Taylor) says to Melanie, "It seems to be a pattern, doesn't it? They strike and disappear, and they start massing again." To his mother, Lydia (Jessica Tandy), who contemplates leaving their home after an attack, Mitch says, "Not now, not while they're massing out there." At the Tides restaurant, a haughty amateur ornithologist named Mrs. Bundy (Ethel Griffies) dismisses the possibility of a "massed attack." An exasperated Mitch, who warns that a "bird war" has been declared, says, "They're out there massing someplace and they'll be back, you can count on that!"

Thus, despite the fact that much of the film takes place in the sleepy seaside village of Bodega Bay, the birds in *The Birds* are strongly linked with the modern, urban crowd. As Melanie Daniels crosses a busy Powell Street at Union Square in the opening shot of the film, we hear streetcars, car horns, revving engines, and the clip-clopping of Melanie's quickened, high-heeled steps. But what dominates the soundtrack here is the sound of the chirping seagulls overhead. While we were given a preview of this terrifying mass of birds in the title sequence, the opening shot establishes the birds en masse as an aural accompaniment to a typical urban scene. And it is interesting to note that Melanie is not the first to notice the source of this noise. After a clever pan, which links the location shot of Union Square with the studio shot of Davidson's Pet Shop, a young boy whistles at Melanie. At this precise moment, a Japanese couple walking by look up into the air, the gentleman of the couple looking twice. Only when the couple leaves the frame does Melanie stop and look up to see the birds. In the point-of-view shot that follows, we see the mass of birds, circling high above Dewey Monument, topped by a statue of Victory holding her trident.

Leslie Abramson devotes several pages of her book *Hitchcock and the Anxiety of Authorship* to this film, seeing it as Hitchcock's greatest testament to the inherent violence of a beholding force. "Among the regimes of cumulative spectatorship that amass throughout Hitchcock's cinema," writes Abramson, "nowhere is the audience more darkly envisioned than in *The Birds*."[32] But for Abramson, the birds above Union Square are merely "innocuous spectatorial figures." Only when the birds arrive in Bodega Bay do they become "darker, magnetized spectators."[33] As we can see, however, there is nothing innocuous about that crowd circling Dewey Monument, claiming "Victory" as their own. Regardless, Abramson is correct to see in *The Birds* the violence inherent in the beholding crowd—an interest I argue Hitchcock sustains throughout his career.

In Hitchcock's fiftieth film, *Torn Curtain*, we have a crowd scene reminiscent of both versions of *The Man Who Knew Too Much*, *Sabotage*, and *The 39 Steps*. Dr. Michael Armstrong (Paul Newman) and his fiancée, Sarah Sherman (Julie Andrews), attend a ballet, in the hopes of avoiding the East German police and making their way safely to Sweden. On a tip from a resentful ballerina, the police arrive. While Roger Thornhill dazzles us with his elaborate and smug put-on when he disrupts the auction in *North by Northwest* (a woman says to him, "We know you're no fake. You're a genuine idiot," to which Thornhill replies, "Thank you"), Michael simply takes a page right out of one of the better-known pieces of constitutional law and yells, "Fire!" Mass hysteria ensues, allowing Armstrong and Sarah to slip away.[34]

Had this panic scene occurred in the United States, Michael (if caught) would no doubt have been charged with a criminal offense: falsely yelling fire in a crowded theater. Yet his defense could very well be twofold: he could argue that he saw what he took to be a real fire on stage, during the ballet performance of Tchaikovsky's *Francesca da Rimini*. A second, less convincing but nevertheless intriguing line of defense could come from a section on panic in the influential study *Crowds and Power*. Here, Elias Canetti describes a curious phenomenon that occurs when someone shouts "Fire!" in a crowded theater. First, a man in the crowd who tries to escape quickly finds himself fighting against this crowd; in other words, he is part of the crowd and yet separate from it, casting blows against it in his effort to push his way toward the exit. When this happens, says Canetti, "the crowd assumes the character of fire. It originated with the unexpected sight of flames or with a shout of 'fire' and it plays like flames with the man who is trying to escape from it. The people he pushes away are like burning objects to him; their touch is hostile, and on every part of his body; and it terrifies him."[35] It is true that Hitchcock photographs the panic sequence as if a real fire were, in fact, spreading throughout the theater. As Brigitte Peucker has suggested, the red and orange glow from the stage performance, the warm yellow of the electric candle wall sconces, and the deep red exit doors, together form a color scheme that calls to mind the fires of hell.[36] Yet the crowd itself appears less like fire than water. Michael and Sarah are swept away by the raging rapids of panic-stricken people desperate to reach the exit. After being separated from Armstrong, Sarah must fight the powerful current of bodies and swim upstream to reach him. *Torn Curtain* has many faults, but it convincingly conveys the volatility of the crowd, the powerful density of bodies, in this climactic sequence. It is thrilling, even breathtaking.

Hitchcock's next film, *Topaz*, has perhaps the largest crowd sequences in the director's lengthy career—though they were not shot by Hitchcock himself. The title sequence comprises several shots of an actual military parade in Moscow, shots that are reminiscent of Leni Riefensthal's *Triumph of the Will*. Later in the film, we see footage of a real pro-Castro rally where hundreds of thousands of Cubans have gathered. Shots of the real Fidel Castro and Che Guevara are cut with Hitchcock's shots of Rico Parra (John Vernon) and the hulking Hernández (Carlos Rivas), who, quite impossibly, spots André Devereaux (Frederick Stafford) in the crowd. It is not surprising that Hitchcock has no ownership of such footage, as conventional as it is.

With his next film, *Frenzy*, Hitchcock returns to his fascination with large urban crowds drawn to the spectacle of sexual violence: in this case, a large crowd has gathered to hear the mayor's speech about the successful cleaning of the River Thames, only to see the naked corpse of a young woman wash up on its banks, the latest victim of the Necktie Murderer. In his final film, *Family Plot* (1976), there is but one crowd sequence: a church congregation is thrown into confusion when Fran (Karen Black), dressed as an old widower, collapses near Bishop Wood (William Prince), who stops to give her assistance. He is joined by Arthur Adamson (William Devane), dressed as an altar server. Adamson injects the bishop with a narcotic, the bishop instantly collapses, and Adamson and Fran whisk him away while a puzzled and fumbling congregation looks on. It's a comical scene, one that demonstrates the crowd's capacity for inaction and inertia. And *Family Plot* is very much a comedy, one that relies less on grand spectacle than on the chemistry between the film's two principal stars, Barbara Harris and Bruce Dern.

Hitchcock's health had deteriorated badly enough that the filming of his next project, *The Short Night*, became impossible. But had he survived long enough to complete this project, he would have treated audiences to a deliciously Hitchcockian crowd scene. This scene occurs during a lengthy conversation between the protagonist, Joe Bailey, and Paul Zelfand, who tries to convince Joe to find and kill Gavin Brand, a man responsible for the death of forty-two people, including Joe's brother. When Joe arrives at the 21 Club in New York to meet Zelfand, the restaurant is empty save for Zelfand, who is seated at a table. In the script by Ernest Lehman, the conversation between Joe and Zelfand is a single long take following this screen direction: "During the scene, we will hear, but not see the room slowly filling up, off camera." The long take, shot 41 of the film, would surely have lasted more than four minutes. Shot 42 is a different angle of Joe abruptly leaving Zelfand, and it is a wide shot of the restaurant. The script reads, "The tables are filled now." As David Freeman, author of *The Last Days of Alfred Hitchcock*, explains it,

> Throughout the action of the scene, the off-camera tables are filling up. That means slowly building the sounds of waiters, diners, and clanking dishes in the background. The standard way to do that is just lay in a sound track of restaurant noises, soft at first, and growing louder. Not a chance. Hitch planned to hire 21's waiters, busboys, and captains, and then add to that two dozen *unseen* extras into the scene. He planned to record it all live. No sound effect tracks. In addition to the scene we've been watching, there's been the parallel action—a wholly different and competing scene—going on, off camera. The main scene—Joe and Zelfand, might be a stock one, but Hitchcock would find a way to make at least part of it interesting, even if only to himself.[37]

In this lengthy compendium I have deliberately sidestepped two of Hitchcock's important crowd films, perhaps the two most important: *Sabotage* and *North by Northwest*. Each presents us with curious examples of what is best described as a magical, even supernatural, transformative force shared by both crowds and cinema. While only the earlier film includes an actual cinema crowd, both *Sabotage* and *North by Northwest* help us understand that the relation between crowds and cinema is far too complex, far too intimate and corporeal to be reduced to the simple formulation of spectators→spectacle. What follows is a case study of a particular—and peculiar—kind of crowd sequence, in which a close association between crowds and cinema is forged, where both crowds and cinema reveal their remarkable transformative powers in a dynamic, even mythic relation. We shall see what might be called Hitchcock's *cine-mana*: a magical, supernatural cinema that merges with the crowd, shares its properties, and with characteristic fluidity diffuses in the crowd's various manifestations.

Sabotage: Hitchcock and the Moving Picture Crowd

> Who has not watched the shifting, changing panorama of the streets? The hurrying to and from, the bustling crowd? And who has not said, "I would like to see this scene again, I would like to study its many interesting phases?"
>
> —Publicity catalog for the Jenkins Phantascope (1896)

> Isn't it a fascinating design? One could study it forever.
>
> —Alfred Hitchcock, speaking to François Truffaut (1962)

Antonia Lant has pointed out that during the first decade of cinema history it was virtually impossible, due to technological limitations such as slow film stock and limited aperture control, to photograph a crowded movie theater. Only in 1907 did it become possible "to shoot a collective theater audience indoors."[38] In the interim, however, the moviegoing crowd was often the subject of "journalists, graphic artists, and painters."[39] In such representations, the movie theater audience is the very opposite of Le Bon's "unruly miscellany."[40] Indeed, it is the ideal crowd: well-behaved, respectful, quiet, attentive, and engaged. The cinema is there for the crowd, and the crowd is there for the cinema—the two come together in mutual recognition. What structures the opening moments of *Sabotage* is the very absence of alarm and uneasiness in the crowd, despite the efforts of Karl Verloc (Oskar Homolka) to create panic by putting out the lights in London with a bit of sand in the city's power generators. Rather than riot and loot, the crowds of the London Underground emerge to street level and form a comic candlelight vigil, with matchstick men grinning at their profits. In a series of four shots, we see an elderly man light a match and hold it high above his head as general laughter explodes around him; three women follow, and they too are laughing. A third shot follows two smiling women who pass a candle between them. The fourth shot is a close-up of a younger man; his face illuminated, he looks up—as if at the flickering images of some magic lantern show. Indeed, these four shots establish the necessary link to what follows: the crowd at Verloc's Bijou.

The scene begins after two establishing shots, the first being a low-angle shot of the exterior of the Bijou, followed by a high-angle shot of the crowd assembled just outside its doors. In the second, the camera singles out two nuns, their bleached white cornettes twice illuminated by a flashlight beam, and pans right to follow them. The moviegoing throng comes across as so polite that it fails to discourage the holy sisters from coming near it. Indeed, despite Mrs. Verloc's concern that the crowd is "getting nasty" and "making a terrible row," it is anything but: an older man stands at the ticket booth operated by Verloc's wife (Sylvia Sydney) and, in the quietest and most sensible of terms, asks for his money back: "I know how the law stands. You broke a contract, therefore you broke the law." Two flickering candles, one on either side of the booth, frame Mrs. Verloc, who responds to the older man, "But it's everywhere, look at the street!" A voice in the background adds, "I pay my money to look at the pictures!" Hitchcock here cuts to a man who is singing an old Irish parlor tune, "Love's Old Sweet Song." As he fiddles with his candles, we hear him sing this line: "Just a song at twilight, when the lights are low." The line that follows, "And the flickering shadows softly come and go," although not sung in the film, neatly echoes the shots immediately prior to the scene at Verloc's Bijou and affirms the idea conveyed by the opening of *Sabotage*: the natural affinity between the crowd and the cinema. Even in a London blackout, the crowd is charmed by flickers of light.[41]

Lesley Brill begins his book on crowds with this bold but exceptionally apt statement: "Movies are crowd machines."[42] The point here is not simply that the sole purpose of the film industry is to generate large moviegoing audiences. Nor is it simply that the cinema is better suited than any other form of representation—including photography—to document the crowd, to capture its psychological and social dynamics. Brill's line of thought seldom drifts far from either of these obvious points, yet he believes the relationship between crowds and the cinema is extraordinarily rich and complex, far more so than is generally acknowledged. Following the work of Elias Canetti, specifically his influential *Crowds and Power*, Brill concentrates on how movies exploit their unique technical properties to visualize metamorphosis, partly as a means of contemplating the nature of crowds: "Movies are a literal art of image-ination. Their power to transform people and the world, moreover, is directly connected with their ability to represent crowds."[43] Brill immediately turns to the choreographed routines of Busby Berkeley, specifically the closing routine in Lloyd Bacon's 1933 musical, *42nd Street*. But he devotes an entire chapter to *North by Northwest*, where he shows how transformation is catalyzed by movies' ability to create and portray crowds.[44]

Yet the relationship between crowds and cinema, as Hitchcock's films persistently demonstrate, is more complex still. While Brill is right to point out the numerous ways movies represent crowds, we should also recognize the ways crowds represent movies. To concentrate and build on Brill's general observation, I argue not only that Hitchcock's movies are "crowd machines" but, perhaps more startlingly, that Hitchcock's crowds are "movie machines." To return to the opening sequences of *Sabotage*, Hitchcock shows the relationship between crowds and movies to be dynamic, fluid, and reciprocal. When the Bijou goes dark and its crowd disperses, we see a remarkable transformation: the movie patrons gather themselves, reassemble, and produce their own flickers of light. A movie within a movie is created, as the patrons spontaneously exchange witty banter, culled straight from a "light" comedy. A detective named Ted (John Loder), who posed as a greengrocer to spy on Verloc, now poses as defense attorney for Verloc and his wife:

TED: It's an act of God, I tell you.
MAN: And what do you call an act of God?
TED: I call your face one, and you won't get your money back on that! Now if a plane were to come along and drop a bomb on you, that would be an unfriendly act within the meaning of the act. But if the juice dries up of its own accord, that's an act of providence as laid down in the act of William IV where an act is defined as any activity actuated by actual action.
WOMAN: No wonder the blinking lights went out!

And so a movie about crowds depicts crowds making a movie . . . about a crowd: Ted's rhetoric takes a sudden turn from Grouchoesque legal double-talk to crowd psychology: "You're all ignorant! Now if you take my advice, you'll go off home because there's nothing doing here. Now go on, get off." And just when we think the crowd will be separated once and for all from the cinema, Mrs. Verloc returns and offers to give everyone their money back. The crowd reassembles around the ticket booth, and as if by magic, power is restored and the Bijou fills again with patrons. The movie begins again. Or did it never really stop?

That is, could it be possible that the Bijou never really shuts off in the opening sequence of *Sabotage*? That is, what if we said the strangeness of Verloc's dilemma is not that the blackout is a failure in spite of its success (the lights go out, but the Londoners are amused rather than terrified), but that the blackout fails *because it never occurs*—or, more accurately, the blackout does *not* shut down the Bijou. Tom Cohen, in his lengthy and provocative reading of the film, suggests as much when he says (perhaps out of exasperation) that the London crowd emerging from the Underground "laugh as if they were in a movie house" (148). The alliance of crowds and cinema here is telling, and it is proved apt when, at the aquarium, Verloc says to his contact, "I hope you were satisfied with last night's show." Of course Verloc cannot in such a public place overtly mention his act of sabotage—putting out the lights in London—so in a curious bit of collusion the blackout becomes a movie screening. Such is the capacity, both human and cinematic, for transformation.

And here one might say that it is Verloc who fails to register, fails to read or experience or respond.[45] "It's not my fault they're such fools," he says. His contact reminds him, "Londoners are not fools. They laughed because they realized what happened was laughable. They did right to laugh."[46] This newsflash shakes Verloc to the core, and Bijou owner that he is, he projects onto the glass of the aquarium tank a preview of coming attractions. In a stunning display of the transformative power of cinema, the crowded aquarium tank dissolves into a movie screen, on which we see the crowded London streets of Piccadilly Circus—"the center of the world" (figures 1.3–1.5). The image of the giant Bovril sign is something of a Hitchcock signature during his

Figure 1.3. *Sabotage* aquarium scene: The aquarium

Figure 1.4. *Sabotage* aquarium scene: Becoming Piccadilly

Figure 1.5. *Sabotage* aquarium scene: Cinema as transformation

British years—twice before, this same crowded scene has appeared in his films: in *Blackmail*, when Alice White wanders the city at night after having killed her rapist, and in *Downhill*, after Roddy Berwick completes his own dazed, nocturnal perambulation. Here, now in broad daylight (another failed blackout?), we hear a thudding explosion, and the crowd in Piccadilly Circus slowly decomposes into its inherent nitrate film base, then becomes a crowd once more: a school of fish. Hitchcock's love of a good dirty joke is well known, and here he dedicates this moment of dazzling cinematic transformation with a telling one-liner: A young boy, hoping to impress his date, says, "This bivalve's rate of fertility is extremely high. After laying a million eggs, the female oyster changes her sex." To which his date replies, "Hmph! I don't blame her."

Roger Thornhill: A Man of the Crowd

> Would it not be strange, in a city of seven million people, if one man were *never* mistaken for another . . . if, with seven million pairs of feet wandering through the canyons and corridors of the city, one pair of feet *never* by chance strayed into the wrong footsteps? Strange, indeed.
>
> —Ernest Lehman, unused narration from the shooting script of *North by Northwest*

The opening of *North by Northwest* gives us perhaps the best example of just how crowded a Hitchcock film can be. One might argue that its first four and a half minutes, which strikingly resembles the opening sequence of *Rich and Strange*, tells the tale of the man of the crowd. Lesley Brill describes Roger Thornhill, perhaps Hitchcock's best-known man of the crowd, as "at once a member of crowds and their master. . . . In each role, Thornhill depends upon crowds for much of his identity. Among them he is comfortable, commanding, and safe. When he is threatened with assassination at the auction, he engineers his escape by joining and then manipulating the gathered crowd of bidders."[47] Thornhill is at his best when people surround him. And if there are no people to be found, things and places will do. To be sure, one of the most intriguing features about *North by Northwest*, and Hitchcock's films in general, is that "things" function less as pointless props than as nonhuman agents—or, in Bruno Latour's term, "actants." The matchbook, the crop duster, the newspaper—these are Hitchcockian objects. And *North by Northwest* makes memorable use of some pretty remarkable places as well, such as Prairie Stop, Highway 41, the United Nations building, and Mount Rushmore. The things and places Thornhill needs most, however, are the things and places that most resemble the crowd. "Crowds," argues Brill, "appear in *North by Northwest* almost continuously. Even in such isolated settings as Prairie Stop and the top of Mount Rushmore monument they are present by proxy."[48] Standing in for actual crowds, such locations become what Elias Canetti calls "crowd symbols." Thornhill will take refuge in some of these crowd symbols, such as the pine forest. He will also find safety in numbers when he dives into the rows of corn during the crop-dusting sequence: "When the attacking airplane descends on Thornhill like a giant hawk, how does this man of crowds respond? He flees into a field of standing corn, hoping to lose himself among the massed stalks."[49]

One crowd symbol that Brill does not mention but which is, as I argue in chapter 2, impossible to ignore in Hitchcock's crowd scenes is the newspaper, which Roger Thornhill stops to purchase in the film's opening sequence. As he and his assistant, Maggie, make their way through the crowd, we see people brush alongside Thornhill, across and in front of his path, and to his left and right. They stream past him, gushing forward like roaring rapids. Not the fastest man of the crowd, Thornhill is nevertheless the steadiest and the surest. And the instant Maggie asks to take a taxi, the two are already halfway out of choppy and uncertain waters. To snatch a taxi from a fellow bystander, Thornhill uses his newspaper, now folded in his hand, like a shield and pushes away the man in a *faux* act of chivalry: "I have a very sick woman here—you don't mind, do you?" In fact, everything about Thornhill—his attitude, his words, the way he moves through the crowd—suggests that he is a man protected by armor or, more accurately, a stimulus shield. To use Georg Simmel's term, Roger Thornhill is the epitome of the blasé attitude.[50]

Once inside the taxi, Thornhill opens the newspaper and gives it more of his attention, which leads the viewer to half-suspect Thornhill is struck by an ad for a weight-reduction product (Reduco?), for his next words are "Do I look heavyish? I feel heavyish." He then asks his secretary to jot down his new motto: "Think thin." One is also led to half-suspect that Thornhill cannot stop thinking about his work. He appears to be studying the newspaper, perhaps analyzing the effectiveness of its advertising. Better still: like the ideal consumer his own copy aims at, he is *processing* newspaper advertising. Or maybe Thornhill is simply illustrating Bruno Latour's point that, for the modern man, reading the daily newspaper is another form of prayer.[51] At any rate, one can hardly say Thornhill is actually *reading* the newspaper; rather, he scans the crowded columns of the *New York World-Telegram* not unlike the way he strides through the crowded sidewalks of Manhattan. As David M. Henkin notes, speaking of the rise of the public newspaper in antebellum New York, "Perusing the columns of the major dailies resembled and paralleled walking down the city's major thoroughfares."[52] If one suspects this point's relevance to Manhattan during the Cold War, one need only consider Henkin's subsequent observation, made only a few lines later, and ponder its relevance to the adventures not only of Roger Thornhill, but of Marion Crane, Marnie Edgar, Melanie Daniels, and a host of other Hitchcock figures who trade risk and reward as they pass through the crowded Hitchcock landscape: "Like streets, news sheets were spaces in which anonymous strangers could gain easy access to information, make quick public impressions, expose themselves to the gaze of others (a gaze that is itself implicated obliquely in the scandalousness of the gesture), and expect to meet one another again."[53] Given the confidence with which Thornhill strolls through streets and sheets, one can be forgiven for assuming, when the taxi arrives at the Plaza Hotel at Fifth Avenue and 59th Street and Thornhill jumps out, that his sudden turn back to the taxi, which has already pulled away, is because he realizes he has left behind his newspaper. With his guard now suddenly down, Thornhill is vulnerable to anything—like a good kidnapping.[54] Unless Thornill can find a crowd to join, he doesn't have a prayer.

Brill's reading of *North by Northwest* is attractive—particularly when he points to features of Hitchcock's film that have eluded critics for too long. For example, Brill notes how critics have drawn a stark contrast between the bustling streets of Manhattan that open the film and the desolation of the Prairie Stop sequence, failing to consider the latter as an extension of the film's opening: "Viewing this sequence with an eye to its crowd symbols also brings into focus its harmony with other actions and enriches our understanding of its underlying logic. The regular geometry of fields and fence posts echoes the architectural lines already associated with crowds."[55]

Although Brill is right to focus his attention on how crowds and crowd symbols saturate the film, I argue that they are more than mere *subjects* of the film. Even within the film's first few minutes, the viewer of *North by Northwest* is struck full force by the strange association of crowds and cinema. The opening shot of the film, the façade of a building upon which are superimposed the opening credits, designed by Saul Bass, is perhaps the single most representative image of this alliance. It is not surprising, then, that the shot is reminiscent of a film made by another great crowd director, King Vidor. After giving us a bird's-eye view of the busy New York streets in the opening of his 1928 film *The Crowd*, Vidor superimposes crowd images, creating what Andrew Uroskie calls "an unrecognizable visual cacophony."[56] Vidor then gives us another superimposition,

> this time of a busy intersection, where ghosted cars and pedestrians seem to pass through one another unscathed. Yet as Vidor's camera pans right, we see this cacophony was simply the result of an intervening windowpane, casting reflections from another street. The street ahead is relatively clear and orderly, its perceived chaos merely the result of an intervening screen.[57]

Hence the opening shot of *North by Northwest*: the busy, congested street below with its ghosted cars and pedestrians reflected in the façade of a glass building. Like the shot of crowded Piccadilly Circus reflected on the aquarium glass and becoming melting film stock, the opening credits assert even more explicitly the idea that, in Hitchcock, not only are movies crowd machines and crowds movie machines, but often one cannot tell one from the other.

For what, exactly, is the "intervening screen" here? Recall that, after the appearance of the MGM logo (drained of all color but green—as if we were all a bit still hungover from *Vertigo*), the screen goes blank. Green still, but now with lines appearing diagonally from the upper right corner and crisscrossing (south by southwest, oddly enough) with lines moving up from the bottom. The effect is one of engineering or architecture, an odd visual amalgam of blueprint (green print) sketches and construction beams. A third element is introduced when the words *Metro-Goldwyn-Mayer Presents* emerge from below, hoisted up like a cable elevator. The words align almost perfectly with the crisscrossing beams, as if fitted with a drawing ruler. The unusual angle of the lines and text is disorienting—it calls attention to itself as a movie screen but one not set to our vantage point. The uncanny effect is that we are watching a movie being projected *in* this movie, or *on* this movie. After a sixth credit emerges ("In Alfred Hitchcock's"), the title of the film appears. Then the green screen gives way to what seems like a reflection of a crowded urban street. Our instincts were correct: what has been forming before our eyes for the past several seconds is a skyscraper, a cathedral to the urban crowd. And onto it, a movie is projected. Or is it the other way around? Common sense suggests that what has been forming is the movie itself, *North by Northwest*, producing—green-screening—images of a crowded city street behind its opening credits. Yet it cannot be seen purely as one or the other, a movie emerging from a crowd or a crowd emerging from a movie.

The crowd scenes that follow the film's opening credits are no less confounding, and we don't have to wait for Thornhill's kidnapping to feel the strangeness of *North by Northwest*'s crowds. Before and just after Hitchcock's cameo appearance, Hitchcock repeats a shot of people entering and exiting a building (once at approximately 00:01:45, and again at 00:02:12). That this repeated shot has, as far as I can tell, gone unnoticed except by one other critic and me is not surprising. We are not meant to notice it, any more than we are supposed to notice the striking similarity between what we see at a crowded intersection (say, Madison Avenue and 60th Street) from one instant to the next. Standing across the street from the C.I.T. Financial Building during its busiest hours, would we be able to say with any certainty whatsoever that we did not see the exact same person exit its front door more than once? In spite of its seeming innocuousness, the repeated shot prompts further scrutiny of the entire sequence. The first time the shot appears, the standard Hollywood disclaimer can be read across it: "The events, characters and firms depicted in this photoplay are fictitious. Any similarity to actual persons, living or dead, or to actual firms, is purely coincidental." This disclaimer, I argue, has the unnerving effect of putting into question any possibility of it being pure coincidence that, less than thirty seconds later, similar persons (living? dead?) can be seen entering and exiting a similar firm. And yet if we are to take the disclaimer's claim seriously—that any similarity, from one shot to the next, of actual persons and firms is purely coincidental—then we are free to assume that what we apprehend in both shots are not similar people but the same people, buzzing in and out of the same firm.

How to explain this? If we examine closely the shots of the opening sequence, we find that a curious loop effect is created: in one shot, taken at street level, we see a crowd of workers exiting a building onto the busy sidewalk; in the next shot, taken from above, we watch as people descend a stairwell that takes them below street level; in the next shot, taken at street level, we see people crossing a busy intersection; in the next shot, taken from a building interior, we watch as people descend stairs.[58] A few seconds later, after we watch two women fight over a cab and then Hitchcock miss his bus, we see repeated the shot with which the sequence began. Or is it not a repeated shot? Is it possible that this is simply repeated action? Are the people who crowd the streets and offices of Manhattan stuck in a rut (or R.O.T.), trapped in a cinematic spool that forever projects them walking out of their buildings, through the streets, down subterranean stairwells that take them back up to their buildings, from which they once again are sucked, only to descend once more and be pumped back up again?[59] Are the two older women locked in a perpetual struggle for the same taxi? And is the director condemned to miss the bus for the rest of eternity? And, most interestingly, is Roger Thornhill doomed to be kidnapped over and over and over again? Or am I but mad north-north-west?[60]

There is at least one critic who might prove me sane: Sara Blair spots the loop as well. In her essay, "Hitchcock on Location: America, Icons, and the Place of Illusion," she notes how the opening sequence of *North by Northwest* functions to establish the spatial systems of the film. Further, in a note that gives more detail of Saul Bass's title design, Blair points to the relation between crowds and cinema that I am trying to establish here: "Not only is the city here a space of image-making; it is itself inseparable from the image of the world it creates. Indeed, the façade of the building becomes a surface for the projection of moving images of city life on the streets below."[61] It is here that she points out the odd loop, the repetition of the shot of people leaving a building of unknown location. Interestingly, Blair does not dismiss the loop as sloppiness, as evidence of Hitchcock's failure to get enough coverage for the title sequence. Rather, she reads the loop as a crowd effect: she invokes two theorists of urban modernity—Georg Simmel and Walter Benjamin—and their suggestions "that cinema not only captures the felt effects of urban experience but shapes the very act of perception to its own rhythms and intensities."[62] The loop, then, is not an error on George Tomasini's part (or Saul Bass's); rather, the loop alludes to the extraordinary impressions of the urban experience: of the doppelgänger, the chance encounter, the fleeting glimpse, the touch of the unknown. One might add to Blair's short list a third theorist, Siegfried Kracauer, who went farthest in associating the cinematic effect with the modern, urban crowd. For Kracauer, the crowd is the ideal subject, "the very meat," of cinema.[63] But Kracauer saw the association as much more complex than this.

Interestingly, Kracauer often spoke of the crowd in protocinematic terms. The Paris crowds of Baudelaire's *Les fleurs du mal*, for instance, "function as stimuli which call forth irritating kaleidoscopic sensations."[64] For Kracauer, the crowd is by its very nature cinematic. Not simply in the sense that the modern, urban crowd is the cinema's perfect subject—which it is: the medium is uniquely equipped to capture street life, that "unfixable flow which carries fearful uncertainties and alluring excitements."[65] But this is just to say that the cinema is *photogenic* in the most mundane sense, and Kracauer sees the relationship between cinema and crowds as more complex. To be more precise, the properties of the cinema and the properties of the crowd share certain "affinities." They form a bond, a marriage; they are blood relations; they share a chemical attraction; they form a compound.[66] For Kracauer, as Graeme Gilloch notes,

> both film and city are the manifestations of the modern collective unconscious. This is the key to their elective affinity. The 'architecture of the instant,' the unconscious patterns and constellations formed out of the crowds, traffic, lights and colours of the city, these unconscious phenomena are what fascinated Kracauer, and film is the medium which brings the content of the unconscious, of the city, of its makers, of its spectators, to light.[67]

Crowds, cinema, and the phantasmagoria that make up our experiences of each, form what Gollich elsewhere calls a "thematic constellation." It is, Gollich says, central to Kracauer's work.[68] And I am arguing here that this "thematic constellation" is central to Hitchcock's work as well.

Thus to fully understand Hitchcock's fascination with crowds, one cannot limit one's analysis to crowd scenes—though, as I demonstrated earlier in this chapter, crowd scenes proliferate throughout his career. But as I have also demonstrated, Hitchcock was attracted not simply to crowds but to the act of crowding—invading another's territory, applying a kind of intense emotional pressure in confined spaces. Further, to again use Lesley Brill's term, Hitchcock's films create a landscape of crowd symbols, such as the newspaper, which, if one follows its tangled journey through so many of Hitchcock's films, reveals itself to be always something other than itself, something like the phantasmagoric.

There is more to be said of Hitchcock's newspaper—indeed, there is more to be said of a countless number of nonhuman agents that not-so-secretly operate in the Hitchcock landscape.[69] As we see in the following chapter, the newspaper—the very emblem of the crowd—is a privileged object in Hitchcock's films. What is required is a way of treating Hitchcock's objects as much more social, much more involved in the course of action than previously thought. The repertoire of actors in Hitchcock's films includes not just Cary Grant, Grace Kelly, Ingrid Bergman, and Jimmy Stewart, but also the newspapers and house keys, the train compartments and women's purses, the chickens and the eggs, the dogs and the birds. Perhaps Hitchcock was not being smug at all: maybe actors *are* like cattle. But this, as Hitchcock insisted, is by no means an insult. Perhaps we can learn from Hitchcock and open our critical allegiances to include not simply persons of interest but all matter in motion. In doing so, we may find that our view of the social changes in ways that are both instructive and frightening. Instructive because we can now trace social connections in Hitchcock's films that have been ignored. Frightening, as Bruno Latour might suggest, because such a journey will not be "risk-free" and "smooth." But is there a better way to describe the Hitchcock landscape than this? A world of "risky attachments and tangled objects"?[70]

Chapter 2

✦

Hitchcock's Newspaper

A Thing of the Crowd

In an illustration by the well-known English caricaturist Philip William May, *Man Reading Newspaper in Crowd* (figure 2.1), we see a corpulent gentleman, sporting a top hat and carrying under his arm an umbrella, holding in two hands a rather fat newspaper whose bulky sheets threaten to envelop a young boy.[1] Given its substantial dimensions, we can safely assume the gentleman's newspaper is not a penny daily. Easily twenty-four inches wide, the newspaper is very likely a respectable six-penny journal—not exactly the sort of newspaper one spreads wide open in a crowd, hence the look on the young boy's face, which seems to betray slight surprise at the gentleman's unmindfulness. This comic scenario reminds us that the newspaper is the very emblem of the modern urban crowd. Sold in sidewalk newsstands, purchased by bus and railway passengers, and left discarded in the streets, where it is picked up again, the newspaper is found wherever there are crowds. Further, the newspaper layout itself creates a kind of crowd effect: its stories are crammed into columns that stand shoulder to shoulder and give to the physically dislocated and radically separate events they depict the illusion of order, coherence, and simultaneity. As Philip Fisher puts it, "The front page of the newspaper is itself a crowd, a mass of individuals who remain strangers to one another."[2] Further, the shape of the newspaper is always changing. It can be folded, rolled up tightly, even ripped apart. And when the newspaper is opened fully in a crowd, its presence is not only seen but felt. Consider in addition to May's illustration, the opening scene of Alfred Hitchcock's *Rich and Strange* (1932), when, with umbrella under arm, Fred Hill opens his newspaper on a crowded train, much to the visible irritation of his fellow passengers.

Or turn to our second image (figure 2.2), from Hitchcock's *Foreign Correspondent* (1940), which bears comparing with May's illustration. In it we see a similarly rotund man, also reading a newspaper, making his way through the crowded city (whose streets will be teeming, moments later, with umbrellas). Of course, the two images are not without significant differences—the

Figure 2.1. Philip William May, *Man Reading Newspaper in Crowd*

Figure 2.2. Hitchcock's cameo in *Foreign Correspondent*

most notable of which is that this second man is unmistakably a man of the cinema: he is the director himself, making his customary cameo appearance. And it cannot pass unnoticed that his newspaper is making its own cameo (in a film that takes the newspaper as its subject) at the moment of a rather obvious process shot. The use of rear projection, however much a studio technique, is one of Hitchcock's better-known signature effects. Hitchcock does not appear in the projection itself but in front of it, just as he does for his cameo in *Stage Fright* (1950). However, there is another man reading a newspaper who does appear in the projection, thus creating an odd doubling effect. Further, this particular cameo calls to mind another: from *Lifeboat* (1944), in which Hitchcock can be seen on a sheet of newspaper, hawking the "obesity slayer" Reduco.[3] There are two images of Hitchcock in this newspaper: the first image is as his former, fatter self; the second as a slimmer, sadder self. The cameo itself is a mini-story, told in pictures.[4] In *Foreign Correspondent*, Hitchcock is not in a crowd, though one is projected behind him while he reads a newspaper. In *Lifeboat*, Hitchcock is not in the film but is projected onto a newspaper.

A strange association is established: the crowd, the newspaper, and the cinema. It is an alliance forged as early as Hitchcock's first films, though we have yet to take the full measure of its strength, its durability as a central trope in Hitchcock's work. In one of the few essays to make note of Hitchcock's use of newspapers, Ina Rae Hark focuses on *Foreign Correspondent*, *Saboteur* (1942), and *Lifeboat*. As we shall see, however, the newspaper's presence is everywhere in Hitchcock, from *The Lodger* (1926) to *Frenzy* (1972). Thus, unlike other well-known objects in his work, such as the lighter in *Strangers on a Train* (1951), the newspaper is not limited to a single film.[5] Further, Hark deemphasizes the newspaper as such to stress what it is meant to invoke: the democratic freedom of the press and the threats posed to it by the rise of fascism. Even as she maintains that the newspaper is a privileged object throughout Hitchcock's career, she sees its function within his work as habitually narrative: "A newspaper's displaying a front-page photo of a wrongly accused man is a recurring trope, both before, during, and after the war years. In this regard newspapers err by regarding the ever-bumbling legal authorities as competent."[6] Treating the newspaper as a "metonymy for the functioning of democratic governments" or assigning it a plot function, Hark largely neglects the close interaction, both perceptual and tactile, between the newspaper and its handlers.[7]

It is true that Hitchcock's newspaper is something to read (for us as well as the characters in the film). *The 39 Steps* and *North by Northwest* give us two of the more memorable examples of such a newspaper (in the former, Hannay spots the story of Annabella Smith's murder on the train as a fellow passenger eyes him suspiciously; in the latter we see a photo of a knife-wielding Thornhill underneath a headline reading, "Diplomat Slain at U.N."). What is interesting in Hitchcock's films is the way their plots keep appearing in newspaper headlines and columns, almost always in distorted form (we know better, or think we know better, based on what we're privileged to witness). Even more interesting, however, is that Hitchcock's newspaper gets considerable hands-on attention. It is treated as more than a receptacle of narrative information: it is reshaped and torn apart, scratched, rolled up, used as a disguise, as a shield, as a telescope. In other words, Hitchcock's newspaper is enigmatic; often when it does appear, it appears not just as a newspaper but as something else as well. When, for instance, in *Psycho* (1960), Marion Crane buys a newspaper in a vending machine at California Charlie's used car dealership, the newspaper first appears to be nothing more than itself—a social product not at all out of place, or what Bruno Latour calls "a matter of fact." Then the newspaper begins to change. By the time Marion arrives at the Bates Motel, the newspaper is no longer just a newspaper; it has been altered, recontextualized. Now the newspaper is what Latour calls "a matter of concern."[8] Marion wraps what is left of the stolen $40,000 inside the newspaper—the very place she looks to find news of her crime. The link between Marion and her newspaper becomes even stronger moments later, when Norman (Anthony Perkins) wraps Marion's corpse in the shower curtain. Now evidence of Norman's crime, Marion herself must be wrapped up and hidden from view. Both she and her newspaper are placed in the trunk of her car and sent to the bottom of the swamp. Think, too, of the newspaper in *Shadow of a Doubt* (1943). Like the ring that is exchanged between Uncle Charlie (Joseph Cotten) and his niece, the newspaper circulates. But unlike the ring, the newspaper is in a state of continuous variation. As it passes from Mr. Newton, to Emma (Patricia Collinge), to Uncle Charlie, then to Charlie, it undergoes changes: first it is the dependable home newspaper, then it is ripped apart, then it is folded into a toy barn, and finally it resurfaces intact in the Santa Rosa Public Library.

What follows in this chapter is an attempt to recall that thing of the crowd, the Hitchcock newspaper, to keep it front and center and not allow it to "disappear into the messages it transmits."[9] We cannot know too much about this singularly unusual Hitchcock thing, and it is the purpose of this chapter to determine its many vocations, not just its most prominent ones. One might argue that one of the newspaper's vocations is to act as a front for none other than Hitchcock's camera—for its "murderous gaze," to use William Rothman's well-known phrase. Like Hitchcock's camera, the newspaper is a harbinger of violence and death.[10] We often spot the newspaper at murderous moments in Hitchcock's films. In *Rear Window* (1954), Jeff uses a pair of binoculars to spy on Lars Thorwald (Raymond Burr), who is seen standing before his kitchen sink, wrapping a saw and a large knife in a newspaper. But as this example suggests, we can link the newspaper not only with murder, but with technologies of surveillance and spectacle (not simply because Jeff (James Stewart) is spying on Thorwald but also because he is a photojournalist).[11] The newspaper is indeed murderous, but again like

Hitchcock's camera, it is also spying, scrutinizing, knowing, dissimulating, and dissembling. For this reason, we ought to consider the many ways the newspaper functions at critical moments in Hitchcock's films, to attend to its conspicuous visibility and, as importantly, to its shape-shifting materiality.[12]

I'd like to begin this journey with one of Hitchcock's most unusual crowd scenes in which a newspaper figures prominently. It comes from *Marnie* (1964), at the Atlantic City Race Course, where Marnie unexpectedly encounters a man in the crowd, a stranger from her past. The scene begins with a curious sequence of shots. The first is a medium close-up of the unidentified man (Milton Seltzer). Behind him are spectators fitted with a variety of ocular prosthetics: not just the usual ones, such as eyeglasses and sunglasses, but binoculars as well. We don't know what the stranger, who stands front and center in the frame, is looking at, but he is most certainly not looking at the race. We think he is looking at Marnie, who has come to the racetrack with Mark Rutland (Sean Connery). However, in the reverse shot that follows, which we can only assume is the stranger's point of view, neither Marnie nor Mark can be seen in the crowd. We cut back to the stranger, to find him holding a most unusual ocular prosthetic: a tightly rolled-up newspaper that he holds up to his right eye and looks through (figure 2.3). The next shot, again his point of view, is through the newspaper, which forms a slightly misshaped iris through which we see Marnie seated at a table watching the race (figure 2.4).[13] Across from her is Mark, who is looking through a pair of binoculars. There are a number of striking things about this particular shot. First, Marnie is seen turning around, away from the track, looking almost directly into the camera. What gets her attention is unclear, though one suspects she has the feeling of being watched—there is, after all, a small army of lookers behind her, and one half-wonders if others might be also not watching the race.

What is more striking is the telescopic effect the rolled-up newspaper produces. Marnie and Mark are seen much too close up compared with our previous point-of-view shot. The newspaper doesn't appear to be hiding a telescope, so how is it possible that it could produce such a view? This is not as odd a question as it seems, for the power of the newspaper is frequently given ocular, even protocinematic, qualities. As early as 1838, Galpin and Sturtevant's penny daily, *The Age*, claimed that a small sheet of newspaper is like "a camera obscura, which gives you the objects that pass before it the smallest possible compass, and yet in full perfection."[14] Consider, too, Frederick Knight Hunt, who, in 1850, writes: "The newspaper is a great mental camera, which throws a picture of the whole world upon a single sheet of paper."[15] What is unusual about these metaphors—the newspaper as camera obscura, the newspaper as *mens mentis obscura*—is that in spite of their conceptual clarity, they do little to help us understand how, technically not figuratively, these newspapers work in such a way. Hunt's metaphor is barely interpretable. Is the newspaper both camera and projector? This seems to be the image Hunt asks us to see. But the newspaper is also a single sheet

Figure 2.3. *Marnie*: The stranger's newspaper

Figure 2.4. *Marnie*: The newspaper as telescope

of paper, upon which the picture it records and projects is printed. Like the Lumières' *cinématographe*, the newspaper is capable of undergoing multiple transfigurations: it is camera, printer, and projector all in one. And yet the newspaper is somehow more: though protocinematic, it has no technical properties, no moving parts—or, more precisely, its moving parts are found in a great mind, a collective brain. As Gerald Stanley Lee put it in 1913, the newspaper is both "mass machine" and "crowd thinker."[16] If Hunt's description of the newspaper wasn't baffling enough, consider Lee's newspaper: it is a moving picture produced by crowds.

Hence the most striking thing of all in this scene from *Marnie*: the newspaper held by the stranger is more than just impossibly telescopic, for it seems to produce Marnie and Mark out of thin air. If we are to trust the first reverse shot, Marnie and Mark are not in the stranger's line of view. The image we view through the newspaper is the visual equivalent of a non sequitur: this view of Marnie and Mark does not follow. Yet we are all the more confident that the stranger does indeed see the two, for he then approaches their table. After Mark leaves to place a bet on the horse Lemon Pudding, we cut to a shot of Marnie, seated alone at the table. The stranger enters from the left, but we do not see his face, as it is out of frame. All we see of him is his torso, in front of which he carries the rolled-up newspaper. Fingering the newspaper with his right hand, he asks, "Pardon me, but you're Peggy Nicholson, aren't you?" Marnie is visibly rattled, but it is not clear who rattles her more: the stranger or the man of whom he speaks, a Frank Abernathy ("You remember Frank," he croons). Why is the newspaper so prominent at the beginning of this exchange? Why do we not see the stranger's face? And why, more importantly, is he holding the newspaper like that, middle and ring finger in the hole, gratuitously to the point of stylization? It hardly matters that, in a subsequent shot, he switches fingers (to index and middle); the point is that he is fingering this newspaper while probing this Miss Nicholson person.

When Mark returns to the table, we expect him to put the matter to rest. Yet he only adds to the confusion—about the identity not simply of the stranger (who simply should be dismissed as a pest) but of the woman as well. Marnie asks the stranger to leave, and he responds, "Aw, come on now, honey, you're trying to pull my leg, aren't you?" At this moment Mark interrupts the awkward exchange:

> MARK: Now why should any young lady want to pull your leg?
> STRANGER: Oh, sorry. I thought I recognized this lady.
> With these words, the stranger begins to gently stroke the inside of the newspaper with his two fingers.
> MARK: [to Marnie] Did he recognize you?
> MARNIE: No.
> MARK: [to Stranger] You did not recognize her.
> STRANGER: I said I thought I recognized her. I said I'm sorry.

A curious line of questioning here: rather than assure the stranger that the young lady is not pulling his leg, is pulling no one's leg, is not a leg puller, Mark instead asks the stranger why any young lady should want to pull his leg. It seems Mark is suggesting that the stranger is an ugly little man that no young lady would want to look at, much less touch. Yet Mark is, in effect, also telling the stranger, "Excuse me, but the young lady is pulling my leg, not yours." Mark then turns to ask Marnie, "Did he recognize you?" But why does Mark not ask the more likely (or more appropriate) question in a situation such as this: "Do you recognize him?" It's as if Mark is determined to rid Marnie of the obnoxious stranger without letting her off the hook. But if Mark's question is misdirected, Marnie's response is practically self-incriminating ("He thought he did, but he was mistaken" would be the best defense). By responding no, Marnie leaves open the possibility that she is someone to be recognized by a stranger. Mark's final remark to the stranger, "You did not recognize her," hardly puts the matter to rest. Quite the opposite: Mark has more or less implied the following: "You did recognize her, but perhaps you had better pretend you did not." Thus what the stranger's newspaper zeroes in on (literally, as it creates an iris effect in figure 2.4) is Marnie. In doing so, the newspaper shows us the considerable danger Marnie is in by having so many identities. One danger, of course, is that by having multiple identities she has no identity at all. This danger becomes lethal if we consider the real possibility that having no identity means any man could have his way with her and suffer no consequences. It doesn't matter to the stranger that she does not answer to the name Peggy Nicholson. Indeed, this gives him all the more reason to keep probing, to keep fingering. It takes a final threat of violence from Mark to put the stranger away for good. In probing too deeply, the stranger presses his luck.

There is another newspaper in this film, one that is visually linked not only with the stranger's newspaper but with the suggestive line of questioning that comes with it—and not just the stranger's line of questioning but Mark's. Earlier in the film, we see a different finger gently stroking the inside of a newspaper, and it is Marnie's. She is scanning the classified ads of the *Philadelphia Inquirer*, searching for a position as payroll clerk. In one column we see multiple female occupations stacked one upon the other: seamstresses, pantry workers, receptionists. Next to it is another column, this one full of ads for housekeepers. The newspaper has a hundred empty positions, all of them waiting to be occupied. It is the woman with no identity who can fill them all, and this is exactly what raises the threat of violence that Marnie faces in a crowd of watchers—a threat made very clear on her newspaper's front page. We get a good look at it when Marnie emerges from Pennsylvania Station and walks toward the camera. She pauses, and we see the newspaper in her right hand in perfect balance with her purse, which she clutches under her left arm. As is the case with so many newspapers in Hitchcock's films, this one cannot pass unnoticed. Indeed, we are meant to read its headline:

"Crash Kills 118." This headline predicts Marnie's own literal crash, when her beloved horse, Forio, trips over the wall and throws Marnie to the ground. But Marnie's newspaper is also linked to the stranger's, which is rolled into a magic telescope through which we probe the woman with multiple identities—though perhaps not as many as 118. Further, the stranger's newspaper links the stranger to Mark, whose baffling line of questioning can hardly be considered a gallant effort to ward off cruel and hurtful watchers. Mark may be humiliating the nosy pervert, but he is also exposing himself as a somewhat sleazy correspondent. Mark also probes the mystery that is Marnie, and his probing is more persistent, and more cruel, than the stranger's. To be sure, if there is a hint of sexual violence in the stranger's line of questioning, it is Mark who carries out the violence.[17]

As strange as these scenes from *Marnie* seem, they are by no means the only scenes in Hitchcock in which the newspaper plays multiple roles in the modern, urban crowd—as a thing to be read, a thing both probed and probing. We may recall a similar scene in *Notorious* (1946), in which Devlin (Cary Grant) and Alicia, also at a racetrack, are spied by a jealous Alex Sebastian (Claude Rains). From high above in the box seating, he is looking through a pair of binoculars while his mother sits next to him pretending to read a newspaper. One might argue, of course, that Mme Sebastian (Leopoldine Konstantin) is reading the newspaper, and that the newspaper is nothing more than what it appears to be. This is why we feel Alicia is at least partially safe as she speaks in confidence with Devlin: the two aren't being watched. But we later learn, when Alicia does, that they are being watched. This casts some doubt as to whether Mrs. Sebastian's newspaper, like Alex's binoculars, is being employed for the most obvious of means. In the movies we can almost always spot the spy: he's the one reading the newspaper. I have in mind *Topaz* (1969), in which spies read newspapers and also pretend to read newspapers as they spy. Think, too, of the scene in *North by Northwest* outside the cafeteria at Mount Rushmore National Monument. The Professor (Leo G. Carroll) is sitting and reading a newspaper while Roger Thornhill stands next to him, looking through binoculars at the crowded face of Mount Rushmore. Of course, the Professor isn't really reading the newspaper.[18] He is using the paper to disguise the fact that he is carrying on a conversation with his newly enlisted spy.

Perhaps the most famous newspaper of all in Hitchcock is the newspaper at the Newton family home in *Shadow of a Doubt*. The question when we consider this newspaper becomes "What is the social connection between a home newspaper and the city newspaper and, more generally, between the home and the urban crowd?" Indeed, no newspaper in Hitchcock undergoes more change, attains more significance, moves more deceptively, or travels more distance than the *Santa Rosa Republican*.

The newspaper in *Shadow of a Doubt* foregrounds a combination of visibility and vulnerability that is in tension with Hitchcock's complex and ambivalent understanding of crowds. Uncle Charlie's great blunder is in failing to appreciate the enigmatic power of the newspaper: he rips out an incriminating story from his brother-in-law's evening newspaper—a column about the Merry Widow Murderer—in the mistaken belief that this will give him cover. But reading the newspaper is not always a private, solitary activity, as it is for Joe Newton. It can also be, as Ann (Edna May Wonacott) will remind her older sister, very public. Despite the Newton family rule that the newspaper belongs to Joe and to no one else ("You've got Papa's paper," says Roger [Charles Bates] to Uncle Charlie, to which his sister Charlie adds, "You know that's Father's newspaper"), a copy of each daily edition of the *Santa Rosa Republican* can be accessed from the archives of the library. Uncle Charlie's private act of concealment is pointless because the story is already in public view. The newspapers in *Shadow of a Doubt* remind us that Santa Rosa is not a closed-off little world, blissfully ignorant of and free from the urban nightmares of its larger neighbors. As many critics have noted, Hitchcock's film exploits elements of film noir, a style we associate with films that take place in big cities (New York, San Francisco, Los Angeles). Robin Wood insists in his celebrated reading of this film that we attend to its thematic oppositions: "The 'innocence' of small town American life; the apparent opposition of that innocence to a corrupt, perverted, and dangerous 'under-world.'" And Wood goes farther: like David Lynch's *Blue Velvet* (1988), Hitchcock's film reveals that "innocence" and the "under-world" "are in fact intimately interrelated and interdependent."[19] I will show here that it is the newspaper that links the small town with the underworld—or, more precisely, with its underworld. When night falls, Santa Rosa gets perverted and corrupted. But it also gets very crowded.

The first newspaper we see in the film is not, it so happens, the *Santa Rosa Republican*. We catch a glimpse of an unnamed newspaper early in the very first scene in the film. We can't tell what newspaper it is because we can't see enough of it, nor may we even hazard a guess since we don't know what city we are in. All we know is that we are in a dark and shabby room in a boarding house. It is likely we are in Philadelphia, the place Charlie remembers being her uncle's last city of residence. Yet it is just as likely that her uncle has moved on. Indeed, we may never know where we are in this opening scene or what newspaper Uncle Charlie has next him on the bedstand.[20] But we do know this: stacked upon that newspaper is a wad of cash—the money he has stolen from the Merry Widows he has murdered—so large that some of it has tumbled to the floor below. Also on the newspaper is a bottle of water, two glasses, an ashtray, an open wallet, and a few of Uncle Charlie's personal effects: the very clues to the Merry Widow Murderer's identity that the newspaper seeks. We know Uncle Charlie is on the run, and now we begin to sense that it is just a matter of time before a story of the Merry Widow Murderer breaks.

At first glance, the Newton family newspaper, the *Santa Rosa Republican*, seems unaware of the Merry Widow murders, occupied as it is with news of the war. We first see it lying flat on the bookshelf near the front door, as

Joe goes to grab it. It's in his hands for no more than eight seconds before Emma snatches it from him and gives it to her little brother. During this brief moment, one can barely make out its headline, "New Major Sea Battle in Solomons as Japanese Attack" (which suggests the film takes place sometime during the first six months of 1942). At this point, the *Santa Rosa Republican* is nothing more than a typical newspaper, a fixture in Joe's after-dinner habits. But as soon as it is in Uncle Charlie's hands, it begins its transformation.

In a perceptive essay that examines maternal desire and American domesticity as represented in both *Shadow of a Doubt* and Hitchcock's remake of *The Man Who Knew Too Much* (1956), Elsie B. Michie makes a good deal of the newspaper in the former film:

> On his first night in the Newton household, Uncle Charlie appropriates Joseph Newton's newspaper, ostensibly to make it a playhouse for Ann (a perfect image of Uncle Charlie's desire to turn the written word into an emblem of domesticity for the girl child). Charlie's ulterior motive in playing this game is, however, to destroy the section of the paper that contains an article referring to himself. It is this paper that, when she steals it back, becomes the means for Charlie to discover her uncle's secret.[21]

Later in the essay, Michie echoes Rothman's point that it is when Charlie reaches the public library and reads the missing headline that her knowledge, and ours, of what the ring's inscription ("To TS from BM") means for the first time coincide: "We see the text of the newspaper article displayed on the screen, read the information contained within it, and understand the inscription of the ring at the same moment that Charlie does."[22] Michie is absolutely right, I think, that the true horror of the newspaper is not that it reveals Uncle Charlie's identity as the Merry Widow Murderer, but that Charlie finds in its lines her own story: a bright, talented young woman (Thelma Schenley, the "TS" on the ring) desires to strike out on her own but must, inevitably, as it was with her mother, become a wife (as Emma says, in the film's most heartbreaking scene, "I got married and . . . you know how it goes, you sort of forget you're you . . . you're your husband's wife"). However, I think we begin to understand this story well before we read the incriminating headline. Our knowledge, I argue, coincides with Uncle Charlie's, when he finds himself in the evening newspaper.

True, we are unable to read the incriminating headline when Uncle Charlie first finds it, as this pivotal shot begins just as Uncle Charlie turns the page of the newspaper so that the headline faces him, not us. Had Hitchcock not cut on this precise action, we might have caught a glimpse of the headline. Instead, we must wait until his niece Charlie finds it in the public library. Still, we register *something* when he turns over the newspaper—and not just the devilish plume of smoke that emerges from behind it. And although we

Figure 2.5. *Shadow of a Doubt*: "Santa Rosa Social and Club News"

cannot see exactly what Uncle Charlie reads, our eyes probe the page of the newspaper that is now visible to us, the page Uncle Charlie has just finished reading: the "Santa Rosa Social and Club News" (figure 2.5). What we see is also something of an incriminating story: in the left column, there is a photograph of a young woman (of Charlie's age) in modern dress and a sporting hat. She is moving forward, it seems, with confidence. In the right column, there is a photograph of a couple, perhaps newly wed. The woman in this second photograph is turned in the opposite direction of the woman in the first and clings adoringly, almost helplessly, to a man in uniform. In this way, the newspaper presents in stark visual terms what Michie rightly calls Uncle Charlie's "Manichean splitting of the world" into independent women and "true wives."[23] The "Santa Rosa Social and Club News" displays for us both the reasons for Uncle Charlie's crimes and his potential victims.

The next morning, we see the newspaper again when Uncle Charlie is reading in bed. Once more, the page visible to us is the "Santa Rosa Social and Club News." As his sister Emma enters with breakfast, Uncle Charlie sets the paper down next to him, with the "Santa Rosa Social and Club News" section lying face up. Why has Uncle Charlie returned—or rather, why has Hitchcock returned us—to this same section of the newspaper? Why hasn't Uncle Charlie disposed of the newspaper entirely? Is he wrong to think he's in the clear after simply removing a page or two? What follows in this bizarre scene may help us understand more fully what this section of the *Santa Rosa Republican* is telling us, and why it is essential that we "read" a Hitchcock newspaper more carefully. As Emma pampers her little brother, she tells him that while he was sleeping, "the newspaper called up for an interview" with Uncle Charlie—and not just Uncle Charlie but the whole Newton family.

Uncle Charlie becomes visibly disturbed and asks Emma why the newspaper happened to pick this particular family. We cut to a shot of Emma as she says, "I told them we aren't a typical family." It is a near full shot, and to the right of Emma we see the photograph of Uncle Charlie's niece that hangs on her wall. It is a photograph that Uncle Charlie had inspected closely when he first checked into his niece's bedroom, in a spooky shot in which he see his ghostly face reflected as if superimposed on the photograph. In this earlier shot, Uncle Charlie has a kind of bemused disdain for his niece, at least as she is depicted in the photograph. She is at the head of her high school class, and easily destined for, if not greatness, then certainly independence. As Emma's words suggest, Charlie is not "typical." But she is real, and there is a growing number of her kind out there, more than her uncle likes ("Emmy, women are fools!" he says). We see the photograph several more times, and each time we do, Emma speaks of the whole Newton family being in the limelight. Indeed, Uncle Charlie's visit has caught the attention of not just the Women's Club but the newspaper, which called the Newton home asking for an interview. Emma also says that a man named Graham has rung the Newton household and that he wishes to ask questions, take pictures, and report his findings to the American people. Uncle Charlie tries to persuade Emma to turn down the offer, but she assures her brother that it would be no intrusion at all for the survey man to take their pictures: "Oh, he doesn't want us to dress up or anything . . . he just wants us to act the way we always do." The problem for women, of course, is that there is a big difference between the way they want to dress, the way they want to act, and the way they should. While the photograph depicts Charlie as one of three young women dressed for success, the cinematographic shot in which the photograph appears in turn depicts Emma as dressed to pamper men.

For Charlie, there is only one way for a woman to dress and act, and he enforces this view with ruthless violence. With his buttery voice, it sounds like he's only teasingly scolding his sister, "Why expose the family to a couple of snoopers?" But as he says these words, he points a knife at Emma, and says, "You ought to have better sense." At that moment, Charlie enters the room, dressed in an apron like her mother. Indeed, as the camera moves right to reframe young Charlie between her uncle to her right and her mother to her left, we see the physical similarity between the two women. On the wall directly above Uncle Charlie we see a drawing of two women in Victorian-style dress. The older of the two is seated, tending to the dress of the younger woman, who stands next to her. The satisfied look on Uncle Charlie's face tells us that there is something reassuring in this picture of traditional femininity, and he is reassured all the more by the picture in front of him, of his doting sister and niece. The idea that Charlie's story may end up being her mother's after all is, however, complicated by that other picture hanging on the wall, the photograph of the "not typical" woman, Charlie. Indeed, the two pictures are not just walls apart but worlds apart. If Charlie strikes out on her own, then she may after all fulfill her mother's own repressed desires and, in doing so, remind us that there is more to her mother's story that needs to be told.

The final horror of the *Santa Rosa Republican*, as Michie rightly shows, is the news of unbearable violence suffered by female victims. For this reason, we may do well to look more carefully not just at what happens when the newspaper passes through Uncle Charlie's hands but at what happens when it passes through a woman's hands. To begin this analysis, let us return to the events of the previous night, when Uncle Charlie reads about himself in the evening newspaper. Michie says Uncle Charlie has "appropriated" Joe's paper, though it is important to recall that Emma first appropriates it from her husband, taking it from Joe's hands and giving it to her brother, whom she settles comfortably on the sofa with the words, "There now, lead a life of luxury." Joe and Herb leave the living room and go out to the front porch to continue their ongoing discussion about the perfect murder. When we return inside, we appear to be alone with Uncle Charlie. He lifts the paper up, obscuring from us the look on his face as he reads the incriminating story. The devilish cloud of smoke emerges from behind the newspaper, which slowly falls away to reveal Uncle Charlie's face and a drooping cigar. He looks about the room and sees only his niece Ann, who is kneeling before a chair upon which her book rests comfortably. She is facing away from him, so there is no reason why Uncle Charlie can't quietly excuse himself and dispose of the newspaper elsewhere, in a discrete manner. Instead, he calls Ann over and asks her if she's ever seen a house made of newspaper. She approaches her uncle and stands next to him, visibly unimpressed. Luckily for her, it takes Uncle Charlie less than fifteen seconds to complete it. Like the telescopic newspaper in *Marnie*, the *Santa Rosa Republican* seems to have a magic of its own. It becomes a house instantly.

But Uncle Charlie hasn't finished yet: he tears off a small piece of the newspaper, which is the incriminating story about him. As he does so, he says, "Rip the door . . . right off." Now we have a house with no door. But if this is meant to be the Newton home, or any home for that matter, there needs to be a door. Without one, anyone may gain inside access—whether it's Herb or a pair of police detectives posing as survey men. I'm with Ann here: this seems to be a pointless exercise, particularly for Uncle Charlie. After all, it is he who, only moments later in the film, scolds his sister for allowing strangers in the house: "I'm just a visitor here," he sternly tells Emma, "and my advice to you is to slam the door in his face." Of course, it's very likely the police detectives will find a way into the Newton home door or no door (and so will

Herb). The important point here is this: Uncle Charlie thinks he can disappear in Santa Rosa. But he doesn't. After all, his visit is big news—and not just to the Newton family. His fame is what makes Uncle Charlie's newspaper game so peculiar. His aim is to rid the newspaper of an incriminating story, to make himself disappear from its headlines; but in doing so, he makes the newspaper, and himself, the center of attention.

And he doesn't stop. Roger enters the room, and before the boy can cry out, "You've got Papa's paper!" Uncle Charlie has already presented it to him, but this time as a "nice little red barn."[24] The more changes the newspaper undergoes, the more eyes are on it. Now Charlie enters the room, and sure enough, the first thing she notices is the newspaper, whose sheets are on the table, strewn upon the floor, folded and torn apart. Despite Uncle Charlie's efforts, the newspaper is now very much on Charlie's mind. And for the next several sequences in the film, it is very much in her hands. Moments after Uncle Charlie's "little game," we see her climbing the stairs carrying a tray with a bottle of water and a glass. She walks to her bedroom, where her uncle is staying, and knocks on the door. Unbeknownst to Charlie, this scene has happened before, when Uncle Charlie's landlady knocks on the door at the beginning of the film. Then, as now, he replies with a faint "come in." And we should be reminded that we first saw a newspaper in this earlier scene, close to a bottle of water and some glasses, and wads of too much cash. One could say that Charlie's knowledge at last coincides with ours: there's something in that newspaper that Uncle Charlie is hiding. She sets down the water and, turning to leave, spots the missing pages of newspaper in her uncle's jacket. "Well, now I know there was something in the evening paper about you," she tells him. Uncle Charlie calmly says she's right, that there was something in the evening paper he didn't want anyone to know about, a story about someone he used to know. Charlie impulsively grabs the newspaper from her uncle's jacket and, proudly unfolding it, declares, "There!" But there is no there, there. Uncle Charlie has ripped the story out, leaving a gaping hole. So there is no reason for Charlie to dispute anything her uncle might say to fill the hole. But rather than put the matter to rest with a simple explanation, Uncle Charlie leaps at his niece and grabs her violently by the wrists. After regaining his composure, Uncle Charlie resumes his little game: he tries to deflect attention from the newspaper, only to ensure Charlie's growing interest in it. His last words before he says good night to her are "Not for you to read . . . forget it."

The words, of course, have the opposite effect: the story is for her to read, and she will not forget that newspaper. In fact, she will not let go of it. After returning home after a long and troubling talk with Detective Jack Graham (Macdonald Carey), the first thing she does is search for the missing pages. She finds them ripped apart and crumpled up at the bottom of a trash can and takes them back to her sister's room, which she has been sharing during Uncle Charlie's visit, and places them on her bed. When Ann asks Charlie what she is doing, Charlie, posing as good housekeeper, tells her she is looking for a recipe. Ann replies, "They have papers in the library, new ones and old ones. Miss Cochran will get them out for you. She won't even notice if you cut out a little bitty recipe." Ann is wrong to think, as Charlie no longer does, that something about a newspaper can pass unnoticed or be forgotten. But Ann is right to point her sister in the direction of the library, where newspapers are on full and very public display. The camera follows Charlie as she races down the steps of the back stairway and begins her desperate flight to the public library, which is about to close, and we see her clutch the pieces of newspaper in her hands, twisting them ever more tightly into a ball. As she makes her way through the surprisingly crowded streets of Santa Rosa (this is no sleepy little town!), the ball of crumpled newspaper is still visible, if only barely, in her hand. I am certain she still grips it as she weaves her way through traffic in the next few shots but less certain it is in her hands when she finally arrives at the steps of the library. When she reaches the front door, she spreads both hands on the glass. Her newspaper has somehow vanished.

Inside the empty library, however, Charlie will find her newspaper replaced and restored among dozens of other city newspapers, stacked up on shelves and neatly draped from newspaper sticks. She lifts a few of these sticks, then turns to the shelves to find the *Santa Rosa Republican*, yesterday's evening edition. She sits at a table and scans its pages. What follows is one of the most extraordinary shots in the film: the close-up of the missing headline, "Where Is the Merry Widow Murderer?" The dramatic crescendo of Dmitri Tomkins's score adds a good deal of drama to this newspaper's entrance, but more striking is the extremity of the close-up. For much of the film, we strain our eyes to read the *Santa Rosa Republican*. Now it seems too close. This shot is, in fact, the first of three extreme close-ups in the film, all of which can be linked: the two others involve the end of Uncle Charlie's frightening monologue about "faded, fat, greedy women," and the ring on Charlie's finger as she descends the stairs near the end of the film. Taken together, the three extreme close-ups virtually close the case: the headline tells us that the ring ties Uncle Charlie to the murder; the dolly in to an extreme close-up of the ring shows that an incriminating piece of evidence is now in Charlie's hands; the extreme close-up of Uncle Charlie answers the headline's question: the Merry Widow Murderer is right here in the Newton house.

What remains open, however, is the question of what happened to that piece of crumpled newspaper Charlie was holding tightly—so much so that it is hard to imagine it slipped from her fingers on her way to the public library. It is a question that cannot be easily dismissed as, for example, a negligible continuity error. One answer, which seems dismissive, is that Charlie doesn't need those pieces of newspaper. They do her about as much good as it did Uncle Charlie to rip them out in the first place. The *Santa Rosa Republican* is a city newspaper; where there is one copy, there are ten thousand or more. What Charlie finds in the public library is not only yesterday's edition of the

Santa Rosa Republican but dozens of other city papers. And if we associate the newspaper with the crowd, we might say that the culmination of Charlie's search for the truth about her uncle takes place in a crowd of newspapers. Indeed, not since *The Lodger* have so many newspapers appeared in a single shot in a Hitchcock film. It's not surprising, then, that Hitchcock would fill the streets of Santa Rosa during Charlie's flight to the public library. Looking carefully at the sequence, we see the streets teeming with people. The idea for crowding downtown Santa Rosa was not simply to create obstacles for Charlie, as Hitchcock did for little Stevie in the infamous bomb sequence in *Sabotage*. By doing so, Hitchcock does create suspense (will Charlie get to the library in time?), but he also reminds us of the newspaper's ties to the city. Joe Newton's newspaper may be an emblem of domestic tranquillity (under threat, of course) but only when we see it at home. When Charlie runs to the public library, carrying pieces of the newspaper, we are reminded that the *Santa Rosa Republican* is also a city paper, a very public thing, and an emblem of the modern, urban crowd. We are also reminded that, for all his talk about the good old days of small-town Santa Rosa, Uncle Charlie is a modern, urban killer.

✦

> The home newspaper is your policeman. It warns against frauds and swindles. It's worth the money and you ought to pay in advance.
>
> —*Official Bulletin: Ohio Department of Agriculture* 1, no. 1 (May 1909)

I wish to conclude this discussion of Hitchcock's newspaper, that conspicuous thing of the crowd, by reemphasizing its close association with the cinema, and with Hitchcock's camera in particular. Given this close association, we should pay particular attention to those moments in his films when a newspaper is present. I'd like to close with a brief discussion of *The Lodger*, not simply to insist that Hitchcock's interest in crowd/newspaper/cinema was there at the outset, but to suggest that no other Hitchcock film gives us a clearer example of this rich and strange figuration. Let's begin with the scene in which the policeman, Joe Chandler (Malcolm Keen), discovers a valise belonging to the lodger (Ivor Novello) locked in a dresser drawer. In this valise, he finds several items that seem to confirm his suspicion that the lodger is the serial killer known as the Avenger: a pistol, a map of the murders (which Joe calls "a plan of the murders"), several newspaper clippings, and a portrait of a beautiful, fair-haired girl. Significantly, Joe seems especially troubled by the newspaper clippings.

Hitchcock's camera lingers the longest on a small collection of clippings from the *Evening Standard*. No less circumstantial than the other items, these newspaper clippings nevertheless all but confirm the lodger's guilt in Joe's mind. To be sure, Joe has discovered what Charlie could never find until her flight to the public library: the truth in print. And whereas Charlie beheld only one breathtaking headline, Joe takes in several. Taken together, these headlines create the film's second quasi-documentary (the first being the sequence that opens the film). With compelling sequential logic, we see, writ large, the story of *The Lodger* itself: "Stabbed. Murdered in Brother's Arms at Coming-Out Ball. Avenger Triangle Clue. Work of a Maniac? Third Avenger Murder. Fair-Haired Waitress Killed at Charing Cross Station. Police Clues Fail. Avenger Still at Large."

What follows is a curious demonstration of the effect that the second quasi-documentary has on Joe. We see him in close-up, standing bent over the table, his face hidden by his fedora. As he slowly turns his head to the right, the fedora continues to mask his face. Finally, Joe lifts his head and reveals to us a look of unshakable resolve: he will name the lodger the Avenger. Yet even without the knowledge revealed in a subsequent flashback, there is every reason to believe that Joe is dead wrong; and with Joe's next gesture we can appreciate the lodger's growing sense of utter hopelessness. Joe pulls one final item from the valise: a portrait of a beautiful, fair-haired girl. "Your first victim, eh?" he says. The lodger's response, "My murdered sister," connects by association to the first headline of the *Evening Standard* that Joe reads. So why does Joe get it so wrong? In his reading of this scene, Rothman raises the question that is at the heart of not only *The Lodger* but the world of Hitchcock's films: "Can innocence be recognized? If so, by whom and under what circumstances, and how are we to account for the fact that the guilty routinely pass for innocent and the innocent for guilty in Hitchcock's world as in our world?"[25] But there is something else going on here, something else besides the blindness of love (and the blindness of jealousy), which causes the misrecognition of innocence and guilt in the world of Hitchcock. It is as if the newspaper clippings do more than engender the contagion of suspicion in the lodger; they induce in Joe what might be called a crowd mentality. This is why he says, after he learns of the lodger's innocence, "Quick—before they tear him to pieces!" Joe thinks like the crowd, knows that the newspaper creates the crowd, fuels it, and sustains it.

Hitchcock depicts the full force of this crowd mentality early in *The Lodger*. The film opens with the sequence of shots that follow the lights flashing three times, "*TO-NIGHT 'GOLDEN CURLS.'*" The body of a young woman is seen lying on the street. We then see an old woman, a witness to the murder, describing the man we will moments later learn is the Avenger. The next shot is of a policeman writing down the woman's description. We then see a journalist who is looking to his left, at the policeman's report, and writing down the story. There is a cut to a crowd of people that has now gathered, just to the right of the crime scene where the journalist, the policeman, and the old woman are standing. A few shots later, we see the journalist racing to a phone booth. The crowd follows the policeman and the old woman to a nearby coffee stand, and as the journalist dictates his story over the phone, the old woman, now revived by a cup of tea, once again describes the murderer by placing a hand over her face, just below the eyes: "Tall he was—and his face all wrapped up," she recalls. As a joke, a man standing in the nearby crowd pulls his coat over his face, mimicking the old woman's description. She sees his face, a spitting image of the murderer she has just described, reflected on the coffee stand's shiny steel container. The old woman screams, and the prankster is scolded. The next shot is of the journalist in a phone booth, furiously dictating the story, which is then telegraphed, printed, and sent out to the newspaper-reading public. Thus in a long sequence of shots, a series of textual relays is established: through the telephone, to the newspaper office, onto a telegraph device, through the printing presses onto news sheets, into trucks and onto crowded streets, across a news ticker and through the crowd, and finally over the radio. From this quasi-documentary, Rothman singles out what he calls "three characteristic touches":

> First, Hitchcock personally appears as an extra in an editorial office. (He appears again at the film's climax.) Second, as a truck carrying bales of newspapers drives into the depths of the frame, two heads, visible through oval windows, swing back and forth . . . as though they were the newspaper van's eyes. Third, a crowd is shown looking upward, all eyes moving in unison—to all appearances, an audience viewing a film. . . . When Hitchcock cuts to the crowd's point of view, we realize that these people are reading a huge electric sign spelling out the *Evening Standard*'s report of the latest Avenger murder.[26]

Rothman's argument here is that the newspaper-reading public's appetite for murder is what draws them to Hitchcock's film.[27] More broadly, one might argue that the opening sequence of *The Lodger* shows us that, in a sense, the crowd is always already at the movies. By Rothman's account, what precedes the "quasi documentary" of textual relays is mere reportage or word of mouth. Yet before the journalist has a chance to send the description of the Avenger to the *Evening Standard* office, the old woman in the crowd sees it projected on a silver screen. The hidden face of the Avenger is already making its way through crowds. Perhaps this is what Rothman tries to suggest after all, for Hitchcock's aim here is to "plant the image of the Avenger in the spectator's mind," therefore making it almost impossible to discriminate between the innocent and the guilty.[28] As Gustave Le Bon, who gave us the first study of the psychology of the modern, urban crowd, writes:

> A crowd thinks in images, and the image itself immediately calls up a series of other images, having no logical connection with the first. We can easily conceive this state by thinking of the fantastic succession of

> ideas to which we are sometimes led by calling up in our minds any fact. Our reason shows us the incoherence there is in these images, but a crowd is almost blind to this truth, and confuses with the real event what the deforming action of its imagination has superimposed thereon.[29]

One can easily associate what Le Bon describes in the above passage with a typical evening at the Lumière *cinématographe*, where the spectator perceives a series of images calling up another series, with no logical connection from one to the next—a succession of "views" that the spectator, through the deforming action of imagination, may confuse with the real event (an arrival of a train at the station, for instance). What is interesting about the above passage is not the swift and suspect manner in which the crowd is condemned (as scholars of crowd psychology have noted, the success of Le Bon's work "is attributable more to his way with aphorism than to rigorous sociological analysis").[30] Rather, it is the protocinematic power that Le Bon reluctantly grants the crowd, which is not only assembled by purveyors of images but itself has the power to assemble images and to superimpose itself upon them as well.

If we find the crowd to be the most peculiar of Hitchcock propensities, it is because the Hitchcock crowd so frequently exploits the power Le Bon here describes. The Hitchcock crowd is not only assembled by movies but is itself a "movie machine"; it conjures images of itself and—with its most trusted purveyor, the newspaper—conspires to expose us all. This strange but telling figuration that I am calling "crowd/newspaper/cinema" is captured wonderfully in *North by Northwest* in a frame conjoining a crowd (the faces on Mount Rushmore), a newspaper (which the Professor holds in his hands), and the cinema (the optic device through which Thornhill looks) (figure 2.6). And as I have argued, this figuration appears throughout Hitchcock's works. Once we choose to follow the newspaper on its tangled journey from *The Lodger* to that film's distant cousin, *Frenzy* (1972), we are not so much surprised to discover that the Hitchcock landscape is overcrowded with media as struck with a feeling most uncanny that it is overmediated by the crowd.

Figure 2.6. *North By Northwest*: Crowd/newspaper/cinema

Chapter 3

Hitchcock's Apartment Plot, or "The Case of Mr. Pelham"

> The poet rejoices in this incomparable privilege, that he can, at will, be both himself and another. Like a lost soul searching for a body, he enters when he wishes into any character. For him all is vacancy.
>
> —Baudelaire, "The Crowd," from *Paris Spleen*

> Could a man actually be in one place doing one thing and still, in his mind, be elsewhere doing something else but so vividly, with such detail, that this is the real, the living part of his life to him? Do you think?
>
> —Albert Pelham, in "The Case of Mr. Pelham"

The last place one expects to encounter one's double is in one's own home. Even one of the most famous doubles of all, Poe's William Wilson, was never so discreet. He preferred to ambush his baffled victim, the story's narrator, in public (at a card table surrounded by spectators and at the carnival). "Scarcely had I set foot in Paris," the narrator tells us, "ere I had fresh evidence of the detestable interest taken by this Wilson in my concerns. Years flew, while I experience no relief. Villain!—at Rome, with how untimely, yet with how spectra an officiousness, stepped he in between me and my ambition! At Vienna, too—at Berlin—and at Moscow!"[1] The double's domain is the urban crowd, not the urban apartment. One might assume that the apartment provides an escape from the thirsty crowd. It's a place of refuge.

That the double might penetrate the private space of the urban apartment suggests two equally frightening possibilities: first, that the urban apartment is permeable and unsecure; and, second, that the person who occupies it is vulnerable and insecure. Viewers familiar with the Hitchcock-directed episodes of *Alfred Hitchcock Presents* will immediately recognize that this is the plot of "The Case of Mr. Pelham" (1955). Let's begin with a person, named

Albert Pelham (Tom Ewell), and a place, his elegant apartment on East 63rd Street, in the Upper East Side neighborhood of Manhattan. Pelham heads his own firm, Albert Pelham Investments, where he employs two female secretaries. He is single, and when he is not working or in his apartment being tended to by his man Peterson, Pelham can be found at a gentleman's club.

Based very loosely on a story by Anthony Armstrong—a story he would expand into a novel two years later—and adapted for television by Francis Cockrell, "The Case of Mr. Pelham" might seem simply to be another in a long line of stories about doubling in the Hitchcock corpus, for Pelham's "case" is that he fears someone is impersonating him and that, more frighteningly, this imposter is making his way into Pelham's life.[2] Thus the episode is really about two people, two Pelhams who, quite to the shock of the first, are occupying the same place, the apartment on East 63rd. We can add to people and place several "things" of note: a key to the apartment and its double (a spare), as well as a necktie and its double (one worn by Pelham, the other by his double). A third necktie might be thrown in for good measure—a hideous and (thank goodness) one-of-a-kind tie that only a Bruno Antony would admire and only the real Pelham will wear.

While the theme of doubling in "The Case of Mr. Pelham" is indeed important and will be given due consideration here, it is the doubling theme's relation to homosexuality that will be of utmost interest. What follows in this chapter is an attempt to treat "The Case of Mr. Pelham" as an important work in Hitchcock's career (it earned him an Emmy nomination in the Best Director in a Televised Film Series category), as well as an important addition to the "apartment plot" defined by Pamela Robertson Wojcik. However, I wish to consider first how, like many of Hitchcock's films, this episode unsettles our grounding both spatially and temporally—in fact, "doubles" down on its efforts by dislocating us in both space and time. In a second and related move, I show how Mr. Pelham's efforts to validate his identity, to prove to himself and others that he is the real Mr. Pelham, are literally a matter of location and timing—a matter of being at the right place at the right time. In a word, Pelham needs an alibi. The cat-and-mouse game Pelham plays with his double—or that his double plays with him (such is the logic of the cat-and-mouse game, or as Philip asks in *Rope*, "Which is the cat and which is the mouse?")—is an effort to both catch and elude his identity. As we shall see, Pelham finds himself trapped in a perpetual "elsewhere" (the word *alibi* is Latin for "elsewhere"). In this way, "The Case of Mr. Pelham" couples the anxiety induced by spatial and temporal dislocation with male hysteria, or more specifically, homophobic paranoia.

Presenting Alfred Hitchcock

Hitchcock directed seventeen episodes of *Alfred Hitchcock Presents* and one episode of the short-lived *Alfred Hitchcock Hour*, as well as two stand-alone episodes, one for the anthology series *Suspicion* ("Four O'Clock," which aired September 30, 1957) and another for *Startime* ("Incident at a Corner," which aired April 5, 1960). While long ignored by scholars, the episodes directed by Hitchcock are beginning to receive close critical attention.[3] Perhaps the most compelling argument for the significance of Hitchcock's television work is to be found in Thomas Leitch's essay "The Outer Circle: Hitchcock on Television." In it, Leitch amends Andrew Sarris's notion of three concentric circles designating the roles of the director (technician, stylist, and auteur) to include a fourth, outer circle: the director as celebrity. In doing so, Leitch makes the case for the importance of the television episodes not in and of themselves but rather insofar as they help us understand Hitchcock's public persona. While appreciative of Hitchcock's noncinematic work (not just the television episodes but the interviews, mystery magazines, literary anthologies, etc.), Leitch argues that the point is "to reconcile Hitchcock the director with Hitchcock the public figure, a persona much more closely congruent with the host of *Alfred Hitchcock Presents* than with the director of any number of masterpieces of cinema."[4] In other words, Leitch wants to explore the relationship between outer-circle Hitchcock—the man who bid us "good evening" each week—and inner-circle Hitchcock: the auteur behind *Rear Window*, *Vertigo*, and *Psycho*.

While the advantage of this approach is that it complicates in interesting ways our theories of authorship, the disadvantage is that it deemphasizes the content of the television episodes, favoring who presents over what is presented.[5] To be sure, Leitch believes—quite rightly—that Hitchcock's role as host of *Alfred Hitchcock Presents* is the show's "defining feature."[6] Thus far, however, I have suggested that we look beyond what we take to be the defining features of Hitchcock's work to expand the Hitchcock landscape—in this case, to include not only Hitchcock's opening and closing monologues but what he directed in between.

Hitchcock was fond of repeating, in speeches he gave toward the end of his career, variations of this line: "One of television's greatest contributions is that it brought murder back into the home, where it belongs."[7] The line is ponderous in a number of ways. It seems to be a reference to *Alfred Hitchcock Presents* in particular, which featured numerous episodes in which murder took place at home (most memorably, perhaps, in the episode based on the Roald Dahl short story, "Lamb to the Slaughter," which Hitchcock directed). Indeed, the first time Hitchcock used the line was in 1955 when speaking about the program's debut. Then the line read a little differently: his new program would be "bringing murder into the American home, where it has always belonged."[8] It is not surprising that Hitchcock would not get the line just right when he repeated it later in his life. But it is a curious rewrite (or error of memory). To say that television in general and *Alfred Hitchcock Presents* in particular brought murder *back* into the home is to suggest that murder had been, for a spell, in exile. Yet the rewrite is curiously apt.

Hitchcock had known, long before the debut of *Alfred Hitchcock Presents*, that for murder there is no place like home. *Shadow of a Doubt* is the film that brilliantly bears out this logic. And while Hitchcock staged domestic murders prior to *Shadow of a Doubt*, this was the first Hitchcock film that brought murder to an American home—perhaps *the* all-American home, the Newton residence. *Rope*, made five years later, was even more macabre. And while Brandon and Phillip's apartment is hardly all-American, it is the scene of an actual murder. In a subsequent Hitchcock film, however, murder did indeed leave home: Miriam's murder in *Strangers on a Train* takes place on the "Magic Isle" at the fairgrounds in Metcalf (and while Bruno had set the terms for a domestic murder, Guy broke them—and not to Bruno's surprise). Yet murder didn't stay away from home for long. Two years later, in *I Confess*, the prodigal son returns. And it would stay home for the back-to-back films *Dial M for Murder* and *Rear Window*, both made in 1954, the year before the debut of *Alfred Hitchcock Presents*. And while 1955's *The Trouble with Harry* locates murder outdoors once more, in the colorful Vermont countryside, Hitchcock had by then embedded murder permanently in the American home, where it belongs.[9]

Hitchcock's Apartment Plot

"The Case of Mr. Pelham" is not about murder, of course, as Hitchcock himself informs us from the get-go. "Due to circumstances beyond our control," he begins, "tragedy will not strike tonight. I'm dreadfully sorry, perhaps some other time." But Hitchcock, good host that he is, assures us we'll be provided with a worthwhile alternative. "However, I have just witnessed a sneak preview of this evening's story. I found it simply frightening. Sometimes death is not the worst that can befall a man. And I don't refer to torture or any type of violence. I mean the quiet little insidious devices that can drive a man out of his mind. Like putting bubblegum in someone's coat pocket." While Hitchcock is clearly invoking madness here, one wonders, once physical violence is struck from the list of possibilities, what else might remain as contender for the worse-than-death scenario—besides putting bubblegum in someone's coat pocket. What other horror might "befall a man," a horror so unthinkable, so unspeakable, that death may seem a worthwhile alternative to him? This chapter proposes that the fate worse than death which Alfred Hitchcock presents is having no alibi. It is worse because Pelham has no attachments except to his "man" Peterson, who cares for him and his apartment. And even Peterson fails him at the crucial moment when Pelham lays claim to his apartment and thus his identity.

One of the "insidious devices" Hitchcock invokes is the imposter's ability to infiltrate Pelham's apartment when he is not there. Indeed, like *Dial M for Murder* and *Rear Window*, "The Case of Mr. Pelham" belongs to a genre that Wojcik calls "the apartment plot": "'The apartment plot' is any narrative in which the apartment figures as a central device. This means that the apartment is more than setting; it motivates or shapes the narrative in some key way."[10] In other words, the place of the apartment has a certain *agency* in the narrative. It is, like so many people, places, and things in Hitchcock, a knowing, willful agent. The *bachelor* apartment, in particular, plays host to the rather queer scenario in which "one's identity is not stable or essential but determined by location"; recall it's the *coziness* (to use Janet's description) of the apartment in *Rope* that raises the specter of its occupants'—Brandon and Phillip's—homosexuality, and it's the permeability of their apartment (the unexpected return of a suspicious Rupert) that threatens to out them.

For Wojcik, the key apartment plot film is *Rear Window*. While she acknowledges the importance of work on the film that sees it as an example of self-reflexive cinema, as an important example of the dominance of the male gaze in cinema, and as one of the primary achievements of an auteur, Wojcik focuses on on the film's modern urbanity. *Rear Window* is about "an animated urban neighborhood, one that is porous, dense, and permeable.[11] Like other films that utilize the apartment plot, *Rear Window* maps an urban geography through which it "navigates tensions between public and private, work and home, privacy and community, loneliness and density, contact and entanglement—tensions that are specific to the domestic urban setting."[12] These tensions are established with the film's first few shots—back-to-back camera pans, right to left, across the courtyard and into Jeff's apartment. The first of the two pans begins with the camera following a cat darting up some stairs below, leading the camera to the far right of the courtyard. The cat leaves the frame, and the camera then pans upward, with the composer's apartment just out of frame to the right. The camera then begins to pan left, giving a full view of the four-story complex directly across from Jeff's apartment. Most of the windows are open; a family of three is standing outside on a porch; an older couple is asleep on a fire escape. Yet while, as Wojcik tells us, we see much of what goes on in these busy apartment complexes and the courtyard they surround, "there is much we do not see."[13]

That space is both exposed and concealed in the apartment plot is only one of its many unsettling features. This narrative is also characterized by surprising coincidences, chance encounters, false identities, and role-playing. For these reasons, Wojcik coins the phrase "public privacy" to describe the "indeterminate space" of the modern, urban apartment of the apartment plot film.[14] *Rope* is an illustrative film in this regard, and although Wojcik devotes some pages to the film, she does not discuss the film's climax, which begins with Rupert's unexpected return to Brandon and Philip's apartment after he has left the dinner party with the other guests. Both Ned Schantz and George Toles have remarked upon Rupert's return as unwelcome guest, and both have found it suggestive of queer identity. For Toles, Rupert engages in a masquerade of good hospitality when he leaves the party, only to return moments later under the pretense of having left behind his cigarette case. "Interestingly," writes Toles, "after making a great show of departing with other guests, he adopts the venerable amorous pretext for returning to the penthouse to retrieve something that he left behind."[15] Schantz probes deeper into the motives behind the curious, and sudden, return of Rupert. Rightly pointing out the strangeness of returning without the police—of returning alone—Schantz suggests two possibilities: Rupert's "ambiguous night call" reveals, as Toles also suggests, that his intentions are amorous. That Rupert's return actually induces tension hardly removes any doubt about a potentially amorous intent. But the tension could not have been unanticipated on Rupert's part, which leads to Schantz's second possible motive: the reason Rupert returns is "ultimately suicidal," as he knows that returning alone to Brandon and Phillip's apartment means repeating David's fate.[16] So while the apartment plot frequently stages moments of exposure and vulnerability for the tenants, it also stages these moments for the guests—uninvited or not.

This is also the thrill of *Rear Window*'s climax, which dramatizes the "public privacy" of the modern, urban apartment.[17] First Lisa sneaks into Lars Thorwald's apartment while he is out so she can look inside a purse that belonged to Mrs. Thorwald. Thorwald returns unexpectedly and discovers his unwanted guest. After a brief exchange with Lisa, Thorwald realizes that he is exposed and threatens Lisa with physical harm. In a panic, Jeff, who has been helplessly watching the whole frightful affair from his apartment across the courtyard, calls the police. They arrive just in time to ensure Lisa's safety, but during police questioning, Lisa signals to Jeff that she is wearing Mrs. Thorwald's wedding ring. Thorwald sees this and, in a sudden turn of the tables, looks across the courtyard into Jeff's apartment—indeed, right into the prosthetic eyes that have been spying on him the whole time. Now it is Jeff who is exposed. Stella has gone to bail Lisa out of jail, leaving Jeff alone. Only moments before, Jeff watched as Thorwald played bad host to an uninvited guest in his apartment. Now Thorwald plays uninvited guest to Jeff's terrified—and extremely vulnerable—host.

All of the elements of the apartment plot I have discussed thus far—closeted male desire, unfixed identity, and public privacy—can be found in "The Case of Mr. Pelham." And while any one of these elements can be found in any given episode of *Alfred Hitchcock Presents*, only "The Case of Mr. Pelham" can be said to have them all, and it is the only episode directed by Hitchcock to feature an apartment.[18] This episode, then, is the only apartment plot in the Hitchcock-directed episodes of his television anthology.

"As a Matter of Fact Quite Gay"

The episode begins with Pelham arriving at a gentleman's club he frequents. We know he is a regular because as he approaches the bar, the bartender asks him if he wants the usual glass of sherry. Pelham is a little early (the bartender says, "Good morning") and looks utterly distraught. He refuses the feminine (though not necessarily effeminizing) glass of sherry and orders a very masculine whiskey.[19] In a story about a man who is a creature of habit, who is comfortable only with the familiar, one wonders why the sudden change of order. Further, the serving instructions are doubled: "Straight," he says, "I believe I'll have it straight." There is something queer about this repetition. The first instruction is given without hesitation: "Straight." The second instruction, however, seems performed. It's as if Pelham is instructing himself, not the bartender. To the queer critic, the line should prick up the ears. Of course neither the line nor its delivery proves anything about Pelham's sexual orientation. One can argue easily that Pelham is rattled and needs something stronger than sherry. Yet, as D. A. Miller has argued in his essay on *Rope*, the dominant signifying practice of homophobia is connotation, which elaborates homosexual meaning even while eliding it.[20] While it cannot bear the burden of proof, suffering as it does from "semiotic insufficiency," connotation can proliferate and provoke.[21]

And proliferate and provoke it does in "The Case of Mr. Pelham." After downing his very butch shot of whiskey, Pelham stops another member of the gentleman's club who has just arrived (also a little earlier than usual), a Dr. Harley (Raymond Bailey).[22] Pelham asks him to share lunch. "I need to talk to you," sputters Pelham, like a man who is simultaneously speaking to another and speaking to another about *how* he is speaking: with few but loaded words. Harley responds in kind, using what might be a professional, "go-to" coded language: "About a 'friend' with a . . . psychosis?" Pelham and Harley stand close—if not too close—to one another. Of course Pelham asks for discretion, but there is a kind of knowingness the men share, and their physical proximity only heightens our sense that this may be one of "those" conversations.

Pelham cannot keep the straight talk straight, and he tells Harley, "It's not a friend, it's myself." As if to stall any further uncomfortable disclosures, Harley says, louder than either had been speaking before, "Well, thanks very much, Pelham. I'd be delighted to lunch with you!" The shift in tone, however, has the effect of calling too much attention to the encounter. By speaking more loudly than necessary, Harley manages to alert us that the two were, until just then, speaking more quietly than necessary. Harley then swigs from his glass of foamy beer with a bit more gusto than necessary, and the two sit at a table Pelham has selected, which Harley admires with a bit more gusto than necessary ("Fine! Fine!"). A space that is excessively homosocial, like this gentleman's club, seems to require such broadcasts of reassurance.

The mirroring/doubling motif conveyed in the mise-en-scène is suggestive as well, as connotation is not limited to nuances of dialogue but includes the things that adorn this place. Hitchcock's camera has Pelham and Harley in a medium two-shot, framed at the waist. The shot lasts nearly a minute,

Figure 3.1. "The Case of Mr. Pelham": The inverted Brouwer

allowing the viewer to scan the image. On either side of the wall hang similar portraits, each of a gentleman facing the right. Above each portrait hangs a pair of light sconces. The mirroring/doubling motif that decorates the gentleman's club suggests the male desire for physical intimacy, close companionship, hearty competition. Framed between Pelham and Harley there is a statuette of two nude men boxing, and they appear to be on the verge of an amorous clinch. The statuette is placed beneath a large painting (figure 3.1)—a somewhat amateurish reproduction of Adriaen Brouwer's *The Smokers* (ca. 1636), but it is reversed (figure 3.2). In other words, what hangs on the wall at the gentleman's club is a mirror image of the original and a far inferior copy. The painting on the wall in the gentleman's club, in brief, displays for all to see what, precisely, the nature of Mr. Pelham's case is: he is to come to the conclusion that he is actually an inferior copy of himself, and an "inverted" one at that.

But is this, in fact, his case? The well-known Flemish artist is known to have captured moments of human comedy, and in *The Smokers* some unknown companion is lighting a match underneath Brouwer's buttocks (Brouwer has painted himself and still-life painter Jan der Heem into the scene). The

Figure 3.2. Brouwer's *The Smokers*

smokers' den is a space of homosocial interaction—including, it seems, the staging of lewd pranks (Pelham will tell Harley that he thinks what troubles him is the result of a "senseless jest"). It is a Rabelaisian space, one that delights in exploiting the lower bodily stratum. The prankster companion in the original Brouwer, who acknowledges us with a wink and a finger to his nose, invites us to share in this bit of bawdy fun.[23] Brouwer's lively reaction is a combination of surprise and pleasure, suggesting that pranks zoning in on the male buttocks are both wicked and welcome in this space.

Ordinarily at home in this gentleman's club, Pelham is now anxious and distracted. When Harley says he prefers to deal with personal matters in his office, Pelham says, "I will come later if you want me to . . . lie on the couch, whatever's necessary." While these words may seem perfectly sensible when spoken to a psychiatrist (it is never stated that Harley is a doctor), one cannot dismiss entirely their homosexual meaning. And when Pelham proceeds to describe himself to Harley, he does so in such a way that his queerness is, to use Miller's words, "elided even as it is elaborated."[24] Pelham says, "I have my own little company, Albert Pelham Investments. I'm single, have an apartment on East 63rd with one servant, Peterson. I have no deep attachments, no demanding relationships, no responsibilities. Nothing unusual at all about me really." The problem, of course, is that Pelham's description of himself also suggests there is nothing *usual* at all about him. In fact, what remains of Pelham's profile once we deduct the attachments, relationships, and responsibilities, is that he lives in an apartment with another man.

Pelham then tells Harley when his worries began: when an acquaintance named Tom Mason mildly rebuked him for giving him the cold shoulder. In the first of several flashbacks (a rarity for Hitchcock), we see Pelham dining at the club with another man when Mason approaches. "I'm glad to see we're on speaking terms again," he says to Pelham (a reference to a love quarrel?). Puzzled, he asks Mason his meaning, and Mason responds, "The day before yesterday, you cut me dead right out here at the corner." Pelham claims not to have seen him, but Mason insists. "You saw me all right. Looked me right in the eye." Pelham pleads not guilty and assures Mason he was in Philadelphia at the time and could not have been on the corner. Pelham then describes a similar incident, when the club's hall man handed him a carton of cigarettes and told him Harry the billiard room attendant sent them up, that he had left the cigarettes at the club the night before.

In the second flashback, we see Pelham confronting the billiard room attendant—indeed, we see him *bribe* the billiard room attendant. "You know Harry, I don't remember ordering those cigarettes. In fact I suspect someone's playing a joke on me. For I don't even recall being here at all last night." He suggestively hands Harry a dollar bill and says, "That, eh . . . might just . . . *possibly* be it, wouldn't you say?" But the bribe doesn't take, as Harry insists Pelham *was* in the billiard room. "You can check with Mr. Mason, you were playing with him," he says, adding, "You made a crack about that crazy hop, skip, and kiss-you-twice carom you made that time. Who else would know about that?"[25] The queer boast is something of a calling card, and Pelham is convinced enough by Harry that he decides to take action and rushes to his apartment hoping to catch the imposter.

It is our first look at Pelham's apartment, and it is hardly what one would call a bachelor pad. It is elegantly furnished, with late nineteenth-century European décor. Portraits of women adorn the walls, and there is very little in the way of the masculine iconography one associates with the playboy aesthetic. The apartment is, in a word, soft. Rather than conveying an enthusiastic heterosexuality, Pelham's apartment conforms more to the aesthetic of a married man's apartment, or what Wojcik calls "the feminized home" (93).

In her discussion of *The Tender Trap* (dir. Charles Walters, 1955), Wojcik describes the apartment occupied by Charlie Reader (Frank Sinatra) as a typical bachelor pad, through which "a parade of beautiful single women" come and go.[26] But when, by the end of the film, Charlie proposes to Julie Gillis (Debbie Reynolds), "we sense that the aesthetic of Charlie's apartment will change" and become more like Julie's apartment. "In contrast to Charlie's hip modern apartment," writes Wojcik, "Julie's apartment is decorated in a much more old-fashioned and feminine manner. Where Charlie has sleek lines, she has curvy Louis XIV chairs."[27] Pelham's apartment would no doubt please Julie and serve as a perfect model for how to make over a bachelor pad, how to send the proper signal to that parade of beautiful single women: "He's mine, ladies." Pelham's apartment has just what Charlie's apartment now needs: "Wall-to-wall 'womanization.' "[28]

While Pelham is not married, his live-in butler Peterson attends to all his needs like the stereotypical 1950s housewife. He prepares Pelham's meals, lays out his nightclothes, takes his phone calls, and—presumably—all of the remaining chores that make up daily domestic living. Moreover, Pelham and Peterson behave as if they are in a marginally unhappy marriage, with Pelham playing the role of aloof husband. Twice Pelham calls home to explain to Peterson that he will be late for dinner. In the second instance, when Pelham comes home to find that his late dinner is not waiting for him in the living room, he stamps on the servant bell and angrily calls Peterson's name. Peterson enters, wearing only a shirt and pants with suspenders, and is baffled. Pelham barks, "Peterson, what is the matter with you? Where's my supper?" Alienating Peterson emotionally might seem unwise, given that he is the only one who can vouch for Pelham: "*Keep your man close, and the next time someone says he saw you at the fights, just* habeas alibi—*produce Peterson.*" Yet the fact that the double can freely enter and leave Pelham's apartment while he is away effectively disqualifies Peterson as an alibi.

Pelham need not produce a man as his alibi, as a reliable story would suffice. But Pelham is not a very skillful storyteller. In one instance Pelham tells Harley that he did not go to work one morning because he was feeling jumpy, on edge. "I decided to go to a picture or something of the sort." As alibis go, this is one doesn't quite pass muster. Under scrutiny, Pelham would have to be a little more exact: Was it a picture or something else? And if he did go to a picture, which one? Harley, in fact, does press Pelham, asking him, "Were you with anyone you know?" Pelham shakes his head no, adding, "But I remember the picture, and it's the one running at that theater, I looked it up this morning!" Unable to produce a person to vouch for his whereabouts, Pelham gives an account that lacks coherence and credibility. If he remembers the picture, he shouldn't have to look it up—and anyway he doesn't say what picture he saw, only where it is running. And even that narrative tidbit is too vague to be of any use. Pelham's "narrative alibi," to use Justin Weir's phrase, is a bit of a shambles.[29]

Of course, as a man of "no deep attachments," it is unlikely that Pelham has had much practice telling stories about himself, about his comings and goings. He is a man of routine, and he enjoys the luxury of routine because he has not suffered the unexpected intrusions that might disrupt it. One of the key ingredients of Wojcik's apartment plot is that the apartment is accessible to visitors (often unexpected) and that the apartment dweller is visible to neighbors (often nosy). One might say that before the double walked into his life, Pelham was a man with no story. And now that the double has walked into his *apartment*, a narrative alibi will no longer suffice.

"Cat and Mouse, Cat and Mouse," or *Le grand alibi*

This section takes its title from two Hitchcock sources. First, as I noted above, "Cat and mouse, cat and mouse" is a line uttered in *Rope* by a very drunk Phillip, who is fed up with the prolonged and prolonging conversation game in which Brandon and Rupert are engaged. Second, *Le grand alibi*, as many know, is the French title for Hitchcock's 1950 film *Stage Fright*. Christian Metz applauds this intelligent translation, since the film begins with a fake flashback—a "grand alibi" for both the villain and the film itself. While the latter film invokes the alibi in its legal context, *Rope* endows it with a psychosexual dimension. What I am proposing is that the macabre apartment plot of *Rope* stages a relation between the alibi and what Miller calls "a heterosexuality configured entirely in terms of men."[30] To borrow the language of Roland Barthes, the cat and mouse game that Brandon and Rupert play "exactly reproduces the physique of the *alibi* (which is, as one realizes, a spatial term): in the alibi . . . there is a place which is full and one which is empty, linked by a relation of negative identity ('I am not where you think I am; I am where you think I am not')."[31] In the cat and mouse game between Brandon and Rupert we see the grand alibi at work: it is the homosexual fixation that determines, if not a hetersosexuality, then a *nonhomosexuality*.[32]

The conversation game in *Rope* begins more or less when Rupert, having returned to the apartment to find his "forgotten" cigarette case, asks for a drink—not a short one but a long one. Here the conversation begins; or more precisely, this is when it picks up where it had left off, which is to say that Rupert's return is a return to the vexed question "What have you done with David?"—the question at the very heart of the film. It's a vexed question for two related reasons: one, because Rupert cannot ask it outright; and two, because Brandon can endlessly postpone having to give the question's only correct response. In postponing, Brandon ensures that Rupert's questioning will continue—and it does. But there is a wrinkle here, for Brandon finds himself in need of an answer to a question *he* cannot ask outright, which is "What are you getting at?" Rupert too can postpone the question's only correct response, the only one that will put the matter to rest. So the conversation game is, in Roland Barthes's phrase, "a sort of constantly rotating turnstile." Further, as with a constantly moving turnstile, we are not sure who leads and who follows, which question runs the game. Cat and mouse, cat and mouse. An example:

> RUPERT: I always hate to leave a party. Especially when the evening has been unusually stimulating. Or strange, like this evening.
> PHILLIP: What do you mean strange?
> RUPERT: Did I say strange, Brandon?
> BRANDON: You often pick words for sound rather than meaning.
> RUPERT: Well, I don't exactly know what I meant. Unless I was thinking about David.
> BRANDON: What was strange about David?
> RUPERT: His not showing up. You don't think anything really did happen to him, do you?
> BRANDON: What could have?
> RUPERT: He could have been held up, or run over.
> BRANDON: In broad daylight?

And so on and so on. Even Philip's exasperated outburst cannot put an end to the game, and as he pours himself still another drink Brandon and Rupert resume the chase. Only after two weapons are brought to visibility—Brandon's pistol and the length of rope used to strangle David—does the chase end. Only the threat of force can bring the turnstile to a halt. Tired, frightened, and now armed, Rupert calls it quits. But as Miller has noted, even after Rupert has renounced Brandon and Phillip's crime and summoned the police, "the charged atmosphere of *Rope* never quite dissipates." What remains, which Miller calls "this residual tension," is the homosexual fixation that structures the film. To be sure, Hitchcock's bold technical experiment—to realize the fantasy of a film with no cuts—both distracts from and zeroes in on the very question *it* can't pose outright: "Are Brandon and Phillip gay?" To put Miller's argument another way, the fussiness (ours, Hitchcock's) over *Rope*'s technique functions as a grand alibi for the film's homosexual fixation.

Thus the film's apartment plot proves to be considerably complex. To paraphrase Wojcik, *Rope* is a closet plot contained within an apartment plot. Rupert's unexpected return to Brandon and Phillip's apartment after the party has ended not only suggests that the apartment is easily penetrable, but it stages the film's impossible fantasy of seeing just what goes on in this apartment when no one is watching. Most important for our purposes here, however, is how *Rope* invokes the fantasy of the grand alibi as a defense against a worse-than-death scenario: that one's heterosexual identity is a fiction. Conjured for the purposes of settling that score once and for all, the grand alibi rewrites the apartment as a clearinghouse.

It is telling, then, that the final skirmish in "The Case of Mr. Pelham," over who is the real Pelham and who is the fake, with Peterson playing the role of adjudicator, should occur in Pelham's apartment. One of the main features of the apartment plot is that it locates identity, however fluid, within the space, however permeable, of the apartment. In *Rear Window*, the identities of Jeff's neighbors are inextricably linked with their respective apartments and what they do inside them. A young woman is seen dancing half-nude in her apartment (or dance studio), and she is identified as Miss Torso. An older woman is seen pining for an unnamed lover in her apartment (or theater), even staging a fake romantic rendezvous, and she is identified as Miss Lonelyhearts. As Jeff stares into the Thorwalds' apartment, he reflects not only on Lars Thorwald's identity but on the future of his own, telling his editor Gunnison over the telephone, "Can't you just see me? Rushing home to a hot apartment to listen to the automatic laundry and the electric dishwasher and the garbage disposal and the nagging wife." Lisa's identity is to a large degree tied to how she discloses—and disguises—herself in Jeff's apartment.

In "The Case of Mr. Pelham," the relationship between identity and place is considerably more complex. In a way, the episode anticipates *North by Northwest*, insofar as Pelham's efforts to outmaneuver and expose an imposter require being at the right place at the right time. Pelham uses this logic to assert self-identification. The first incident he reports to Harley concerns an acquaintance of Pelham's who claims he saw Pelham at the Garden, watching the fights. "But I hadn't been to the Garden the night before, " he tells Harley. "In fact I never go to fights." When Mason tells Pelham he saw him on the street corner around two o'clock, Pelham replies, "Not guilty. I was in Philadelphia the day before yesterday. Didn't get back 'til six-thirty." And while Pelham is accused of no crime, he follows state statutes, codes, and cases of common law by saying he was "not guilty" because he was in another place.

After one home invasion, Pelham asks Peterson if he noticed anything peculiar about him. Peterson says no, that Pelham seemed "as a matter of fact quite gay" and that his "quip about that taxi driver was most curious." For the second time, the alibi—or lack thereof—is closely associated with homosexuality. This association is not unique to "The Case of Mr. Pelham" but characterizes several of Hitchcock's feature films, notably his best film about "doubling," *Strangers on a Train*. While Robert J. Corber has shown that the film raises the specter of a "homosexual menace" that threatened to corrupt straight American males, and it therefore spares no effort to extricate Guy from his ties with Bruno, the film goes further by making explicit the danger of being alone in a confined space with another man.[33] On two occasions, Guy finds himself in a train compartment with another man.[34] First, and most famously, Guy is alone with Bruno in his private compartment. The second time, Guy is alone in a lounge car with a professor from Delaware Tech named Collins (John Brown)—a man, it will turn out, whose testimony could exonerate Guy of Miriam's murder. Creating a visual allusion to Guy

Figure 3.3. *Strangers on a Train*: Guy's other close encounter

tapping Bruno's foot, the gesture that sets the two off on their "criss-cross" journey, Hitchcock shows Guy and Professor Collins in a wide shot, their outstretched legs hovering close together (figure 3.3).

Guy is reading a newspaper, and he is amused by Collins's drunken croon, "He loved that goat, indeed he did. He loved that goat, just like a kid."[35] He turns to Guy and asks, "What's your opinion?" Guy, taking the question to be directed at the man's singing, jokingly replies, "Well, you'll never make the Metropolitan." Collins introduces himself, then proceeds to give Guy a flash lecture on integral calculus. "In differential calculus, a function is given and its differential is obtained. Understand?" Guy, with as much conviction (and as little caution) as he showed Bruno when asked about swapping murders, tells Collins, "Sure, I understand." If we were to read this scene of Guy and Collins as "doubling" the earlier train compartment scene with Guy and Bruno, then Guy has quite possibly struck—however inadvertently—his second bargain. But with whom, and for what? Is the "function" the professor gives Guy some kind of spy code? Or is it just as likely that the professor is coming on to Guy?[36] What makes Guy so vulnerable—and in Corber's view, a threat to national security as well—is his failure to be on full alert to either possibility.

Whatever the threat may be—gay code or spy code—it is intensified when two men are alone in close quarters. It is as if the encounter itself is the threat. When Guy calls him before Captain Turley (Howard St. John) as a potential alibi, Collins expresses no memory of their encounter: "I'm terribly sorry, but I really don't remember meeting this gentleman. Unfortunately I remember very little about our trip from New York, you see we . . . we had a little celebration." When Guy reminds Collins that he was singing a song about a goat, Hitchcock cuts to a medium close-up of Turley, whose expression combines doubt and distaste. The scene ends with an exasperated Guy appealing to sound logic: "Captain, is it so important whether or not Professor Collins remembers me? Surely the important thing is I've been able to name a man who was on a train with me, you've been able to find him. Isn't that proof of where I was at 9:30 last night?"

We learn in the next scene, however, that Captain Turley was unconvinced. "When an alibi is full of bourbon," he tells Senator Morton, "it can't stand up."[37] It may seem unlikely that Collins should black out so completely. More unlikely, even, than the possibility that Collins *does* recall the encounter but fears being outed. When alone in a place with another man, one shouldn't be singing about goat love and chattering about integral calculus. It's, well, unseemly—as demonstrated by the expression on Captain Turley's face when Guy presses Collins with the details of their encounter. Thus, in *Strangers on a Train*, the transference of guilt between men is not limited to Bruno and Guy. By failing (or refusing) to be Guy's alibi, Collins can recuperate his heterosexuality (and patriotism). In doing so, he forces Guy to bear the burden of guilt for Miriam's murder. This is the paradox of the alibi in Hitchcock: a man must have one to clear him of any suspicion of guilt. But to produce an alibi, he potentially accedes to another form of guilt, that of being alone with another man.

In this way, sexual guilt is broadly associated with private encounters with men.[38] Such encounters are given a special strangeness in Hitchcock, as in the scene from *The Paradine Case* (1947) in which Andre Latour (Louis Jordan) pays an unexpected visit to Anthony Keane (Gregory Peck) late at night in Keane's room. It is an erotically charged encounter—not in spite of but because of each man's denial that it is one. When Keane asks, "What is it you want with me?" Latour replies, "Beg pardon, sir, but I thought it was you wanted to see me." Keane then insists, "Remember this, Latour, you forced yourself on me, I didn't seek you out." Such an encounter is the inverse of the alibi. Whereas the alibi exonerates the accused by testifying that he was with him *elsewhere* at the time of the offense, the private encounter with another man *is* the offense.[39] This would explain why Collins finds himself in such a bind: to be Guy's alibi is to admit to the offense of being alone with a younger man in the observation car, drunk and crooning about a man who loved his goat just like a kid.

A similar sort of double bind ensnares Pelham: the need for a "paranoid-associated homophobic alibi" ("I was not where you think I was" and "I was not with whom you think I was") exposes Pelham's exceptional and exceptionally deep attachment: his apartment and the man he lives there with, Peterson.[40] In the first of two similar sequences, Pelham returns to his apartment only after his double has just left. The first return is prompted by a strange telephone call Pelham places to Peterson: "Hello, this is Mr. Pelham . . . no I don't want to *talk* to Mr. Pelham, I *am* . . ." Suddenly realizing that Peterson thought he was home, Pelham races back to the apartment. He finds the apartment empty and calls out to Peterson. The two confront each other in the hallway. Peterson tells Pelham, "Changed your mind, sir? You were going out for the evening, you said." Puzzled, Pelham turns and walks a few steps to his bedroom. Hitchcock cuts to an over-the-shoulder shot as we watch Pelham open the door, revealing, only briefly, the interior of his bedroom, which is neatly arranged. Pelham walks back to Peterson and says, doubling his words, "When you . . . when you let me in, did you . . . did you happen to notice anything different about me?" Peterson says, "But I didn't let you in, sir, you let yourself in." Peterson returns to his bedroom to find that his spare key is still where he left it, then puts both his key and the spare in his jacket pocket. He tells Dr. Harley that the next morning he had the lock on his apartment door changed and only one key made.

In the second sequence, Pelham returns to his apartment late, around 10:00 p.m., expecting to find his supper laid out for him. Irritated when no supper is to be found, he calls for Peterson. A baffled Peterson tells Pelham that he ate his supper and shows him the dishes, as well as the last half-bottle of claret. Then, just as in the previous sequence, Pelham turns and walks to his bedroom. Hitchcock cuts once again to an over-the-shoulder shot, and we see Pelham's bedroom, with his nightclothes laid out neatly on his bed. He turns back to Peterson, who is standing in the hallway. He asks Peterson the same question he asked in the earlier sequence: "Peterson, when you let me in . . ." And just as he did in the earlier sequence, Pelham repeats himself: "Did you . . . did you . . ." Yet now, Hitchcock cuts to an extreme close-up of Pelham's right hand reaching into his pocket as we hear Peterson interrupt: "But you let yourself in, sir." The extreme close-up lingers for several seconds as we see Pelham produce from his pocket a key—the only one to the new lock. It tumbles gently through his thumb and fingers.

This key has many cousins in Hitchcock. As Michael Walker notes, the key is one of Hitchcock's most frequently used motifs. While it is given dramatic focus as early as the British films, Walker claims that the key becomes an elaborated motif only later, beginning with *Notorious*, then *Under Capricorn* and *Dial M for Murder*. In these three films, argues Walker, the key is "linked to tensions in a marriage." As Walker examines the key and traces "the details of its operation" in these films, he finds that it is a symbol of patriarchal control.[41] A woman gains access to keys only with the permission of the head of the household. So when a woman gains possession of the key without permission, she usurps patriarchal control and thus puts herself in physical danger (as when Alex discovers Alicia has taken the key to the wine cellar, where the uranium ore samples are hidden, prompting him to conspire with his mother to poison Alicia).

In "The Case of Mr. Pelham," however, the keys never leave Pelham's possession. The double, it seems, has no need for them. Locked doors are no impediment to him; he comes and goes as he pleases. Though formally similar to other close-ups of keys in Hitchcock (clasped in Alicia's hand at the end of the dazzling crane shot in *Notorious*, in Tony's hand as he embraces a distressed Margot after the attempted murder in *Dial M for Murder*, in Marnie's hand just before she drops it down a drain in *Marnie*), the extreme close-up of Pelham's key signals only its ineffectiveness *as* a key. In its brief moment to shine, the key shows off only its irrelevance. It's as if the extreme close-up of the key is nothing more than a cruel mockery of the logic that structures the doppelgänger genre: *there can only be one*.

Because securing the apartment now proves to be an ineffective way of preventing his double from interfering in his life, Pelham tries a different plan of action. He decides to follow Harley's curious advice, which is to break his predictable routine so that he won't be as easy to match. He decides to forgo his usual, bland, unfussy necktie in favor of a garishly patterned one ("An exclusive model, no two alike, you won't see another," the clothing salesman tells Pelham). Pelham thinks that by switching to the ugly one-of-a-kind model, he will be one step ahead of his double. After taking the morning off, he arrives at his office and is greeted by his secretary, who takes no notice of the tie. She tells him she didn't expect him to return, having worked so hard all morning. Pelham is shocked to learn that while he was away from the office shopping for ugly ties, his double was hard at work, being more efficient—and more routine—than Pelham himself.

Instantly struck by the idea of placing a call to his apartment, we hear Pelham blurt, "Peterson!" Reading actor Tom Ewell's lips carefully, however, one can see that he in fact blurts, "My man!" The line "Peterson" is looped.[42] It is a telling edit, for when Pelham dials the number and hears a voice at the other end of the line, he halts, realizing that the voice is not Peterson's but his own. "Is Peterson there?" he asks. The reply is "*My* man?" This sequence is queer in a number of ways, most obviously in the way it stages the question of who has sole access to Peterson—the double's curious emphasis on *my* suggests that access may be contested—but also in that this little telephone drama unfolds the same way many stories of infidelity do. Pelham calls Peterson and another man answers, or calls home and learns that another man is there. The twist, of course, is that Pelham's double is the "other man," so no blame can be attached to Peterson. Stranger still, the imposter on the phone complains that he has told Peterson he is not supposed to be called on his telephone, the implication being that Peterson has in the past taken personal calls at Pelham's apartment. Pelham's reaction is especially strange, as he instructs the twin Pelham to inform Peterson that he won't be home until late, if at all. Strangest of all, the twin Pelham has no reply. This sets the stage for the final showdown, when Pelham shows up unexpectedly—in his own apartment.

The final showdown in Pelham's apartment begins with Pelham arriving to find Peterson on his way from the kitchen carrying a cocktail tray. Seeing Pelham at the door, Peterson stops dead in his tracks, and utters—sputters—a line that is quite apt for the apartment plot: "What is this, what's going on? Going out, coming in and my never hearing it!" Indeed, what keeps the apartment plot lively are unexpected comings and goings. Until the double began infiltrating Pelham's apartment, neither Pelham nor Peterson was subject to the quirky perks of apartment dwelling (in the way that, say, C. C. Baxter is in Billy Wilder's *The Apartment*), what with Pelham's routine being so routine. When the double emerges from the parlor to confront the real Pelham, flummoxing Peterson all the more, he opens the possibility for what could be a truly bizarre turn in this nascent apartment plot: what if this apartment could happily accommodate two Pelhams? Could this promise a frolicsome future for both its occupants, as well as Peterson? Double your Pelhams, double your fun?

The doppelgänger genre, however, cannot accommodate this possibility, so "The Case of Mr. Pelham" doubles down on routine by way of an object. Pointing to Pelham's garish necktie, the double tells Peterson the real Pelham would never wear such a ghastly tie. Peterson brightens at the idea, and says, "No sir, that's the truth . . . you haven't got one like it! What's more, you wouldn't buy one!" He turns away from Pelham to look at the double, widens his eyes, licks his lips, smiles, and says, "You're the real Mr. Pelham, all right." The necktie plot, it seems, has brought an end to the apartment plot just as it was getting started. Curiously, however, the *real* clincher comes after Pelham loudly begs, "No, Peterson, I only bought it to prove I had something he couldn't duplicate!" The double calmly interrupts Pelham and says, "Please don't shout. No good can come of that, you know." Peterson then turns to the double, smiles, and says, "You're the real one all right. I've heard you say that many times, sir, just that way." One can only begin to speculate under what circumstances Pelham has said to Peterson, "Please don't shout. No good can come of that, you know," but it is a telling fact of apartment life that shouting is routinely overheard by neighbors, nosy or not. Pelham's chiding of Peterson is just the routine management of the apartment's sonic landscape.

Suffice it to say, Peterson's fond memories of the many small domestic dramas played out in this apartment tip the scales, suggesting that the apartment plot lingers, if only as a possibility, or as a threat. Satisfied nonetheless, Peterson smiles at the double: "Just ring if you want me, sir." "Yes, I will," is the double's reply. Now alone with his double, Pelham asks, "Who are you?" The double replies, "Why, I'm Mr. Pelham . . . you're mad, you know." The scene ends with a close-up of Pelham. As the shot fades to black, he casts his eyes upward and smiles, lost perhaps in the baffling thought that he is in exile in his own apartment. Home but elsewhere.

What follows is a curious epilogue. It's now more than a year later, and we are back at the gentleman's club. The "new" Pelham is playing billiards with

Mason, who asks if Pelham is in the millionaire bracket yet. "Oh, possibly," he responds drily. Indeed, this man is no cowering worrywart. The "new" Pelham is positively blasé. And he has every reason to be. Apparently, it has been a good year. He asks Mason "if I seem to have changed any, since I started to get ahead." Mason replies that Pelham seems "to sort of [have] taken hold of things more is all," commenting that the incident with the imposter settled him down or something, allowed him to "take a grip on things." Then, in perhaps the most bizarre gesture in the episode, the "new" Pelham mounts the billiards table, his left leg stretching over the bumper and straight backward, as Hitchcock's camera tracks in slightly. He then aggressively strikes the cue ball.

Mason's assessment of this "new" Pelham, punctuated by the latter's bold body language, suggests an image of decidedly confident and successful nonhomosexual masculinity. This is a man with a firm grip, a man who knows how to get ahead. It is as if the "old" Pelham finally has an alibi, someone who can vouch for him. No longer under the strain of homosexual panic, the "old" Pelham can smile dreamily in his padded cell, knowing the "new" Pelham will proudly strut about, sure of his visible, public nonhomosexual identity, confident that others will notice and approve, and even admire. No wonder, then, that Hitchcock places a portrait of a male lion perched atop his rival on the wall behind the "new" Pelham as he is perched atop the billiards table. This aggressor, this athlete, this champion, is the king of the jungle, cock of the walk. He is the bold nonhomosexual; he is the grand alibi.

✦

Of course, the question of "madness" persists. In the closing monologue, we see Hitchcock, wearing a garish necktie (not Pelham's but a different model), being dragged away by two men in lab coats. "But I'm Alfred Hitchcock, I am, I can prove it!" he pleads. After this man is dragged off camera, we pan to the left to find another Alfred Hitchcock, who assures us that while the man we just saw "carried off the impersonation brilliantly," he was no Alfred Hitchcock. Oddly, it is not the garish necktie that did in this imposter but having bubblegum in his pocket. As Hitchcock told us in the opening monologue, putting bubblegum in someone's coat pocket is one of those "quiet little insidious devices that can drive a man out of his mind." And Alfred Hitchcock wouldn't be caught dead with bubblegum in his pocket. Offscreen we hear a gunshot, an eerie reminder that "death is not the worst that can befall a man." And "The Case of Mr. Pelham" does little to hide from us just what it thinks to a man might be a fate worse than death: to have no alibi in the modern urban world.

Chapter 4

✦

Lost and Found in Hitchcock

> The next job is to create the proper geography.
>
> —Alfred Hitchcock, story memo, October 12, 1961

Cinema and cartography are coextensive. In his book *Cartographic Cinema*, Tom Conley suggests "that in its first shots a film establishes a geography with which every spectator is asked to contend."[1] Consider one of the most common criticisms of a film that fails to cohere technically or narratively: "That film lost me." Consider, too, as I have elsewhere, David Denby's review of the Pixar animated film *Ratatouille* (dir. Brad Bird and Jan Pinkava, 2007).[2] In it, Denby praises the skillful way the kitchen sequences always cohere spatially: "Keeping the space clear and coherent may seem an odd thing to praise in an animated film, but one of the marvelous things about 'Ratatouille' is how well we come to understand the geography of the kitchen in which much of the movie takes place."[3] This chapter demonstrates that Hitchcock's cinema betrays a counterimpulse: to lose us. The complementary themes of homelessness, of aimless wandering, of exposure and vulnerability, of being lost, which haunt Hitchcock's *Vertigo*, are far more common and significant than previously acknowledged.

This chapter charts the unnerving and unstable locations of Bodega Bay, California, and Quebec City, Canada. In *The Birds* and *I Confess*, we experience the paradox of knowing *exactly* where we are while feeling a profound sense of detachment and dislocation, of both psychic and spatial distress. This is precisely what Conley says about the use of recognizable locations in film noir:

> As a general hypothesis it can be said that while it reaches into the deeper swells of psychic conflict, film noir is built upon geographies of uncommon clarity. It underscores, perhaps better than other genres or conventions, what makes cinema a medium that builds upon physical and mental cartographies. The films carefully tell us where they take place at the same time their visual rhetoric causes us to wonder where we are—both historically and psychically—in relation to them.[4]

Though I invoke noir here, I don't intend to explore fully the extent to which some of Hitchcock's films might be considered examples of film noir.[5] Rather, I wish to argue that in both *The Birds* and *I Confess* one might trace a noirish network of contrary impulses: both films continually remind us where we are (Bodega Bay, California, and Quebec City, Quebec, respectively), yet each induces a profound feeling of dislocation and disorientation. To be lost and found in the Hitchcock landscape is to know where you are but not what it means to be there, let alone where you are going. Thus in Hitchcock, psychic tension is also spatial tension. In his reading of Hitchcock's *The 39 Steps*, Conley refers to Hannay's desperate escape to Scotland as "a study of the anxiety of displacement."[6] On the run from the police, Hannay flits from one place to the next, until he finds himself escaping from a train and descending to the foot of the Forth Bridge. We know as well as he does where he is, but this knowledge is useless, and we share his anxiety that he has no idea where to go next. "In a signature fashion," writes Conley, "the film turns a monumental structure and a geographical reference point into a site of anxious anticipation."[7]

Think, too, of the (very noirish) opening sequence of *Vertigo*. In the film's second shot, the camera pans left to follow a man being chased across the rooftops by a police officer and a plainclothes detective. We are given a panorama of a city. And while it is dusk, we can discern, with unmistakable clarity, that we are in San Francisco (to be precise, we are above the Top of the Mark at the Mark Hopkins Hotel, looking east). From right to left, we can spot the bright red neon sign of the Southern Pacific Building, the tower of the handsome Ferry Building, and the Appraisers Building. In the background we trace the Bay Bridge across Treasure Island and off toward Oakland, which sparkles in the distance. Finally, the camera pan ends with a clear view of Coit Tower, one of the film's defining geographical reference points, second perhaps only to the Golden Gate Bridge. As Madeleine will later explain to Scottie, she was able to find his apartment because she remembered it was near Coit Tower. "It led me straight to you," she says (to which Scottie responds, "That's the first time I've been grateful for Coit Tower!").

Of course, Madeleine already knows how to find Scottie's apartment, for Madeleine is actually Judy Barton, enlisted by Gavin Elster to lure Scottie on a series of prolonged and perplexing excursions through the city. So while one of the functions of the opening sequence (and the scene that follows it, in which we are given the same panoramic view of the city through the window of Midge's studio apartment) is to locate us within a specific and recognizable cityscape, the film proceeds to complicate the relationship between space and knowledge, between location and identity. Our journey through San Francisco—its inskirts and outskirts—is a dizzying one; our trajectory is repetitive and circular. Indeed, most critics would agree that the logic mapping San Francisco is the logic of dream and desire—and the two hardly form a reliable GPS. As Ana Salzberg neatly puts it, in *Vertigo* "space itself resists the strictures of ground coordinates."[8] Thus it is possible to trace in Hitchcock's cinema, particularly the films in which a specific location is given a special prominence, the effects of competing impulses: to locate and dislocate, to orient and disorient. In doing so, we might gain a better understanding of the uncanny in Hitchcock—that feeling of being both in exile and at home, both lost and found.

In his Hitchcock book, François Truffaut admits that the French film theorist André Bazin was "not an unconditional admirer of Hitchcock," but he thanks his mentor "for using the key word *equilibrium* in connection with Hitchcock."[9] To be precise, Bazin wrote admirably of a *dis*equilibrium in Hitchcock, of a mise-en-scène that shows "reality only in those moments when a plumb line dropped from the dramatic center of gravity is about to leave the supporting polygon, scorning the initial commotion as well as the final fracas of the fall."[10] Reflecting on Bazin's idea years later, Truffaut suspected this quality of (dis)equilibrium in Hitchcock's work stemmed from the director's fear, due to his weight, "of losing his balance."[11] Perhaps so, though surely this is not what Bazin was implying.[12] Rather, one might say that the quality Bazin thought best epitomized Hitchcock's style was the director's ability to zero in on that instant, so as to sustain it, when the world around you goes out of alignment. Like the instant you realize you're lost.

"The Proper Geography"

The October 1952 issue of *Good Housekeeping* included Daphne du Maurier's story "The Birds," which features Nat Hocken, his wife, his children Jill and Johnny, and his neighbors Mr. and Mrs. Trigg, who hunker down in a Cornish seaside cottage during a mass avian attack. Set nearly eight years after the end of World War II, the story of death falling from the sky surely suggests the sustained and widespread bombing that Cornwall suffered, even though the West Country had been relatively safe from German aerial attack. Several times in du Maurier's story, Nat listens for news on the radio about the birds and their movement, but hears only the crackle of static. At one point Nat thinks the British Navy is coming to the rescue, then realizes that what he sees are gulls rising from the sea. At the end of the story, when all hope is lost, Nat's wife wonders if America will help: "They've always been our allies, haven't they?" she asks. "Surely America will do something!"[13] The silence is broken with the sound of splintering wood and beaks pecking at the door "with all the deft precision of machines," and here the story ends.[14]

This brief summary of "The Birds" may seem to suggest—wrongly, as I will later show—that Hitchcock's adaptation takes little if anything from du Maurier's story. Consider the oft-quoted statement Hitchcock made to François Truffaut about his process of adaptation: "What I do is read a story once, and if I like the basic idea I just forget all about the book and start to create cinema."[15] True, it is all but required of today's scholar to dismiss this statement as sheer disingenuousness—a well-known characteristic of Hitchcock's public persona—and to point out that the director's process of adaptation was far more complicated than this statement allows, that he owed a good deal more to his source material than just "the basic idea" (as has been shown in Palmer and Boyd's recent collection, *Hitchcock at the Source*). Yet if one had to choose a film that failed to prove Hitchcock a liar, it may just be *The Birds*. Indeed, Evan Hunter claims that Hitchcock said to him, "Forget the story now that you've read it, because all we're using is the title and the notion of birds attacking people."[16] In the film there are no Hockens, no Triggs, no son Johnny. There is a daughter, but her name is Cathy Brenner (Veronica Cartwright). Actually, there are two daughters: the aforementioned Cathy Brenner, daughter of Lydia, sister to Mitch; and another named Melanie Daniels, daughter of the wealthy and powerful newspaper magnate Parker Daniels (who does not appear in the film). The birds are the only characters Hitchcock takes from du Maurier's story, and they descend upon a family plot devised not by du Maurier but by Hunter in collaboration with Hitchcock: the perverse love triangle of Mitch, Lydia, and Melanie. The criticism of *The Birds* as adaptation tends to focus almost exclusively on these changes of characters.

But do we even wish to call Hitchcock's film an adaptation? Richard Allen calls it "adaptation in reverse," since *The Birds* adds to du Maurier's story the novelistic details of a conventional romance narrative.[17] But if we head in the wrong direction, I think it is not because Hitchcock's film is not an adaptation, but because we have been distracted by the romance narrative. There are, of course, other changes—the most obvious being the relocation of the story's action from Cornwall, England (where du Maurier spent most of her life) to Bodega Bay, California (not far from where Hitchcock lived, off and on, for almost thirty years). To attend to this important change of setting, however, means we draw our attention away from the family romance added by Hunter and toward the peculiar spatial problem of page-to-screen adaptation. But this is precisely the turn we should take, if we wish to head in the right direction. I argue that Hitchcock is preoccupied less with the family romance than with the cinematic space of that narrative, with the challenge of creating what he calls, in a story memo dated October 12, 1961, "the proper geography." What I propose, in fact, is a turn away from the family romance and toward the importance of spatial location—as well as spatial *dis*location and the anxiety it induces—in *The Birds*. This second turn not only brings a clearer understanding of the technical aspects of Hitchcock's process of adaptation but also allows us to see some overlap, some family resemblances, between du Maurier's story and Hitchcock's film.

To be sure, the clearest family resemblance is that story and film share the same "basic idea": death falling from the sky. Hitchcock's *The Birds* was released only five months after the Cuban missile crisis, and there is no reason to suggest that the idea of death falling from the sky haunted Hitchcock's audience any less than it did du Maurier's readers. Truffaut, in his interviews with Hitchcock, was the first to draw a parallel between the bird attacks and "the ultimate threat to mankind"—atomic warfare.[18] Since then, critical interest in *The Birds* has, with rare exceptions, focused less on the film's Cold War context and more on the film's treatment of human relationships and unconscious desire. Regardless of their approach, most critics of *The Birds* arrive at more or less the same position, which is that Hitchcock's film is *symptomatic* in the richest psychoanalytic sense. In a recent study of the various stages of adaptation undergone by *The Birds*, Walter Raubicheck and Walter Srebnick show that Hitchcock himself was less interested in the explicit political events that Evan Hunter alluded to than in "the social and cultural stresses of the era," less interested in the impact of missiles than in "the impact this turbulent history was having on individual lives and relationships."[19]

But Hitchcock was by no means unaware of Truffaut's association between birds and bombs, and an emergent interest (in individual lives and relationships) does not necessarily diminish other interests (such as death falling from the sky as the ultimate threat to mankind). On February 24, 1962, during a story meeting with Hedren, Hitchcock explained to the actress that the psychological stress triggered by one of the bird attacks is "getting mixed up with [Melanie's] attitudes towards the young man." After struggling with his clarification of what, precisely, she should be experiencing psychologically ("She's getting a bit unnerved . . . the bird attacks and there's something funny her . . . gives her a funny feeling"), Hitchcock comes straight to the point: "It's people beginning to, in extremes, *like in an air raid*, get very emotional. It's a reaction; it's a reflex action, really."[20] There are, of course, countless situations in which groups of people can experience emotional stress, but in *The Birds*, this emotional stress can have only one source: death falling from the sky.

But I wish to attend to another point Hitchcock makes. What is essential to the understanding of human relationships in *The Birds* is not just the fear of the bird attacks, but how the characters *react* to this fear, what their *reflexes* are. In other words, how the characters adjust and orient themselves spatially, as in a feedback loop, is crucial. The idea of death falling from the sky can be coupled with the fear of being lost. In both du Maurier's story and Hitchcock's film, the two ideas catalyze each other: random attacks from the sky radically destabilize an individual's sense of spatial orientation, increasing the urge to find direction while simultaneously making the attempt futile. Thus the fear in du Maurier's story is twofold: certainly the gulls gathering in the bay inspire dread, but the birds induce anxiety in another, more complex way. Early in the story, a line appears that belongs neither to the characters nor to the narrator; it can only be categorized as free indirect speech, hovering above the text as the birds hover above our heads: "Make haste, make speed, hurry and begone; yet where, and to what purpose?"[21] For some time now—surely since Robin Wood's early criticism of the film—scholars have considered why it refuses to answer the second question: "To what purpose?"[22] Hitchcock's film, however, seems more obsessed with the first question posed by du Maurier's text—"Yet where?"—and moreover pays special heed to the text's imperative.

"The basic idea" of du Maurier's story is illuminated in one of the more remarkable moments in the film: the sequence when Melanie delivers the lovebirds to the Brenner home in Bodega Bay. At the suggestion of the postal clerk—presumably an authority on location—Melanie takes a motorboat to reach the dock at the Brenner home rather than traverse the road that curves around the bay. After leaving the lovebirds, along with a note to Cathy that replaces the note she had written to Mitch, Melanie returns to the motorboat and heads toward town. Mitch, after discovering the lovebirds, views Melanie through a pair of binoculars and decides to follow her along the shore in his car. As Melanie approaches the pier where Mitch waits, a gull strikes her on the forehead. The attack comes as a surprise, a sudden rupture in the course of the events. These are almost *non*events—Mitch's unobservable busywork inside the barn, Lydia and Cathy's convenient departure by truck, Melanie's stealthy arrival and departure. But their careful orchestration, the systematic fashion in which they are filmed, suggests a weighty significance, so that when Melanie arrives at the pier, we expect that she and Mitch will have much to discuss. Instead, the gull attacks Melanie.

But it is perhaps the *precision* of the gull's attack that is shocking as much as its suddenness or arbitrariness: to the extent that we are uncertain *why* the bird attacks, we are certain it knows *where* to attack. What we and Mitch witness is a tactical airstrike. Indeed, the gulls' impressive targeting capabilities are discussed later in the film, shortly after a long conversation between Melanie and Annie Hayworth (Suzanne Pleshette) about Lydia. Melanie tells Annie of her invitation to Cathy's birthday party and her hesitation about attending because of Lydia's earlier cold behavior. "Suddenly, into the silence," reads Hunter's screenplay dated March 2, 1962, "comes a THUMP at the door startling them both." Once again, however, it is not just the startling nature of this bird's arrival that arrests the characters. At the sight of the dead gull at her front door, Annie coos sympathetically, "Oh, the poor thing. He probably lost his way in the dark." Melanie responds, "But . . . it isn't dark, Annie. There's a full moon." Annie's impulse is not only to pity but also to anthropomorphize the bird—she gives the pronoun *he* a more emphatic (and more empathic) sense by suggesting that the bird was helpless and wayward, like a child lost in the dark. Du Maurier's story, however, is clear about the profound misdirection of such sympathies:

> In spring the birds flew inland, purposeful, intent; they knew where they were bound, the rhythm and ritual of their life brooked no delay. In autumn those that had not migrated overseas but remained to pass

> the winter were caught up in the same driving urge, but because migration was denied them followed a pattern of their own.[23]

Not only are the birds purposeful and intent, but they also follow a "pattern of their own," which suggests something far more ominous in Melanie's words. She points out that Annie's "he"—her "poor thing"—was not at all lost in the dark; she also uses a decidedly different grammar, speaking of this bird event in an oblique case: "*It* isn't dark outside." That the birds cannot be humanized and made familiar is not necessarily a frightening idea—that is, unless they attack. We cannot know their navigational patterns, for the birds do not abide by our universal coordinate systems. We are, then, all the more vulnerable.

This is part of the reason why the film is obsessed with human navigation—so much so that one might call *The Birds* a film about cybernetics, which is the study of goal-seeking and self-correction. Norbert Wiener, the founder of cybernetics, formulated two concepts that are useful here. The first, *feedback*, is a term used by control engineers to describe the process by which a motion follows a given pattern: "The difference between this pattern and the actually performed motion is used as a new input to cause the part regulated to move in such a way as to bring its motion closer to that given by the pattern."[24] In short, a "feedback loop" is a process by which we send and receive information in a given environment, allowing us to comprehend this environment and to make necessary adjustments as we navigate it.[25] The second concept is *ontogenetic* versus *phylogenetic* learning. According to Wiener, "These two phenomena are closely related to each other, for the first is the basis for the adaptation of the individual to its environment by means of experience, which is what we may call ontogenetic learning, while the second, as it furnishes the material on which variation and natural selection may operate, is the basis of phylogenetic learning."[26] Coincidentally, Wiener refers to the work of Julian Huxley, who demonstrates "that birds have a small capacity for ontogenetic learning. . . . Complicated as the behavior patterns of birds are—in flying, in courtship, in the care of the young and in nest building—they are carried out correctly the very first time without the need of any large amount of instruction from the mother."[27] If, as Mitch Brenner claims, there is a "bird war," it is a war between ontogenetic and phylogenetic learners—between humans, who must constantly adapt and change within a hostile environment, and birds, whose knowledge of this environment is preprogrammed (which is precisely what makes this environment especially hostile to humans).

The turn I'm suggesting, away from the romance narrative in Hitchcock's film to the "basic idea" shared by both film and source text, is a turn away from psychoanalytic theory to cybernetics. In fact, the film begins with a cybernetic moment: Melanie arrives at a San Francisco pet store promptly at 3:00 p.m. to collect a mynah bird she wishes to give to her "veddy prim and straight-laced Aunt Tessa." Worriedly, Mrs. MacGruder (Ruth McDevitt), the pet shop clerk, informs Melanie that the bird has not arrived, probably due to traffic. Melanie then suggests that the mynah bird be delivered to her, and she offers her address. I would suggest that with this opening exchange, in just over three minutes of screen time, the film has established its "basic idea": *Where are the birds, and where am I?*

But this is just the first of several of examples of global positioning and self-correction that occur throughout the film. After Melanie notes Mitch's license plate number, she phones Charlie at her father's newspaper and asks him to obtain Mitch's address from the Department of Motor Vehicles.[28] Shortly after, when an elevator passenger tells Melanie that Mitch is in Bodega Bay for the weekend, Melanie asks him, "Bodega Bay? Where's that?" The man responds, "Up the coast. About sixty miles north of here. About an hour and a half on the freeway, or two if you take the coast highway." When Melanie arrives in Bodega Bay, she asks the postal clerk about the location of the Brenner house, and the postal clerk says, "See where I'm pointing? See them two big trees across there?"[29] Melanie then asks how to reach the house, and the postal clerk tells her to "follow the road straight through town 'til it curves on the left . . . straight through town, stay on your left, right around the bay to the front door" (figure 4.1). Many critics who write about *The Birds* remind us that Melanie attends a course in general semantics at University of California, Berkeley, but they neglect to mention that the course meets only once a week. "I do different things on different days," Melanie tells Mitch. "On Mondays and Wednesdays I work for the Traveler's Aid at the airport." Mitch then asks, sarcastically, "Helping travelers?" To which Melanie responds, "No, misdirecting them. I thought you could read my character."[30] Melanie, it can be said, spends her time in San Francisco acquainting herself not only with "finding new four-letter words," as she puts it, but also with the logistics of ground traffic control. Later in the film, when it becomes clear that Melanie might have to spend the night in Bodega Bay rather than return to San Francisco, Melanie directs herself "across to Santa Rosa," where she'll "come onto the freeway much earlier."

The sheer number of instances when directions are given or solicited is remarkable, but the social awkwardness of these instances is also important. When the man in Mitch's apartment building tells Melanie that Mitch is in Bodega Bay for the weekend, he is most certainly not "awfully sorry," as he claims. Similarly awkward is the scene where Melanie struggles with the cagey postal clerk ("I'm looking for a man named Mitchell Brenner." "Yah." "Do you know him?" "Yah." "Where does he live?" "Right here, Bodega Bay." "Oh, yes, I know, but where?" "Right across the bay, there." "Where?"). More than three minutes of screen time are devoted to steering Melanie in the right direction, but her successful arrival at the Brenner house does not mark the end of local navigation. In the Tides restaurant, a mother wonders (as her child asks, "Are the birds going to eat us, mommy?"), "What's the fastest

Figure 4.1. *The Birds*: Directing Melanie Daniels

road to San Francisco?" Deke, the owner of the Tides, says, "The freeway, ma'am." "Where do I get it?" she asks, and a hard-drinking salesman says, "I'm going that way, lady. You can follow me."

This emphasis on the embarrassment produced by a loss of direction no doubt accounts, in part, for the film's comic tone—the screwball element that Hitchcock appreciated in Hunter's script.[31] After all, a loss of direction does not always result in anxiety. Of interest here is the work of Vivian Sobchack, who isolates three forms of a loss of direction: the first is "the experience of going round in circles," the second is "not knowing where you are," and the third is "not knowing how to get where you're going."[32] The first is more or less a temporal condition, as we find ourselves "repeatedly oriented to the *past* since one finds oneself continually revisiting and relocating there."[33] The second is far more terrifying, as there is neither a future destination nor a past point of origin with which the viewer can feel grounded. It is, argues Sobchack, "the 'black hole' of being lost: the experience of the unmarked Mesopotamian desert and sandstorms of *The Lost Patrol* or of the vast landscape of Death Valley in *Gerry*."[34] But not, it seems, of the parochial environs of Bodega Bay. To be sure, these are no mean streets that Melanie navigates—she may be lost, but she hardly seems ungrounded. It would appear, then, that the instances of a loss of direction in *The Birds* resemble what Sobchack identifies as the third form of being lost, "a more mundane and less threatening form of spatial disorientation":

> Unlike the other two forms of being lost, its spatial structure is linear and *forward-directed* toward a reachable distant point—even if both the direction that is "forward" and its intended destination cannot be

> precisely located. . . . This form of being lost is focused on the real possibility of pragmatic resolution. It presents itself as a hermeneutic problem rather than as a recurrent nightmare or an existential crisis, and its major affective charge tends to be frustration rather than desperation or panic.[35]

Asking for directions is simply a matter of "not knowing how to get where you're going," and the effect of this form of being lost is comic frustration, not existential dread. A case in point is the scene in the hallway outside Mitch's apartment. Melanie's frustration is made all the more comic by the "excruciating politeness" of Mitch's neighbor—Richard Deacon, who was well known by audiences at the time for his numerous appearances (as frustrated desk clerks, aloof hotel managers, and the like) in television situation comedies such as *The Adventures of Ozzie and Harriet*, *The Danny Thomas Show*, and *Leave It to Beaver*.

It is true that misdirection is frequently played for laughs in Hitchcock's films. For example, in *The Man Who Knew Too Much* (1956), Ben McKenna follows a lead from a dying Louis Bernard (Daniel Gélin) and visits the taxidermist Ambrose Chappell at 61 Burdett Street, Camden Town. Ben begins to think he's in the wrong place, and an outrageous melee ensues, with Ben fending off a pack of angry taxidermists and their stuffed animals. His wife, Jo, waiting behind in a hotel room, suddenly realizes that Ambrose Chappell is not a man but a place, Ambrose Chapel—a church located at 17 Ambrose Street, West Two. Of course, a mounted swordfish wielded by an aged taxidermist is no real cause for alarm. The worst Ben suffers is a bite from a lifeless tiger. But the animal attacks in *The Birds* are a real threat, so it seems hardly adequate to call every scene of misdirection nothing more than situationally comic.

Several of the film's instances of global positioning and repositioning occur *before* the threat represented by the birds is made evident: the first attack takes place after Melanie asks for directions to the Brenner house, after directionlessness presents itself as a specific difficulty in the film. Nevertheless, the birds' first appearance in the film—hovering above San Francisco's Union Square Park at the intersection of Geary and Powell Streets—is a moment with its own menace. And what if we were to assume that these are *the* birds—the same birds that will launch several attacks on the people of Bodega Bay, that these birds *follow* Melanie or, at any rate, make the same sixty-mile journey—north by northwest, it so happens—to Bodega Bay? Here a curious scenario presents itself: later in the film, we learn that Melanie chose to take the longer but more direct route to Bodega Bay via the Pacific Coast Highway, rather than the faster, roundabout route along the 101 freeway, which is further inland. In doing so, she anticipates her route to the Brenner home, which is across the water by motorboat, rather than along Westshore Road by car.[36] Like the birds themselves, Melanie takes the straightest route possible (surely it would be against nature for the birds to follow the advice of the man in the elevator and take the freeway—a point made to humorous effect in the shots of the lovebirds swaying to and fro in Melanie's car). But there is a cloud hanging over this scene, in the form of a flock of gulls that has traveled with Melanie and settled on the surface of the calm waters that she, a skilled cybernetic, now navigates. The lines tracing the paths of Melanie's route to and from the Brenner house, and Mitch's chase along the shore, only *appear* to weave a tissue of nonsense. A passage from du Maurier's story intimates that the drive taken by Melanie and the lovebirds up the Pacific Coast Highway is haunted by a dreadful force and is therefore far less canny than it appears: "And like people who, apprehensive of death before their time, drive themselves to work or folly, the birds do likewise; tomorrow we shall die."[37]

What Hitchcock's film presents is a fear to be reckoned with: a fear of exposure. The presence of birds heightens these fears, as they hover above us as well as the characters in the film; the birds are masters of navigation, speed, and precision. If the caged lovebirds mock us with their human-like rocking to and fro, the birds of the air humiliate us by turning us into fools who flap our useless limbs and fumble about willy-nilly. "What we experience in *The Birds*," writes Murray Pomerance, "is a fluttering, extended, directionless, aggressive present."[38] It is *we* who experience directionlessness in the fluttering, extended, aggressive present of Hitchcock's film and du Maurier's story. In the latter, the first fluttering, extended, aggressive attack on Nat Hocken and his family occurs when the birds enter his children's bedroom through the window: "The window was wide open. Through it came the birds, hitting first the ceiling and the walls, then swerving in mid-flight, turning to the children in their beds."[39] After Nat pushes his children through the bedroom door and closes it behind him, he wraps a blanket around his head; blinded, he tries to fend off the birds with his bare hands. "How long he fought with them in the darkness he could not tell," writes du Maurier, "but at last the beating of the wings about him lessened and then withdrew, and through the density of the blanket he was aware of light."[40] In the aftermath of the attack, Nat removes the blanket from around his head: "Dawn, and the open window, had called the living birds; the dead lay on the floor. Nat gazed at the little corpses, shocked and horrified. They were all small birds, none of any size; there must have been fifty of them lying there upon the floor."[41]

This attack on Nat in his children's bedroom corresponds to three scenes in Hitchcock's film. The image of dozens of dead birds scattered upon the floor is recast in a scene after hundreds of swifts descend through the chimney into the Brenners' living room.[42] Mitch, Melanie, Cathy, and Lydia escape unharmed and return later with Sheriff Malone to a room in shambles. The floor is littered with broken glass, plates, teacups, and dead birds. Perhaps a more obviously corresponding scene from Hitchcock's film is the final attack on Melanie. While Lydia, Cathy, and Mitch sleep in the living room, Melanie sits quietly before the fire. She hears sounds of birds fluttering and calls to Mitch, who does not wake up. She decides to make sure the birds have not entered the house. Taking a flashlight from the table (one of the birds has cut the power to the house), she walks up the stairs, opens a door, and enters the room. All is darkness. Looking up, Melanie sees a hole in the ceiling that reveals the night sky. She gasps in shock, then shines the flashlight to reveal dozens of crows and seagulls perched upon a child's bed. The birds launch a relentless and brutal attack on Melanie, who, having fallen backward against the bedroom door, has trapped herself inside the room. Like Nat, all she can do is swing her only weapon of defense—the flashlight—wildly and hopelessly in the dark.

The motif of blindness and directionlessness suggests another scene: the bird attack at Cathy's birthday party. Before the attack, Mitch and Melanie climb down from the dunes after having a drink and discussing Melanie's schedule, which includes misdirecting people at the airport on Mondays and Wednesdays (and going to bird shops on Fridays). It is important to note here how directionlessness is a topic of conversation just before a bird attack. The camera pans right to reveal Annie, who has been watching the birds while the children play Blind Man's Bluff. Annie has just spun a blindfolded Cathy around three times and sent her off with a gentle "There you go." Psychoanalytic interpretations of this attack are as abundant as the birds in the sky, although few note the aptness of this particular children's game.[43] Here I turn to the work of a pair of bird experts Mrs. Bunday may have been familiar with. In their book *Birds of Washington*, W. L. Dawson and J. H. Bowles say this about the nimble and cunning chickadee: "Blind-man's buff, hide-and-seek and tag are merry games enough when played out on one plane; but when staged in three dimensions, with a labyrinth of interlacing branches for hazard, only the blithe bird whose praises we sing could promptly master their intricacies."[44] In other words, we are no match for the birds, whose gifts of orientation and navigation are not simply better than ours but of an entirely different order.

The film ends with Melanie, Mitch, Cathy, and Lydia abandoning a shelter that has failed them. Once the roof of the Brenner home is breached and Melanie is physically injured and emotionally traumatized by a brutal attack, there is no other option but to flee. The plot of *The Birds* has been leading them precisely to this moment. And here we might stop and pose a question not fully explored, much less answered, by critics: as the four make their way from the house to the car, why do the birds, who have assembled en masse, not attack them? To be sure, the film gives us no explanation for why they *won't* attack, and every reason to think they *will*.[45] One might begin exploring this question by noting that there is only one other instance in the film when the birds do not attack, and that is at the very beginning, when Melanie spies a large flock of birds circling above Union Square as she walks to Davidson's Pet Shop, where she will encounter Mitch Brenner and decide to pursue him. Thus if we are to associate this first menacing, though not malicious, flock of birds with Melanie's flight to Bodega Bay—one she navigates with the help of Mitch's neighbor—we could say that the birds that loom with similar menace and lack of malice on and around the Brenner home at the end of the film tell us perhaps what we should have known all along: we make haste and make speed, but with no destination and no purpose. All along, the plot of *The Birds* has led these four characters to where we find them at the end: on the road (in a convertible no less) with nowhere to go.

A film about death coming from the skies above Bodega Bay presents a unique challenge to Hitchcock: to create "the proper geography." In a story memo dated October 12, 1961, Hitchcock tends to the peculiar problem of mapping his film: "We are going to have a special arrangement for this whole setting of the school in relation to its position in the town. . . . A plan will have to be drawn up showing how we can relate these buildings in Bodega to the roadways in the community of Bodega Bay."[46] Hitchcock's approach to the "bird's-eye view" of Bodega Bay is instructive. Significantly, in the story memo Hitchcock addresses the spatial problem of the film: "A site must be found for photographing Bodega Bay high up. This is in order to show the audience the shape of the terrain, and also the distance of the house in the story from the town proper." Ultimately, the solution to this problem was to create a composite of matte paintings and live-action footage shot at Universal Studios. This shot, as William Rothman writes, occupies "an impossible position alongside the soaring seagulls, as if a bird of their feather. The birds that oversee this world are not gods or devils, this shot implies. They are just birds."[47]

But when we, like Rothman and so many critics with him, turn to the question of perspective (is this the point of view of the birds? of God?) we also turn to the question that is posed whenever we behold a map, which is what I take this shot to be: a map, a topographic projection, of Bodega Bay. As Conley makes clear,

> a map in a movie begs and baits us to ponder the fact that *who we are* or whomever we believe ourselves to be depends, whether or not our locus is fixed or moving, on often unconscious perceptions about *where* we come from and may be going. To be able to say who one is depends on believing in the illusion that consciousness is in accord with where it is felt in respect at once to itself and to its milieu.[48]

What needs more critical discussion is Hitchcock's attention to the particular problems of *direction*, in the navigational sense. Indeed, navigating an unfamiliar environment is not simply Melanie's problem in *The Birds* but the problem of cinema itself, one Hitchcock felt acutely during the process of taking "The Birds" from page to screen. All his talk about finding the "proper geography" and showing the audience "the shape of the terrain" makes Hitchcock seem primarily motivated by the need to make his film cohere spatially. Yet his films also bear out a contrary impulse, which is to take advantage of what Sobchack calls the "initial premises" of cinema. Speaking of why there are "fewer scenes of people literally getting lost in the cinema than one might expect," Sobchack says,

> a primary reason might be that since the cinema, itself, is made up of bits and pieces of discontinuous and discontiguous time and space, the goal of both the cinematic apparatus and the traditional narrative is to make these fragments cohere into a coordinated geography the viewer can navigate. Evoking literal disorientation reminds cinema and the spectator to varying degrees of the cinema's initial premises, which are incoherent.[49]

Part of what makes a Hitchcock film so uncanny is the way the cinema's initial premise of incoherence is to a large extent *expressive* of the film's landscape. Like Melanie Daniels, Hitchcock is both expert guide and expert *mis*guide (and for Hitchcock, these roles add up to a full-time, lifelong occupation). If *The Birds* is, as Robin Wood claims, a "culmination," it is a culmination insofar as it demonstrates Hitchcock's obsessive impulse to create a cinema that makes full use of its initial premises.[50]

Confessions of a Streetwalker: Hitchcock's Camera in Quebec City

Having experienced in 1925 a number of shocks and unpleasant surprises during the filming of *The Pleasure Garden* in Italy, Alfred Hitchcock would, for the remainder of his career, prefer the comforts of the studio to location shooting. Yet in spite of this preference, Hitchcock did give audiences memorable scenes of actual locations, small towns and big cities alike—including but not limited to Washington, D.C., London, New York's boroughs of Manhattan and Queens, San Francisco and its nearby environs, and numerous spots along the Côte d'Azur. There's also Paris, Copenhagen, Marrakesh, as well as Phoenix, Arizona, and Craftsbury, Vermont. Yet apart from the extensive writings on *Vertigo*'s San Francisco (and San Francisco's *Vertigo*), there is very little scholarly interest in the unique ties of Hitchcock's films to place (one important exception being Murray Pomerance's *Alfred Hitchcock's America*, which examines various locations in some detail).

But Hitchcock's interest in dizzying geography was by no means exclusive to San Francisco. One might go as far back as 1927's *Downhill* to find what is widespread in Hitchcock's films: the cinematic portrayal of cities both large and small as producing anxiety-inducing feelings of misdirection and disorientation. The scene I have in mind is when Roddy Berwick, having crossed the English Channel from Marseilles, wanders the streets of London in a daze; this is a scene Hitchcock would repeat, and improve upon, in *Blackmail* two years later, as Alice White ends up in exactly the same spot, beneath the Bovril sign at Shaftesbury Avenue and Regent Street, the very first neon sign in Piccadilly Circus. As we've just seen, *The Birds* helps us to appreciate the inevitable fusion of direction and misdirection in Hitchcock, and we have yet to examine fully the strange logistics of ground traffic control in the films that foreground location. As noted above, a fitting name for a study of movement in the Hitchcock landscape is cybernetics—the flow of information that affects control and communication. What is fascinating about the Hitchcock landscape is how frequently things go haywire, how frequently information and place go worryingly out of alignment.

An illustrative example might be retired detective John "Scottie" Ferguson's visit to the McKittrick Hotel in *Vertigo*. He has followed Madeleine Elster to this location, 1007 Gough Street in the neighborhood known as the Western Addition, after a stop at the cemetery at Mission Dolores and the art gallery at the Palace of the Legion of Honor. Now he watches Madeleine get out of her car, go into the hotel, and look out through the window of her upstairs room. Thus far, we might think we are witness simply to what Alexander Welsh says is typical of Hitchcock: "He takes for granted the mobility of modern urban populations and concentrates, by means of the camera alone, on the hurrying urban society of strangers under surveillance of the police."[51] Then a curious thing happens. Not only is Madeleine no longer in her room, but the desk clerk insists she has not been in the hotel at all. "Well, I would have seen her, you know," she tells him. "I've been right here all the time putting olive oil on my rubber plant leaves." Since he has produced for the clerk his detective's badge, indicating that he has the authority to demand knowledge of, and access to, the mysterious lodger, Scottie asks the desk clerk to go up to her room and look. As she does so, something catches Scottie's eye. Robert J. Belton has noted the curious point-of-view shot that follows, of "an enormous light fixture, bristling with jagged glass prisms atop a pole emerging from the newel post at the bottom of the stairs."[52] As Belton notes, the film never follows through with "the possibility of lurking meaningfulness, like some Uncanny threat" that the shot suggests.[53] He offers up a Freudian reading of the light fixture, yet an equally promising line of thought is that the shot answers the look of increasing bewilderment on Scottie's face. The jagged glass prisms that adorn the light fixture suggest spiral movement, as the prisms atop the fixture point outward, while those hanging from its tiers point downward. It's a striking visual metaphor for the vertiginous plunge Scottie will soon take, for the beautiful abyss to which he gives himself.

The point not to miss, however, is the *certainty* Scottie has of Madeleine's exact location, backed by his badge. There is on his face more than a little visible irritation when the clerk contradicts his information. When she beckons from the top of the stairs, "Oh Mr. Detective," it's a sly mockery of the procedural we've been watching. Scottie leaps confidently up the stairs, only to find Madeleine's room empty.[54] Up until this very moment, Scottie has behaved far less like the wanderer he'll soon become and more like an expert in identifying presence and tracking movement ("You're still the hardheaded Scot, always have been," Gavin reminds him).[55] But now, Scottie has lost Madeleine. And this is no ordinary elusion; it is as magical as Uncle Charlie's escape from the two detectives at the opening of *Shadow of a Doubt*, proving he is like Madeleine, who "can move in unheralded ways through physical space."[56] From here on out, Scottie will be more open to forgoing reason (much to Midge's disapproval).[57]

Time and again we see in Hitchcock this discord of information and place. It's as if, in any given location of a Hitchcock film, we are given two views: one totalizing, expository, the bird's-eye view, if you will. This view we associate with cartography, with knowledge and surveillance. Call it the "proper geography." Another view is far less coherent, far less legible, precisely because it is at ground level, on the streets. What I have in mind here is very close to what Michel de Certeau says are two ways of looking at the city: as a voyeur or as a walker. The former strives for the totalizing view of the city, so as to make it readable. The latter moves through the city as if blind; the walker's paths are "intertwining, unrecognized poems in which each body is an element signed by many others," and these paths "elude legibility."[58] These ways of looking at the city coexist and overlap, forming a bewildering ensemble. While in the previous chapter we wrestled with the idea of a person being in two places at once, here we will wrestle with the idea of two places being one: "A *migrational*, or metaphorical, city" that "slips into the clear text of the planned and readable city."[59]

My interest now is to follow Hitchcock's camera as it navigates one of the most unusual locations of his long career, Quebec City, the setting of 1953's *I Confess*. As it is one of the lesser-known Hitchcock films, a brief synopsis may be of some help. A man named Villette is found murdered in his home. A caretaker named Otto Keller (O. E. Hasse) confesses this crime to Father Logan (Montgomery Clift), in whose church he works. Keller accidentally killed Villette while trying to rob him. The morning after the murder, Logan goes to Villette's home, where the police and a crowd of bystanders have gathered. There he meets Inspector Larrue (Karl Malden), who asks to speak with him. Logan is willing to cooperate, but Larrue is immediately suspicious as he watches Logan pace nervously in the street outside Villette's home. Larrue's suspicion is compounded when Logan begins talking with a woman, who he later learns is Ruth Grandfort (Anne Baxter), the wife of Pierre Grandfort (Roger Dann), a respected member of parliament. After Larrue learns from two young girls, who were walking past Villette's house at the time of the murder, that they saw a man in a cassock leaving Villette's home, Logan becomes his prime suspect. Yet Logan cannot exonerate himself because he is bound by his faith not to share information gained from a confession. Things become dire for Logan when Ruth tells Larrue that she was being blackmailed by Villette, who had spotted her in a compromising position with Logan and threatened to reveal this information to Ruth's husband. The film reaches a climax when Otto, who finally confesses his crime, is gunned down by police in the ballroom of the Chateau Frontenac—a historic hotel that is one of Quebec City's most iconic landmarks.

Compared to other locations visited during the making of his other films, Hitchcock made considerable use of Quebec City. According to the production notes for the film, "Eighty percent of the action of *I Confess* was filmed in Quebec, including all of the exterior scenes and a major share of the interiors."[60] This makes Quebec City one of the most prominent cinematic landscapes in all of Hitchcock, second perhaps to San Francisco. As I've shown, directionlessness and disorientation are primary concerns in *The Birds*; yet while Bodega Bay is the place where anxieties about spatial dislocation are laid bare, it is not the town itself that produces them but the birds. In Hitchcock's *I Confess*, however, we see a more intimate dynamic between cinema and city. Hitchcock's camera relentlessly pursues Quebec City's streetwalkers, charting dizzying paths and connections. Hitchcock's camera is, one might say, let loose, unbound, free of any obligation to map "the proper geography" of Quebec City.[61] Yet this unrestrained mobility hardly defines the plot of *I Confess*, which links secret information with movement through the city streets, and calls forth the investigative impulse to make both information and city comport and cohere. It is precisely the zigzag wanderings the camera traces that provoke a hermeneutic activity of cartographic reason, embodied most of all by Inspector Larrue, whose very name links him with urban mapping. But his name is also linked with *allure*, the idea of being lured, enticed, drawn, even misled—an idea that is established at the film's outset and sustained throughout.[62] What follows is a reading of *I Confess* that traces Hitchcock's camera as it *deranges* the geography of Quebec City.

Critics have made note of the peculiar montage that follows the opening credits of the film.[63] The camera is lured by a number of signs reading, in French, DIRECTION, as it makes its way along the darkened cobblestone streets of Quebec City (figure 4.2). Finally we arrive at our destination: the open window of an apartment, through which we see a corpse. It's a classic Hitchcock setup. Here is, in William Rothman's terms, the "murderous gaze" of Hitchcock's camera, luring the unsuspecting spectator to what it rightly suspects the viewer desired (and hoped) to see all along: a grisly death. But why would this director be in need of direction? Is it because we are in—as far as Hitchcock's films go—a foreign land? In the interest of exploring just what, exactly, Quebec City has to do with this film that it hosts, I will follow a literal reading of the film's opening sequence, a reading that is too easily dismissed. Whereas Pomerance tells us that "the word 'direction' is taken to refer not to the orientation of a thoroughfare, but to a moral and general state of human affairs," I suggest we consider the value of a literal reading, in order to tease out some of the ways in which the film conveys, through its

Figure 4.2. *I Confess*: Direction in Quebec City

visualization of Quebec City, the anxiety of *mis*direction, of *dis*orientation that shadows the film's investment in surveying and mapping.[64]

Hitchcock is warning us of what we're about to get into by watching *I Confess*, which is that our tour of Quebec City will be anything but ordinary. By this I mean that the cameo, which comes just after the opening credits of the film, is warning us of the misdirection that may follow. While we are told to move one way (DIRECTION) we find that the director himself is going another way, walking in the wrong direction above L'Escalier Casse-cou, or breakneck stairs, a seventeenth-century stairway that connects Upper and Lower Town in Old Quebec. It's likely Hitchcock continues in this direction along rue du Petit Champlain. Combining the shots of the navigator who founded Quebec City, the DIRECTION signs, and the wrong-way cameo, we see that the opening of *I Confess* is somewhat preoccupied with the city in which it takes place. Indeed, throughout the film one senses the camera's topographic fascination with Quebec City—its desire to chart one's way through the city, to engage in the formal spatial practice of surveying and mapping.

Yet these practices prove to be not entirely successful, given the way cinema can scramble a city beyond the point of recognition. As we begin to think about location, indication, direction, orientation, and mobility in *I Confess*, we find that Quebec City resists mapping—or more precisely it resists the kind of rational cartography that might paint a coherent picture of the city. Hitchcock's Quebec City never quite coheres. While many films take liberties with location, as filmmakers frequently take shots from several different parts of the city and edit them together to create a single imagined space (this is what the Soviet film theorist Lev Kuleshov, whose ideas Hitchcock knew well, called "creative geography"), I argue that something stranger is happening in *I Confess*. Part of the problem lies with the fact that Quebec City isn't really one city but many: Old and New, sacred and secular, pre- and post-Duplessis (the conservative premier of Quebec who was in power in 1936–39 and again in 1944–59). This is of course true of many cities, and while *I Confess* busies itself with disorienting us, it reorients us toward a more complex understanding of the city. It is a view of the city that challenges what we might call the "Google street view" of the city, the impulse to fully map every square inch with a mobile mechanical eye. *I Confess* proves that the city is too complex, too gnarled up with countless itineraries, personal histories, plots, motivations, and memories. With Hitchcock's camera as our guide, we find that we are lost before we even begin.

Take, for instance, Amy Lawrence's reading of the first few moments of *I Confess*: "The film opens on a dark night in a European-looking town. Signs clutter the empty streets as a series of shots show arrows pointing in opposite directions. Hitchcock strolls through, oblivious to the confused space."[65] While Hitchcock's cameo appears before we see any arrows, and further, the arrows do not point in opposite directions, Lawrence's inaccuracies seem somehow apt. What might be taken as an unambiguous formal design, the left-to-right trajectory of Hitchcock's camera, turns out to be as confused as Lawrence suggests. The first image we see in *I Confess*, during the film's opening credits, is of the Chateau Frontenac, viewed from some distance, placing us somewhere on the Saint Lawrence River. The next shot is of Chateau Frontenac but from a much closer angle, suggesting that we have moved east to west or, map-minded, right to left. We are now looking straight up at the statue of the great French navigator, Samuel de Champlain, who founded Quebec City in 1608 (figure 4.3). He appears to be moving in the direction of the chateau while our master of *direction*, Alfred Hitchcock, is seen navigating a very different path (figure 4.4).

Should we choose to follow this streetwalker, we'd find ourselves on rue du Petit-Champlain. But the camera will not allow it and pushes on in the opposite direction, reestablishing a left-to-right vector field. But just as it does so, we are once again reoriented—this time by the arch of the Citadelle wall, which, with its pointed tower, directs our eyes upward. The next shot is of another DIRECTION sign, which curiously leads us to the Cathedral-Basilica of Notre-Dame de Québec on rue de Buade. In the distance, barely noticeable at the bottom left of the screen, is a man who first moves from left to right, but then, as if to confuse or elude us, backtracks and heads in the opposite direction.[66]

Figure 4.3. *I Confess*: One-way Frontenac

Figure 4.4. Hitchcock's cameo in *I Confess*

Perhaps we have glimpsed some random streetwalker who happens to be in shot. If so, he has been allowed to remain for us to see him—this is a very long static shot, and surely Hitchcock and his editor, Rudy Fehr, could have afforded to leave this phantom on the cutting room floor if they wanted to. But the idea of a random accident hardly does away with the desire to speculate in hindsight as to the figure's identity. He could be any number of people—perhaps Otto Keller, perhaps Villette returning home (we have yet to come upon his dead body). It may even be Father Logan, who, in the course of the film, shows himself to be quite a streetwalker: on at least three occasions we find him ambulating through Quebec City.

While seemingly orienting us toward a murder, the opening of *I Confess* actually presents us with a confusing geography. The shadowy streets of Quebec City, scattered with mixed signals, are empty save for the director himself and one shadowy person who seems to be covering his tracks. These two figures suggest the contrary impulses of the film, direction and misdirection: the all-too-familiar silhouette of the director himself, who walks purposefully in one direction, and a man unknown to us, who doubles back as if to confound his follower.

Yet there exists another possibility, which is that the figure is one of two young girls who also happen to be walking the streets of Old Quebec that fateful night and witness the man emerging from Villette's house. Like the cassock the man wears, these girls are essential to the film. Without their eyewitness testimony, it would be difficult to connect the film's two plots, the first being Otto's murder of Villette and his subsequent confession to Father Logan, the second being Villette's blackmailing of Ruth Grandfort, who—we learn by way of flashback—had witnessed what appeared to be Ruth's intimate liaison with Father Logan.

But why the two girls? Presumably it is because the combination of youth and innocence makes their testimony unimpeachable. The girls are much too young to be streetwalking in the immodest sense—though it is not easy to ignore how the film encourages us to make such an association. Just before Inspector Larrue brings the girls in for questioning, his assistant Murphy (Judson Pratt) momentarily piques the erotic interest of Crown Prosecutor Robertson (Brian Aherne) when he turns to Larrue and asks, "Shall I bring the girls in, sir?" And while the idea that the two girls are streetwalkers is dismissed as swiftly as Robertson's hopes for some after-lunch titillation are dashed, we may find it hard not to wonder why they are walking the streets of Old Quebec at this time of night, without a chaperone. A draft of the screenplay, dated May 26, 1952, suggests there is something lurid about the streets of Quebec City at night: the DIRECTION signs are described as forming a "tempting pattern as if they were Pied Pipers leading us toward some awfulness." Anyone familiar with the folktale "The Pied Piper of Hamelin" will recall that the piper lures away all the town's children in retribution for not receiving payment of one thousand guilders for having first lured away all of the town's rats.[67] Lured, then, by a "tempting pattern," the direction of the two girls' movement is determined by desire, not by the need to reach an intended destination or to go from point A to point B. To refer once again to Sobchack's typology of spatial disorientation, the spatial structure of this form of the itinerant is not "linear and *forward-directed* toward a reachable distant point," but haphazard, unpredictable, wayward, and potentially boundless. Like our mysterious stranger who backtracks in the shadows in the film's opening sequence, the girls' movement frustrates any mapping impulse. Indeed, the pair seems to convey less an innocent charm than a sense of temporal and spatial confusion—the cinema's initial premises of discontinuity and discontiguity. Larrue asks what time it was when they passed the Villette house, and the two girls disagree. One girl tells Inspector Larrue that it was 11:00 p.m., while the other insists it was later. To account for their uncertainty, the first girl explains that while they had just finished babysitting, they did not go "straight home."

But Larrue does not ask them *why* they did not go "straight home," nor does he ask how they found themselves at Villette's home at 40 rue Sainte-Angèle. Instead, he imposes his own important detail into their testimony: "Let's say it was between 11:00 and 11:30." What is essential to Larrue is not the substance of the girls' testimony but how the logic of the testimony functions: for him, space operates as a grid of knowledge that works merely by the fact that someone is observed in a particular position (the two girls see someone outside a murdered man's home, Larrue observes Father Logan and Ruth outside a murdered man's home, Larrue has his men follow Ruth as she meets Father Logan on the ferry, Larrue learns that Villette had seen Ruth and Father Logan together under the gazebo, and so on). This is perhaps why Larrue is drawn to the window for a view of the city when he learns the stunning piece of information the girls give him—"He was a priest . . . a priest"—but the news is stunning only because Larrue's way of thinking has made it so. A moment later, Larrue says to the girls, "Tell us exactly," to which the first girl adds that they were, in fact, on their way home—"by the rue Valentin." But rue Valentin is a small, five-hundred-meter stretch of road that runs north–south, and it is nearly twelve kilometers east of Villette's home, a good two-and-a-half-hour walk. Saying they were not going "straight home" is quite an understatement. Larrue should know this, even without the aid of the map of Quebec City on the wall behind his left shoulder, next to the window. This misinformation would be enough for Larrue to question, if not dismiss outright, the girls' testimony (quite simply, one cannot walk past Villette's house by way of rue Valentin).

Yet Larrue is not interested in the route the girls have taken, which, as they themselves admit, is anything but continuous and contiguous. The girls are women of the night. As such, their actions are, in the words of Deborah L. Parsons, "ambiguous and defy interpretation."[68] Larrue appropriates their knowledge as walkers and observers and places it in a new context, where

Figure 4.5. *I Confess*: Larrue and the map of Quebec City

things make sense and cohere. Like the masculinist geographer described by Gillian Rose in *Feminism and Geography: The Limits of Geographical Knowledge*, Larrue demands "an omniscient view, a transparent city, total knowledge."[69] It is curious how quickly things fall into place for Larrue; nothing slows him down—not even the possibility that the girls' testimony should be corroborated or that someone might be impersonating a priest in a cassock. Vigilant and single-minded, it is Larrue who follows the one-way signs.

As if to further add to our sense that *I Confess* is indeed a film about *direction*, about the relationship between space and knowledge, the map of Quebec City makes several more appearances in the film.[70] Following the work of Conley and others, one might say that the map transcends its status as a peripheral object or mere dressing and asks us to reflect upon the spatial histories and spatial geographies of Quebec City. The map first appears in the scene I have just described. Its second appearance comes in the scene in which Larrue and Robertson question Ruth Grandfort about her secret meeting with Father Logan on the ferry on the Saint Lawrence River (figure 4.5). This is the moment Larrue learns of the blackmail plot—a plot easily mappable because blackmail and the scandal it preys upon are both matters of a compromising *position* that can be neatly diagrammed. Like the alibi, blackmail is the coupling of person with place. Yet whereas the alibi can exonerate someone by claiming to have been elsewhere with the accused at the time of the crime, the blackmailer can threaten to reveal information about someone who had been seen with another in a compromising position. Thus the logic of alibi is the inverse of the logic of blackmail: the latter makes the coupling of person and place a liability. A figure of the law, Larrue understands these things. As Welsh has noted in his reading of Hitchcock's *Blackmail*, the police, who make it a practice of bringing incriminating information to the light of day, belong to "the representative institution of what might be thought of as official, ubiquitous blackmail."[71] Thus the map in *I Confess* is aligned at once with knowledge of the comings and goings of people in the city and with a modern, secular epistemology.

Larrue keeps a vigilant eye on Quebec City's topography and the people of Quebec City, who, naturally, are itinerant and mobile. In a well-known shot from the film, we see Larrue's eye shift from Keller, who stands in front of him, to the window outside, where he sees Father Logan nervously walking up and down the sidewalk. As Michael Walker notes, "Larrue's stare signals his alertness: Father Logan, waiting for and then meeting Ruth, is behaving a little oddly for a priest. Here it is essentially ironic that, as Larrue looks at Father Logan, he is distracted from the real murderer in front of him."[72] But to what, and to whom, is Larrue alert? What, precisely, constitutes his "alertness"? As Walker rightly notes, his alertness isn't to criminal guilt, which here stares him in the face. He is alert to streetwalkers—indeed, it is Father Logan's walking back and forth, like our mysterious stranger's backtracking, that Larrue recalls when the girls tell him they saw a priest coming out of Villette's house.

Larrue embodies a kind of cartographic rationality that defines space as made of "boundaries, areas . . . volumes, thresholds, and rooms" or as "distributed into squares, blocks, pyramids, and points of surveillance" (Larrue asks his deputy about Ruth Grandfort, "And you followed her from the ferry to 22 Grande Allée?"); he wields the power of geo-surveillance, security, and discipline.[73] Note, when watching *I Confess*, the map's proximity to Larrue's head—that is to say, to his brain (figure 4.6). One could argue that the map resembles an eye—an eye that is bloodshot from looking too much, without a blink and without rest. Larrue thinks of Quebec City as an ancient does, perhaps as Champlain himself thought of it: to found a city is to pit "reason against desire, the settling of the scattered into a single place."[74] Paradoxically, we find that the secular, modern detective Larrue is no different than the men who built the Citadelle, which encloses Old Quebec. Larrue is a man of the past; he is Champlain mapping an older city.

The problem, of course, is that the city is not the map—any more than the police are the polis. Or, to put it in a better way, the city is made of innumerable maps that overlap, intersect, and coexist in past and present, innumerable maps that chart "itineraries, connections, crossroads, points of contact and intersecting lines."[75] What *I Confess* seems to convey is this tension between

Figure 4.6. *I Confess*: How Larrue's brain works

two ideas of the city: the city as polis and the city as labyrinth—the latter stressing "wandering, vagrancy, anonymity, randomness, the underground, the outlaw, the fugitive, the slave, the alien, the streetwalker, the beggar, the trader, and the exile."[76] Father Logan is many of these things at once. He is intense and itinerant like the outlaw or the fugitive; his path is determined by Eros rather than Apollo, by passion rather than reason, by his heart rather than the mind of the urban planner. He is, to use de Certeau's categories, walker to Larrue's voyeur. And Father Logan carries a secret with him. Indeed, the secret may very well be the reason *why*, toward the end of the film, he takes a long, strange walk. Whereas Larrue represents a secular institution that relies on information circulating, Father Logan represents a sacred institution where information goes to die. When you confess your secrets to a Catholic priest, your secrets disappear. Father Logan may circulate, but not the secret he carries with him.

And so we follow Father Logan on his long, strange trip near the end of the film and find him jaywalking the streets of Quebec City, in blatant defiance of traffic laws (figure 4.7). Such movement is not uncommon in Hitchcock: think of Charlie racing recklessly but determinedly through the streets of Santa Rosa to its public library in *Shadow of a Doubt*; or Jeff watching Miss Lonelyhearts walk through busy traffic in search of a random,

Figure 4.7. *I Confess*: The jaywalking priest

amorous encounter and seconds later seeing the murderous Lars Thorwald getting nearly run over at the same spot as he returns home in *Rear Window* (1954); or the policeman with two naughty boys in tow, whose jaywalking stops traffic at the precise moment when Brandon and Phillip (two very naughty boys indeed!) murder David at the opening of *Rope* (1948). The very premise of Hitchcock's installment of *Startime*, titled "Incident at a Corner," is a combination of all the elements we have traced thus far: a street intersection, a crossing guard, a pedestrian, a chance encounter, a secret past that baffles the present.

Of course, jaywalking may appear to a traffic cop as a violation of how things are supposed to move. To Father Logan, it is simply the direction in which he is headed—his plot transgresses the grid, so to speak. Father Logan's long walk, which follows his dramatic confrontation with Keller, begins as he exits Église Saint Zéphirin de Stadacona from a side door and ends, more than three minutes of screen time later, back at the front entrance of the same church. His roundabout movement takes him from the Gare du Palais, where he jaywalks, to Le Capitole Theatre, which is screening Bretaigne Windust's 1951 film *The Enforcer* (this is no doubt a nod to Robert Burks, who was the cinematographer for *The Enforcer* as well as several Hitchcock films, including *I Confess*). Where Father Logan's long walk takes him next is—and there is no other way to put this—logically impossible. He is seen from behind Station Four (Jesus Meets His Mother) of the Way of the Cross, making his way along Avenue Royale near the Sanctuaire de Sainte Anne de Beaupré, thirty-four kilometers northeast of Quebec City, easily a seven-hour walk from Le Capitole Theatre.

Of course, the footage of Montgomery Clift (or his double) walking beneath the Way of the Cross might be dismissed as simply another example of Hitchcock's use of creative geography. After all, the shot is extraordinary and more than justifies itself aesthetically and thematically, despite the fact it defies topographical logic. We could, however, also indulge another possibility: given that the Quebec City police cannot locate Father Logan—during the sequence, we see two detectives stop a lookalike on the street near the Citadelle—we defensibly can assume Father Logan's long walk has taken him to the city's outskirts. It's a whopper of a trek—some fourteen hours round trip—much longer than the two girls' walk home via rue Valentin. No wonder, then, that Father Logan collapses against the wall just outside his church.

A more interesting alternative to the idea of "creative geography" presents itself if we recall the game of direction/misdirection that the film establishes in its opening montage, as well as the disorienting views of Quebec City that Hitchcock's camera gives us. Employing the visual stylistics of film noir, Hitchcock gives us strange, off-kilter perspectives of the city's church steeples. Like most films noir, *I Confess* presents the city as labyrinth.[77] The topology of Quebec City is chaotic; it never coheres like the city on paper that is the map in Robertson's office. As Murray Smith has said about Danny Boyle's *Trainspotting* (1994), John Smith's *Black Tower* (1987), and Patrick Keillor's *London* (1994), we might say that *I Confess* employs not creative geography but "creative derangement."[78]

So the function of the map in Robertson's office is, paradoxically, to remind us that the city is made of derailings and lost bearings. The bird's-eye view of Quebec City commanded by the map in Robertson's office tells us no more about space and place than what either Ann or Father Logan can tell Inspector Larrue about the tangled intersections of personal plots that make up the narrative of *I Confess*. While the birds-eye view in *The Birds* signals chaos coming down from above, the birds-eye view of Quebec City signals chaos from the bottom up. It signals an idea of the city as both past and present, old and new, an idea of connections and coincidences, of intersections and entanglements, of public records and secret confessions.[79] It also signals that in Hitchcock a *proper* geography means a *suitable* geography—that is, a geography suitable to the film's narrative, even at the expense of fidelity to real ground coordinates. We return, then, to the central paradox of Hitchcock's location shooting: an "uncommon clarity" of place coupled with a sense of dislocation, of being lost. Perhaps this is what we mean by the *unheimlich* in Hitchcock: the disturbing feeling of being both not at home and at home, of being both lost and found.

Chapter 5

✦

Our Old Friend Telepathy

I did know more. I couldn't tell you.

—Charlie Newton, *Shadow of a Doubt*

Tell me, when are you gonna show me your E.S.P.?

—Luke Sanderson, *The Haunting* (dir. Robert Wise, 1963)

"Telepathy," notes Ned Schantz, "is the telephone in a perfect state of dematerialization—no apparatus, no sound waves, no ear."[1] Telepathy is, in part, the nonmaterial transmission of thought. But if telepathy is unbound to any particular "thing," it is also unbound to space and time. One might say the space of telepathy is the infinite, and the time of telepathy the instantaneous. In Robert Heinlein's *Time for the Stars* (1956), Gregory Graham tries but fails to convince that telepathy would be a useless form of interstellar communication since even telepathy must abide by the laws of physics; no signal, telepathic or other, can travel faster than the speed of light. To this, Dr. Mabel Lichtenstein, head of Project Lebensraum, responds: "Telepathy doesn't pay the least bit of attention to the speed of light." Telepathy, she speculates, is not physical. Further, she explains (and she has measurements to back her), "Telepathy doesn't pay any attention to the inverse-square law either."[2] In lay terms, a telepathic signal never loses its strength, no matter how far it travels. Distance is as meaningless to telepathy as time. And although one cannot exactly say telepathy is "people-less," one cannot be certain that telepathy is limited to people. Telepathic communication happens between humans and, as we shall see, between humans and *non*humans. The logic of telepathy, then, is that it abides by no laws of physics. It is an occult logic and is unbound to the laws that we assume bind people, places, and things.

The uncanny experience of telepathy in Hitchcock is the subject of this chapter. By telepathy, I mean more broadly something like occult communication. This includes telepathic communication in the most commonly understood sense but also mind reading, clairvoyance, the sending and receiving of secret codes, fragmentary utterances that seem (only seem) to have no addressee or no addressor.[3] In short, I include any form of verbal or nonverbal interaction that does not follow the normal channels of communication, that may not even pay the least bit of attention to the laws of physics. Call this the "outlaw-speak" of both native and foreign correspondents.

The correspondents in Hitchcock with access to occult communication are, with rare exception, exclusively female: Charlie in *Shadow of a Doubt* (1943), Alicia in *Notorious* (1946), Marion in *Psycho* (1960), Marnie in *Marnie* (1964), and Blanche in *Family Plot* (1976).[4] These are formidable characters, to be sure. Yet they make up only a portion of what I argue is an uncanny network of female correspondents, a network that troubles the boundaries of people, places, and things—boundaries that otherwise struggle to ensure the stability of meaning, of everyday discourse, and the (physical, scientific) laws of powerful men. Like quantum entanglement—the name that physicists have given to the phenomenon of protons and particles hurtling through space independently, yet communicating with each other at distances that defy our laws of physics—this vast network of female voices form an often but not always distant intimacy in Hitchcock, an intimacy of sympathetic whisperings, occult transmissions, and secret codes.

"Imagined as transmitting sympathy and strategy to women beset by patriarchy," argues Schantz, "female networks threaten the gendered circulation of meaning and power in a masculine culture."[5] Focusing on late eighteenth- and nineteenth-century literature, as well as twentieth-century film, Schantz examines the most prominent modes of female network operations: gossip, letters, and telephones. But Schantz also explores what he calls "the far end of the telephonic imagination": telepathy. In his compelling readings of Anatole Litvak's *Sorry, Wrong Number* (1948) and Hitchcock's *Shadow of a Doubt*, Schantz concludes: "What these films share is a powerful sense that the female desire for telepathy is a response to claustrophobic domestic conditions and that it is a desire all the more important when conditions turn gothic, subjecting the heroines to a murderous intimacy with the very men on whom they most depend."[6] In the pages that follow I wish to complicate and expand Schantz's reading of *Shadow of a Doubt* in particular, and Hitchcock's films in general, to show how the desire for telepathy is scattered across the Hitchcock landscape and can be traced to moments in his films when "the earthly laws of conventional reality" seem to give way to "the possibilities of the supernatural."[7] Or, one might say, when Hitchcock is at his most gothic.

One of the deepest ambivalences to be found in the work of Alfred Hitchcock is his mutual (and not mutually exclusive) antipathy toward and sympathy for his female characters. Time and again, Hitchcock depicts female characters in mortal danger, as a result of circumstances sometimes within but mostly beyond their control. And yet, as shown in the work of Tania Modleski and others, Hitchcock does so because of a strong identification with the feminine. His willingness to mete out suffering to his female characters is very nearly matched by his willingness to expand a sympathetic consciousness in his spectator.[8] In achieving the latter, Hitchcock reveals his fascination with *how* women suffer, *how* they respond to suffering, and *how*, even, their resistance to those who would have them suffer undermines the very authority Hitchcock assumes. Writes Modleski, "While most critics attribute this interest [in female victimization] to a sadistic delight in seeing his leading ladies suffer, and while even I am willing to concede this point, I would nevertheless insist that the obsession often takes the form of a particularly lucid exposé of the predicaments and contradictions of women's existence under patriarchy."[9] To paint a kinder portrait of Hitchcock is hardly Modleski's aim, and yet she acknowledges numerous moments in Hitchcock's films where his sympathy for women registers. What follows is an attempt to seek out more such moments—not, as I hope will be quite clear, to "save Hitchcock for feminism," to quote Robin Wood's well-known line, but to enrich our understanding of how Hitchcock was both attracted to and baffled by the female mind.

"Do You Believe in Telepathy?"

In one of the few sustained discussions of telepathy in a Hitchcock film, Schantz turns to its prominent treatment in *Shadow of a Doubt*. His focus is on Charlie (Teresa Wright) and her "pursuit of telepathic intimacies."[10] "He heard me, he heard me," Charlie says to herself as she walks from the telegraph office, where she has learned her uncle is already on his way to Santa Rosa. Yet for all her talk about the powers of telepathy, argues Schantz, Charlie fails to have the communicative intimacy that telepathy promises. As her secret knowledge about her uncle's guilt grows, she finds herself increasingly isolated. At the end of the film, her only potential confidant is Jack Graham, the detective who, with his partner Fred Saunders (Wallace Ford), has been tracking the Merry Widow Murderer on the West Coast (the other possible suspect being somewhere on the East Coast). It is they who strongly believe that Charlie's uncle was the Merry Widow Murderer—a secret Charlie feels obliged to keep from her mother, Emma, who would "die" if she learned the truth about her younger brother. The irony is that this secrecy, which is meant to protect her mother, only alienates Charlie further from her—and the town of Santa Rosa, to whom Charlie surely has lied. "Indeed," writes Schantz, "the whole town will remain the innocent and ignorant place [Uncle Charlie] wants it to be. For want of any penetration into her mother's mind, for want of a little genuine telepathy, Charlie, and through her *Shadow of a Doubt*, passes off a crippling failure as a necessary fiction."[11] Thus Hitchcock's film depicts a female heroine who ultimately fails to see the promise of telepathy come true, who must abandon "the consolations of shared knowledge." By the end of the film, says Schantz, we find little hope in the "limited intimacy" she may find with Jack. Instead, we place our hope in Charlie's escape—even if she must escape alone.[12]

In this way, we might see *Shadow of a Doubt* as a film about private knowledge and the need for women to share it. Further, it is a film about how women's efforts at finding a much-needed intimacy are constantly thwarted by men. The final image of a shell-shocked Charlie, her head cast downward in disbelief and despair, is the image of a woman with too much knowledge—of her uncle, of the world—and no one to share it with. No fellow telepathic travelers around. But while Schantz's argument ultimately turns from telepathy, the fantasy of impossible intimacy, to the fantasy of a fast escape, he believes that the film nevertheless looks beyond itself to a possibility that is hard not to consider—even desire—which is that Charlie will not accept the terms of Jack's deal: a lethal stasis in exchange for a little intimacy: "All we can hope for is that Charlie has the courage to see through this rotten bargain, that her uncle's final act of terror on the train has not scared her into the false safety of stasis. Better to go out like Amelia Earhart, who must have known as well as anyone that there are worse things than flying alone."[13] One cannot deny that Schantz has Charlie Newton's best interests at heart. Indeed, I would suggest we expand the possibilities of a happy ending for Charlie by putting stock back in the nimbleness of her *mind*, by tracing her telepathic activities to get better insight into private female knowledge.[14]

The first moment we see Charlie Newton, her superior intelligence is clearly established. She is lying in bed, brooding over the tedium and conventionality of her family. When her father, Joe, tries to cheer her up by reminding her of his recent raise, she tells him, "How can you talk of money when I'm talking about *souls*?" All Joe can muster in response is a slightly condescending "oh." He shows little interest in understanding his daughter's mental state. He may be proud of his daughter's mind ("The smartest girl in her school," he is quick to remind everyone), but he's not much of a listener—unless, of course, he is in the company of his partner in pretend crime, Herb. In fact, there is no one in the film Charlie can truly call a confidant. Charlie's uncle is not the telepathic partner she thinks he is, and Jack Graham is . . . well, uninteresting. The latter may be attracted to Charlie's mental acuity, but like Joe, he shows no signs of being a true confidant. He lies to her, misreads her level of affection for him, and speaks to her as much out of duty as out of interest (if given a chance, what would Jack say in response to Charlie's wonderful phrase, "I'm talking about *souls*"?).

As for Charlie's uncle, he is unresponsive to his niece's notion about the two of them being twins and indulges it only to use it against her when she turns on him later in the film. Charlie can read minds, but her uncle cannot. And the film suggests in many subtle ways that Uncle Charlie resents his niece's mind, its acuity and its reach. In not so subtle ways, the film suggests that what Uncle Charlie despises as much as mobility is women's access to and sharing of private knowledge. Uncle Charlie's first act of violence against his niece is not in response to her mobility, but in response to her claim, gaily made, that she knows a secret about him. "What secret?" asks Uncle Charlie. "Well, now I know there was something in the evening paper about you," responds Charlie. When Uncle Charlie tells her it's none of her business, she reaches inside the pocket of his jacket and pulls out the story he had ripped from Joe's newspaper earlier in the evening. Uncle Charlie then grabs Charlie's wrist and violently pulls her toward him. Indeed, although we (thankfully) are not witness to Uncle Charlie's violence toward the merry widows, there are several instances in the film when violence is very near the front of his mind (and is actually enacted by him, even if in a far milder form than murder). While his niece is Uncle Charlie's prime target for much of the film, he makes more than a few veiled threats to his sister Emma, who leaves herself vulnerable precisely when she speaks of her participation in Santa Rosa's women's club. "Women's club," Uncle Charlie chuckles with not a little contempt. His demeanor becomes increasingly nasty as Emma informs her little brother that a young man named Graham is to visit the Newton family to conduct an interview for something called the National Public Survey. "There were really two young men," she continues. "One of them takes the pictures." "Oh there were two," Uncle Charlie says nervously. "Yes, Mr. Graham was the nicest. Oh, he doesn't want us to dress up, or anything. He just wants us to act the way we always do." At this, Uncle Charlie snaps: "Emmy, women are fools. They'd fall for anything." Wielding his butter knife, he tells Emma, "You ought to have better sense."

But "better sense" is precisely what Uncle Charlie doesn't want women to have. The idea of Emma "cooking up" anything but supper disgusts him. One wonders here if Uncle Charlie is less angry at the thought that his cover might be blown than he is at women with "better sense"—specifically, his niece Charlie. The photograph of Charlie standing at the front of her graduating class (she has the best sense of all) is conspicuous in several shots during this sequence, and we see it clearly behind Emma's head as Emma moves toward Uncle Charlie's bed to apologize to him for allowing strange men into her home. But Emma's apology is suddenly cut off by the entrance of Charlie, who looks more like her mother and less like the head of the class. Dressed in an apron and ready to dote lovingly on her uncle, she walks directly into the line of fire. From this moment on, Charlie will be, among all the women in *Shadow of a Doubt*, in the most danger—because of her better sense.

And Charlie's "better sense" is perhaps the best sense of all: telepathy. The question that hovers around the film is who her telepathic partner(s) might be. The answer, we shall see, is *not* her uncle. But as we turn to other possible partners, we find that the list is not short. At the top of the list, and not because we are moving alphabetically, is Charlie's younger sister Ann. This telepathic alliance is suggested in the opening moments of the film, when Ann is on the phone with the clerk from the Postal Union Office, Mrs. Henderson.

There is a telegram waiting for Emma, but Ann cannot write down the message because she doesn't have a pencil. Besides, Ann tells Mrs. Henderson, she likes to keep her mind free of things "that don't matter." Leaving it at that, one might conclude that the statement is nothing more than an indication of Ann's lack of interest in family affairs. But Ann has more to say when prompted by Mrs. Henderson, who (unheard) asks why Ann likes to keep her mind free of things that don't matter. Ann continues: "Because I have so much to keep on my mind." "Such as?" is the unheard question that follows. "Innumerable things!" is Ann's reply. When Emma calls Mrs. Henderson to inquire about the telegram, she shouts into the phone, prompting Ann to explain that shouting is unnecessary. In doing so, she reminds us that it was, in part, the desire for psychic abilities that prompted the invention of telephonic communication: "She makes no allowance for science. She thinks she has to cover the distance by sheer lung power."[15] Ann may seem solitary in her reading habits compared with her father—who cannot be uncoupled from his reading partner, Herb—but her mind is clear and wide open. On Ann's mind are books like Sir Walter Scott's *Ivanhoe* and Bram Stoker's *Dracula*, and it is the latter, as Schantz rightly notes, that well prepares Ann for the sudden arrival of a vampire.[16]

James Mclaughlin makes note of the references to *Dracula* in *Shadow of a Doubt* and, further, makes the connection between Stoker's gothic novel and telepathy. He remarks that Uncle Charlie's "most important similarity to Dracula . . . is that Uncle Charlie is summoned by his niece. Charlie stresses the fact that her uncle 'heard' her, that there is a kind of mental telepathy between them."[17] Yet the film gives us ample reason to believe that Charlie's telepathic partner is *not* her uncle. Recall that Uncle Charlie sends the telegram indicating he is on his way ("And try and stop me," reads the message) before we see Charlie lying in her bed. Further, the message is for his sister, Emma, not his niece. Further still, it is Ann who takes the message, and she shows absolutely no interest in it. In short, Charlie only *thinks* her uncle hears her. This is not to suggest that Charlie is no telepath. Rather, one might argue, following the above line of thinking, that Charlie *intercepts* her uncle's signal, that she is a spy, or something like an unlicensed telepath. We need, then, to redirect our attention to the ways in which her better sense is transmitted, how a female telepathic network in *Shadow of a Doubt* broadcasts signals *about* Uncle Charlie but not *to* him.

Still, the *Dracula* parallel is of considerable interest. I would suggest here that we recall how the vampire is defeated in Stoker's novel, beyond driving a stake through his heart and cutting off his head. For what is as indispensible as garlic to nonvampires is a reliable network of private discourse—in this case, the shared journals of Jonathan Harker, Mina, Lucy, and Dr. Seward. The accumulation of secret knowledge about a common enemy, whose prey is innocent young women, gives this alliance the advantage (Mina writes in her journal that "the diary of a doctor who attended Lucy might be something to add to the sum of our knowledge of that terrible Being").[18] More than this, the journals give all concerned some clarity of mind, with thoughts resistant to vampiric influences. Jonathan Harker writes, "When I had written in my diary and had fortunately replaced the book and pen in my pocket I felt sleepy. The Count's warning came into my mind, but I took pleasure in disobeying it."[19] While it is possible here to dispute the telepathic powers of Dracula (could Jonathan be imagining the warning?), there is no disputing the effectiveness of Jonathan's shielding strategy, which is to share his thoughts with others, including of course the women who are the vampire's main prey. It is no wonder, then, that the count burns what he believes to be the only existing copy of the collated journals and letters—for they are, writes Jim Collins, "the principal means of destroying the monster. The writings slowly but surely 'circumscribe' the monster by pulling him within the confines of their discourse."[20] Just as the count destroys what he believes to be the only copy of the collated letters and journal entries, Uncle Charlie rips the headline about the Merry Widow Murderer out of Joe Newton's copy (when thousands of other copies circulate) of the *Santa Rosa Republic*. Unlike the count, however, Uncle Charlie should know better. And sure enough, his niece will find the story when she reads another copy at the Santa Rosa Public Library. But the important point here is that, like Count Dracula, Uncle Charlie fears the shared, secret knowledge that others have about him.

In Uncle Charlie's case, however, it is shared, secret, *female* knowledge that is most threatening, and indeed the communications *between women* structure the film.[21] The night of Uncle Charlie's homecoming, Charlie, who is setting the dinner table, begins humming just as Ann tells her, in the first of two coded, if not secret, messages, "Sing at the table, you'll marry a crazy husband." The phrase, dismissed by her brother (to whom no one listens, ever) as mere superstition, is significant for several reasons. The precise name of the tune Charlie is humming escapes her, although we are reminded, thanks to the extradiegetic shot of couples dancing, that it is Franz Lehár's "The Merry Widow Waltz." After Uncle Charlie tells Joe he'd like to deposit some cash, "Say, thirty or forty thousand," Charlie begins humming again just as Emma utters the words, "The way men do things!" (figure 5.1). We can presume Emma is remarking upon the financial transaction her younger brother is planning with Joe (and banking, and the government in general—a subject about which, Ann reminds her brother, they are not allowed to talk badly). But "things" is casting a rather broad net, and given that Emma's offscreen voice is noticeably louder than it should be, her words have a chilling effect. In what is likely an example of automatic dialogue replacement (ADR), Emma's voice sounds disembodied; and we are meant to hear it as it overlaps with Charlie's humming. That is, "The way men do things" is carrying the same message to Charlie that "The Merry Widow Waltz" does. It is as if Emma—with musical accompaniment—says it all.

Figure 5.1. *Shadow of a Doubt*: Charlie tunes in

The unusual extradiegetic shot bridges this scene with the scene prior, in which Uncle Charlie gives his niece the gift of the wedding ring. In this prior scene, Charlie is uncomfortable accepting anything from her uncle, since it would "spoil things." She feels that she and her uncle, in some strange way, already share a special bond, and that the gift is redundant and unnecessary. What Charlie desires is a bond that is nonmaterial, no things attached. "You're a strange girl," Uncle Charlie tells her. "Why should it spoil things?" Charlie responds, "Because we're not just an uncle and a niece. It's something else . . . we're sort of like twins, don't you see? We have to know." The line is curious; why "*we*"? It would make more sense for Charlie to say, "I have to know." So who is the "we" to which she refers? It can't be Uncle Charlie, for it makes no sense to say he has to know his own secret. It's possible that Charlie misspeaks, but if she does it's quite an apt error, one that casts light on the network of female knowledge invoked by the film. The "we" can be said to refer to the other women in the film or, broadly speaking, to all merry widows, past and present, who make up the nonmaterial network of women. Her refusal of the ring reinforces her telepathy, or her belief in it.

Just then, Uncle Charlie asks for his niece's hand and places the ring on her finger. Thus Ann's warning not to sing at the table comes too late—perhaps not for Charlie, but certainly for Mrs. Bruce Matthewson, the ring's former owner. Indeed, Ann's words for her sister seem not to be a warning at all, but rather a clue. After all, it is unlikely that Charlie makes a habit of singing (or humming) at the dinner table. She uses her voice to defeat boys at debate tournaments, not to entertain. Rather it is Mrs. Bruce Matthewson who very likely did her fair share of singing at the table, if only because she lost her place on the stage after marrying. As we learn later in the film, from the headline Charlie reads at the library, Mrs. Bruce Matthewson was "the former musical comedy star, known to audiences at the beginning of this century as 'the beautiful Thelma Schenley.'" We can only conclude, as Elsie Michie does, that Thelma Schenley's marriage to Bruce Matthewson was more than a career-ending move; it also meant a loss of identity—just as Emma's marriage to Joe Newton meant Emma was no longer "Emma Spencer Oakley of 46 Burnham St., St. Paul, Minnesota, the prettiest girl on the block" but Mrs. Joe Newton.[22] As Emma herself confesses, in a heartbreaking moment near the end of the film, "You sort of forget you're you." Being the latest victim of the Merry Widow Murderer, Mrs. Bruce Matthewson, we can assume, had been seen being courted by a handsome young stranger going by the name of Mr. Spencer. Perhaps she even sang to him. Setting this aside as sheer speculation, we must nevertheless account for the source of Ann's words to Charlie: "Sing at the table, you'll marry a crazy husband." One possibility is that the source is Thelma Schenley herself. The shot of the couples dancing to "The Merry Widow Waltz" that Hitchcock inserts between the two scenes may not be extradiegetic after all, but may instead suggest some sort of psychic bridge between Thelma Schenley, Ann, Emma, and Charlie, who share private knowledge about "the way men do things."

Patrick Crogan has considered, at some length, the "Merry Widow Waltz" images and how they function in the film.[23] For Crogan, the most persuasive possibility is that the image of the waltzing couples "represents the mysterious relation between the strangely doubled characters of Uncle Charlie and Charlie." This "image-sound set," as Crogan calls it, emphasizes the theme of doubling (the image is of couples, the couples resemble each other, etc.). Further, the doubling emerges as "an invisible thirdness" that stands in for "the enigma of the telepathic link" between Charlie and her uncle, an enigma that does not enter the film itself and is not accessible to either Charlie or Uncle Charlie. This reading of the waltzers' appearance, as intriguing as it is, reinforces what the film, in fact, renounces: the telepathic partnership of Uncle Charlie and his niece. No doubt Charlie believes her uncle hears her thoughts, but only at the film's outset. As the film progresses, the fantasy of a telepathic partnership between niece and uncle gives way to a more promising (if not entirely successful) network of private female knowledge.

Crogan himself is interested in the possibility that the image-sound set of the waltzers does *not* stand in for the doubling of niece and uncle. In a footnote to his essay, Crogan entertains the notion that the image-sound set is a communication sent from *elsewhere*. "There are grounds," he suggests, "for arguing that the dancing couples image 'comes from' the dead widow whose ring Uncle Charlie has just given to young Charlie, Thelma Schenley, the 'TS' engraved on the ring which Charlie immediately notices." Were critics to relax their allegiance to the theme of doubling in the film—insofar as it regulates our understanding only of the relation between Charlie and her uncle—they might pursue other telepathic intimacies. I argue that Crogan's impulse to at least consider the possibility of private knowledge shared among women pinpoints what is at stake in the film. The film suggests that it is in Charlie's best interest to use her "better sense"—in fact, for all women to make use of a "better sense"—even at the risk of death.

Surprisingly, Charlie's younger sister, Ann, is under no threat at any point in the film, despite the fact that it is she who first suspects that her uncle is not the hero her older sister makes him out to be. Only seemingly uninterested in her uncle, Ann perhaps senses there is something nasty about him. She senses, if not the content, then the feeling of his guilt. At one point in the film, she refuses to take a seat next to him at the dinner table. More significant is the fact that she is feeding Saunders all sorts of information about the Newton family—including, Charlie perhaps thinks, information about her uncle ("We play games," Saunders tells Charlie. "I ask questions. She knows all the answers," which brings a worried look to Charlie's face). Indeed, Ann may spend much of her time reading books, but there is more than a little to suggest that she spends much of her time reading minds as well. Later in the film, Graham and Saunders are walking with Charlie, Ann, and Charlie's friend Catherine (Estelle Jewell) along the sidewalk near the Newtons' home. It is here that Ann bestows upon her sister the second of the two coded, if not secret, messages. As Saunders leaves Ann and Catherine alone to join Graham and Charlie, who are walking several feet behind, we hear what sounds like another rather obvious instance of ADR: "Step on a crack, you'll break your mother's back." The well-known children's phrase seems to be directed at either Graham or Catherine, who are walking beside Ann. But this cannot be confirmed, since we see Ann from behind as she begins to speak. Further, Hitchcock cuts to a reverse shot of Graham, Charlie, and Saunders just as Ann says, "You'll break your mother's back." Surely the purpose of this edit is to suggest that the phrase is meant for Charlie, who carries the burden of secret knowledge about her uncle that would break her mother's heart if she knew, but must know nevertheless.

Yet Ann's phrase suggests something far more ominous, more violent, and more final than a broken heart. When Charlie first considers the possibility that her uncle is a murderer, she says to Graham, "My uncle hasn't done anything. He knows it would *kill* mother if he did." Later in the film, when Charlie learns the ugly truth, she and her uncle discuss the matter of Emma's ignorance, and the terms are equally serious: "Think of your mother. It'll *kill* your mother," says Uncle Charlie, to which Charlie responds in kind: "Yes, it'll *kill* mother." So on exactly three occasions, the secret knowledge of Uncle

Charlie becomes potentially lethal. Is it any wonder, then, that Ann exclaims, "I broke my mother's back three times!"

Given the curious occult logic of the children's phrase (the suggestion of some telepathic link between a sidewalk crack and a mother's back), it seems this is yet another instance of Ann's ability to get in her sister's head. Far from being entirely isolated, Charlie is plugged into a potentially beneficial network of private female knowledge. Potential, of course, carries Charlie only so far. As Schantz argues, Charlie's search for true, intimate companionship ends in failure. He feels the ending of *Shadow of a Doubt* is "heavy" not because "Charlie will inevitably marry Jack" (something Schantz does not accept) but because the town of Santa Rosa "will remain the innocent and ignorant place [Uncle Charlie] wants it to be. For want of any penetrations into her mother's mind, for want of a little genuine telepathy, Charlie, and through her *Shadow of a Doubt*, passes off a crippling failure as a necessary fiction."[24] In the end, argues Schantz, Charlie trades the possibility of shared knowledge for the promise of escape.[25] I cannot take issue with what is, I think, one of the best pieces of criticism on *Shadow of a Doubt*. I do argue that we can expand that possibility of shared knowledge, playing up its scope without denying its ultimate failure.

One might even consider including in this female network the librarian, Mrs. Cochran (Eily Malyon). Recall that it is Ann who suggests that her sister go to the public library to find a copy of the previous day's *Santa Rosa Republican* (a "thing" I discuss in chapter 2). Once she arrives, it is too late; the public library is closed and the front door locked. Yet through the glass that separates her from Mrs. Cochran, Charlie sends an all-but-silent plea. As much mind reader as lip reader, the librarian allows Charlie access—albeit not without a mild bit of scolding ("You know as well as I do," she tells Charlie in a suggestive phrasing). But the scolding only adds to the sense that Mrs. Cochran is giving Charlie privileged access here. And I think it is of no small significance that the public library appears, because it is after hours, to be a very private and intimate space—for women only. After she reads the headline, Charlie takes the ring her uncle gave her off her finger and once again reads its inscription: "T.S. From B.M." Hitchcock's camera pulls backward and up in a memorable crane shot, making Charlie appear, with her suspicions confirmed, frightened and small—she is both wisened and wizened.

But is Charlie alone? In the strictly literal sense, yes, since Mrs. Cochran is nowhere to be seen. Yet this extraordinary shot of Charlie also suggests, generally speaking, that solitude appears to be precisely what Charlie is destined for.[26] Such a view of Charlie, as I understand it, figures her as something like Stanley Cavell's "unknown woman," who, in contrast to the heroine of the Hollywood comedy of remarriage (from which the genre of the Hollywood melodrama of the unknown woman derives), achieves integrity and transformation by abandoning or rejecting marriage. In four films, *Letter from an Unknown Woman* (dir. Max Ophuls, 1948), *Gaslight* (dir. George Cukor, 1944), *Now, Voyager* (dir. Irving Rapper, 1942), and *Stella Dallas* (dir. King Vidor, 1937), Cavell finds four heroines who, like their sisters in the Hollywood comedies of remarriage, seek integrity and transformation through knowledge or education. In the comedies of remarriage, the woman's education is achieved mutually with (and through) the man's—in the "process of a mode of conversation with the man."[27] In the melodrama of the unknown woman, however, the education of the woman occurs outside this process and instead within the melodrama's "mood of heavy irony, since her (superior, exterior) knowledge becomes the object—as prize or as victim—of the man's fantasy, who seeks to share its secrets (*Now, Voyager*), to be ratified by it (*Letter from an Unknown Woman*), to escape it (*Stella Dallas*), or to destroy it (*Gaslight*), where each objective is (generically) reflected in the others."[28] Charlotte, Lisa, Stella, and Paula, respectively, each in the end recognize their isolation and find in it an integrity that, according to Cavell, transcends marriage.[29] Does Charlie, at the end of *Shadow of a Doubt*, resign herself to unknownness?

To pursue this possibility, we turn to the film's closing scene, in which Jack Graham stands next to Charlie, a few feet below her and holding her right hand. One might assume that Charlie is two steps above Jack, but the effect is twofold: he is striking the pose of a man proposing marriage (indeed, critics like James McLaughlin read this scene as a marriage-to-be). If this is the case, however, then Charlie is most likely rejecting Jack (kindly, affably). One need not rely on the staging of this scene alone to reach this conclusion, as Charlie more or less stated her position on marriage shortly before Uncle Charlie slams the garage door on the two.[30] Charlie does not consent to marriage but instead offers friendship in its place.[31] The other effect of placing Jack beneath Charlie in this final scene is to suggest her superiority to him—or at any rate, her newfound freedom, purchased, as it is, with a necessary sacrifice. And if it is not her superiority, then perhaps it is her "interestingness" that is emphasized. In this way, the film's ending conforms to Cavell's definition of the melodrama of the unknown woman, "in which the enormity of the woman's hidden, anonymous sacrifice is made sublimely large by the stupendous uninterestingness of the man."[32]

But here is where we encounter complications, for Jack may indeed be uninteresting; Uncle Charlie, however, is *not*. We know nothing of Jack and need know nothing. And while this might make it less plausible that Charlie would choose a betrothal to Jack (who, as I see it, knows as little of Charlie as Stephen Dallas knows of Stella Martin), it doesn't make it less plausible that she would choose a betrothal to her uncle. In this way, the so-called union between uncle and niece takes on an especially interesting twist. It is this union that Charlie transcends—and not at the end of the film but much earlier. In other words, her isolation begins in that darkened library, alone with the knowledge that transforms her. It is no wonder, then, that Charlie returns home for a lengthy, irregular slumber: she awakens only at nightfall the following day, just in time for dinner. It is in this prolonged darkness that Charlie fully acknowledges her isolation, her unknownness. "The woman's isolation," writes Cavell, "is associated in the films of unknownness with some register of her relation to the transcendent—grounded in a cosmic symbology of light and darkness, of enclosure and the imagination of freedom."[33] Cavell has in mind, among other unknown women, Paula at the end of *Gaslight*, who stands on a roof under the darkened, clouded sky and says, "It's been a long night." In *Shadow of a Doubt*, we find Charlie's transformation is made legible with similar "symbology": at the film's outset she lies in her own bed, in the afternoon light, imagining a freedom that is, though beyond her grasp, within her range of view. Sending out thoughts of souls, Charlie believes she is heard by—she is in conversation with—her uncle Charlie. Two-thirds of the way into the film, she now sleeps in her sister's room, through the day—that is, past the light and into darkness and isolation. One might say, then, that Jack Graham occupies, at the end of *Shadow of a Doubt*, the position that Brian Cameron (played, it so happens, by Joseph Cotten) occupies at the end of *Gaslight*. He's a friend, to be sure, but not necessarily a potential husband. While Charlie doesn't mind Jack's talk about loving her, her response to his amorous overtures is "I want us to be friends, I know that." One might also say that viewers who insist that Jack and Charlie will be coupled occupy Miss Thwaites's position at the end of *Gaslight*, espying Paula and Brian alone. "Well!" she says, meaningfully—but we can't be certain properly.

If I seem to be unduly concerned with keeping Charlie unmarried, it is only to suggest that one of the many things that make *Shadow of a Doubt* so interesting is that it summons the prospects of Charlie's future. The film calls our attention to it several times, beginning with her earliest thoughts ("What's going to be our future?" she asks her father), to the photograph of her at the head of her graduating class that hangs on her bedroom wall, to her father's complimentary statements about her ("The smartest girl in her class at school . . . she's got brains"). Recall that it is in unbearable stasis where we first find Charlie, a state of affairs she cannot abide. But much to Charlie's shock and dismay, it is not her uncle who rescues her and her family from this rut. Uncle Charlie is not a forward-thinking man—nor is he entirely backward-looking. In a telling moment (one of several in which Uncle Charlie goes into something like a hypnotic trance, in which we are in the presence of an unfiltered Uncle Charlie) he says to Emma and Charlie, "Today's the thing. That's my philosophy. Today." It is a philosophy he presses on his niece at the 'Til Two club, where he implores Charlie to "wake up," to accept the present as the only thing (no past / no remorse; no future / no consequences). "Use your wits, learn something!" he tells Charlie. Just then, Charlie gets up to leave, and the waitress Louise asks, "You goin', Charlie?"

The answer, which I argue the film makes legible, is yes. She is certainly dressed for it by the film's end. While I have suggested other possible readings of the film's final shot than something like a proposal, one need only look carefully at Charlie's outfit to read the ending as both a gentle rejection of Jack's proposal and a recognition of the future, of going places. The outfit, it so happens, is identical to the one worn by the young woman in the "Santa Rosa Social and Club News" (figures 5.2 and 5.3). It is foolish to think this woman in the newspaper is, in fact, Charlie. But it is difficult to ignore the similarity, particularly since the young woman in the newspaper is contrasted with—spatially offset by—the photograph of the couple (presumably newlywed) in the right-hand column. Indeed, the effect is that the young woman at left is turned from marriage, walking away from it.

But to what? If *Shadow of a Doubt* tells a story similar to those found in the Hollywood melodrama of the unknown woman, one might say that Charlie is bound for what Cavell calls a "world of women."[34] As an alternative to a world of Joe Newtons (and Jack Grahams) and Uncle Charlies, this world would not appear entirely unsatisfactory, were it not for the ways Cavell characterizes it: this is a world of limited options, of isolation and solitude; it is a world in which communication (or as Cavell terms it, conversation) is negated. It is a world without networks, without relations. Wit and intelligence may not be scarce in the world of women, but they are also not shared. Charlie, if she is bound for this world, is bound for unknownness. Call this Cavell's world of women's triumphant bleakness.

And while triumphant bleakness casts a shadow over Charlie by the film's end, one cannot shake the feeling that she is bound for something better than unknownness (which is hardly fit to print in the "Social and Club News"). Something better might indeed be marriage to Jack, although there is much to suggest this is not Charlie's only or best option. What is beyond doubt, however, is Charlie's power of sympathy, her better sense. What I have been suggesting thus far—my central concern in this reading of *Shadow of a Doubt*—is that Charlie's better sense is not negated, that her failure to find in her uncle a true telepathic partner is not necessarily a failure of her better sense. As I've tried to show, potential partners—with whom to share her wit and intelligence—abound in the film. I ask my reader to indulge me one last example of Charlie's skills as a mind reader, one last instance in which her telepathic powers are foregrounded, in which we might see her as a survivor in the Hitchcock landscape. It comes in one of the film's most unusual cuts—if not its most unusual. Charlie and Jack have just bumped into Charlie's two friends, Catherine and Shirley. The cut comes abruptly after this encounter. The camera dollies away from a close-up of Charlie to a two-shot of Charlie and Jack, as Charlie says, "I know what you are really, you're a detective. There's something the matter and you're a detective!" What happened just prior to this cut is open to speculation, but it is clear that Jack has *not* told Charlie that he's a detective. In fact, there's every reason to suggest Jack has revealed little if anything about his true identity and motives prior to what can best be described as a mental jump cut.[35] Charlie guesses it all before Jack can speak. Jack says, "Charlie, listen."

Figure 5.2. *Shadow of a Doubt*: the "Santa Rosa Social and Club News"

Figure 5.3. *Shadow of a Doubt*: Charlie, dressed for success

"I won't listen!" is Charlie's reply. As Jack continues, he pleads with Charlie, "Have I asked you a lot of questions? Have I?" Only then does he confess that he is a detective, "a pretty bad one." Presumably Jack says this because he has blown his cover. But it's perhaps more fair to say that Jack is a perfectly fine detective, but Charlie is too smart for him and her "better sense" exposes him. Indeed, it is as if Charlie is not only ahead of Jack but, given the formal strangeness of the scene, ahead of the film itself.

Tania Modleski devotes only a few lines to *Shadow of a Doubt* in her book *The Women Who Knew Too Much*. But what she says about Charlie is revealing about many of Hitchcock's heroines and many of the films she discusses. "Charlie is a typical Hitchcock female," writes Modleski.

> Both because her close relationship to her mother arouses in her a longing for a different kind of life from the one her father offers them and because she seems to possess special incriminating knowledge about men. Charlie's attitude is representative of two types of resistance to patriarchy I have been discussing here—that which seeks to know men's "secrets" . . . and that which knows the kinds of pleasure unique to women's relationships with other women.[36]

This relationship—of shared secrets and sympathy—is, I argue, often occult in nature. As Nicholas Royle has suggested, the word *telepathy* has its roots in the history of sympathy.[37] What I've suggested thus far is that one can trace in *Shadow of a Doubt* a telepathic network that links all its female characters, a network that has Charlie as its principal, and busiest, operator. And while at film's end we see Charlie in the same condition of physical stasis we saw her in at the film's outset, she is now dressed in active wear, dressed for success, dressed for the future.

What, then, is Charlie's future? It's quite possible that she will learn to cultivate the proper telepathic partners and continue to seek the pleasure of company with other women. It's also quite possible to imagine what the "Santa Rosa Social and Club News" might say about Charlie—who she is and where she is going. Charlie's father has given us some hint in this regard. Surely the column would make note of Charlie's skills as a debater (Joe says she won the debate against the East Richmond High School), and to expertly outdebate one's opponent, one must think like one's opponent and anticipate his thoughts—get inside his head, so to speak. Surely the column would indicate that she has graduated at the top of her class (as the photograph on her wall strongly suggests). And surely the column will note that she is a good reader (the librarian knows her by name)—if not as voracious as her little sister. I imagine a column that speaks little if anything of her love life but much of her female companions, how highly she is regarded (the film goes out of its way to suggest as much). I imagine a column that predicts great things for Charlie. I imagine a column that predicts Charlie going places.

Our Old Friend Telephony

A woman on the move is the subject of this next section, and the various ways in which men press into service canny technologies of communication as a means of curtailing her movement, of controlling her and, most of all, getting inside her head. As several scholars have suggested, an impetus behind the invention of various tele-technologies that emerged in the nineteenth and early twentieth centuries is the fantasy of telepathy. J. Hillis Miller writes that "radio, television, sonar, radar, information storage, retrieval, and manipulation on tapes, discs, and in ever more compact and more powerful computers are no more than extensions of the human ability to feel, see, hear, and receive messages at a distance."[38] In his impressive history of telepathy, Roger Luckhurt writes, "Psychical communications were not secondary or degraded analogies weakly propped on proper science. Inventors and technologists often initiated investigations inspired by the promise of rendering 'supernatural' means of communication mechanically possible."[39] The telephone, Luckhurst points out, was in this way the quintessential tele-technology. And it is well documented that Alexander Graham Bell frequented séances, and that his assistant, Thomas Watson, was a medium. Nicholas Royle writes, "It should be clear that 'telepathy' is historically linked to numerous other tele-phenomena: it is part of the establishment of tele-culture in general."[40]

Take as an example the 1911 issue of *Telephony: The American Telephone Journal*. In it there appeared, under the heading "Holding the Line" by Byron Williams, an "advertisement" for the Telepathy Telephone Co., Limited. The purpose of this company, the mock advertisement reads, "is to accelerate the sympathetic affection of one mind by the thoughts, feelings or emotions of another at a distance, without communication through the ordinary channels such as the ante-date telephone, the telegraph, pneumatic tube or via the back-yard fence!"[41] There follows an exemplary exchange between husband and wife, in which the former "telepaphones" the latter to inform her that he will not be coming home for dinner. The wife then "gets the message, sniffs and replies: 'Go ahead, John, and enjoy yourself. Your wife is in the country—but she's coming in to attend a matinee and a bridge party and a dinner at Martoni's. So sorry you have to work like that. Buzz! Buzz!' And she rings off—er, that is, she breaks the connection." Curiously, Telepathy Telephone Co. Ltd.'s new invention is heralded as the inevitable, yet ideal, mode of discourse between husband and wife: "In these parlous days a married man sees so little of his wife as almost to be unable to pick her out in a crowd. The demands of modern business and up-to-date club life are simply unbelievable."[42] In fact, so wondrous is this new, thing-less mode of communication that "a man need never go home unless the lawn demands mowing. He can do all his family confidences by telepaphone—and do it NOW!" So while this weird, wireless company initially promises sympathetic affection, feelings, and emotions, it ends up guaranteeing the man an unlimited amount of freedom away from his wife, "a night off with the boys" whenever he so chooses.[43] All the telepaphone seems to guarantee the wife is to be perpetually stood up.

Yet this spoof suggests (only so) that, with a remote husband, a wife is free to seek out female companionship—just as Emma Newton is free to spend what little leisure time she has with fellow members of the women's club, since hard-working Joe prefers, during his leisure time, the companionship of Herb. While the husband sets the terms of telepaphonic discourse (the telepaphone, it seems, was designed as an instrument for pursuing *his* business and pleasure), one can't help suspecting that the wife will turn the instrument to her own desires and circumvent her husband's "family confidences." There's no suggestion in the ad that the husband might "ring on" anyone but his spouse. When he does, the wife already has other plans. How and when these other plans were made begs some consideration. If we are still willing to purchase the idea that the telepaphone can accelerate sympathetic affection through the thoughts, feelings, and emotions of others, then we might grant the possibility that the wife uses it to pursue alternative intimacies instantaneously. For the husband, the telepaphone is ideal in that it avoids all the interferences that often thwart a caller (the ad promises its user that there is "no 'central' to keep you waiting while she clears the line, no dispute over tolls, no time limit," etc.), yet its application is considerably narrow, restricted to mere point-to-point communication. Imagine, on the other hand, a wife who uses the telepaphone as a means of achieving what the ad promised at the outset: the transmission and reception of sympathetic affection, the arranging of healthy encounters—matinees, bridge games, meals—with other women.

What I am suggesting is that this bit of telephonic/telepathic theater offers a useful way of thinking about what happens to the woman who finds herself in a stifling marriage and with a serious shortfall of companions, a slight female network in a vast landscape. This is where the fantasy of telepathy reaches its highest stake. In the case of Marnie Edgar, we have another female character associated with that "better sense," telepathy. Marnie is a typical Hitchcock heroine, insofar as she is strong-willed and intelligent. But she is typical also because her pool of female companions is severely impoverished, perhaps more than any other female character in Hitchcock. While, like Charlie, she exhibits little interest in marriage, Marnie also exhibits little interest in *people*.[44] Marnie believes in nothing—save, perhaps, horses. And there is one horse with whom she cultivates an intense bond: her stallion Forio. In the novel upon which the film is based, Winston Graham makes Marnie not only close to Forio but also *possessive* of him. When Mark tells Marnie that Forio will be brought to Wykwyn shortly (in the film, Forio's arrival at Wykwyn is a surprise), Marnie thinks to herself, "Forio. I don't think I even liked Mark talking about him that way. Because Forio was a *personal* possession, a personal companion and friend. I wanted him here but I wanted him still to myself."[45]

Marnie's isolation is established with the film's first shot, which presents the graphically stark, modernist image of a woman, yellow purse clutched loosely under her left arm, at a desolate platform of a train station. The shot is, both visually and figuratively, a one-point perspective. Marnie is alone; her destination, a vanishing point. A similar shot, in terms of graphic starkness, shows Marnie in the women's bathroom of Rutland Publishing Company, where she waits patiently in a toilet stall while her female coworkers put on their coats, touch up their faces, make their plans, and leave for the day. It is one of the most arresting shots in the film. Because it lasts fifty-three seconds, and Marnie is, save for her darting eyes, entirely motionless, the spectator is encouraged to take in the full intensity of the shot and the significance of this place we share with Marnie. To be frank, we are standing in a toilet stall with Marnie—separated, most likely, by the commode itself. In *Psycho*, Hitchcock gave us the first glimpse of a toilet in mainstream American cinema; there it was in the place of a grisly murder (and, later in the film, it yielded up the clue in the crime's investigation).[46] Here, in *Marnie*, the toilet stall is one of the many claustrophobic interior places that, as Michele Piso notes, "function less as havens than as torture chambers."[47] Indeed, although Marnie hides in the toilet stall, one can hardly see this place as a safe haven.

This is a bleak scene, one in which we cannot but see and feel the depths to which this young woman has sunk. This is no happy place. Scenes like this make *Marnie*, in Piso's words, "the most unusually severe" of Hitchcock's films: "Absent are those happy spaces, those dwellings and shelters that can inspire daily chat or nocturnal intimacy."[48] Here, in the toilet, Marnie removes herself from daily chats, from potential companionship and conversation with other women. Apart from the expected *good-bye*s and *see you Monday*s, one subject dominates the chatter of her coworkers heard offscreen: the telephone. As we watch Marnie, we listen with her to snippets of conversation from her departing coworkers: "Do you mean we have to hang around and wait until they call?" "I don't know, but let's get home because he may have already called you." "Oh well, if I miss his call that's the way it goes."

What this scene tells us is not simply the lengths to which Marnie will go to steal, the lows of her premeditated theft, but also about her self-imposed isolation—not from all women, but from women who seem "content to stay a wage slave in the same office" all their lives, whose only free time is devoted to being on call, under the command and control of men who use the telephone as one of their principal instruments.[49] Later in the film, Mark will have an impromptu conversation with his sister-in-law, Lil (Diane Baker), just after Marnie rides off with Forio, with whom, thanks to Mark, she has been reunited. Lil tells Mark that she overheard a conversation he had with Marnie, that she is willing to help him if he's in "some kind of trouble." Mark chastises his sister-in-law for eavesdropping—something to which Lil willingly confesses. Then Lil tells Mark that she didn't need to "overhear stuff" to know that there is something wrong. Lil's "better sense" tells her that

Mark needs help, and she offers him her services as "guerrilla fighter, perjurer, intelligence agent." In putting the offer in such terms, Lil demonstrates where and how female knowledge operates in Hitchcock: it is marginal, tactical, willfully duplicitous (if need be), and covert. Mark asks for option number three, intelligence agent, and Lil tells him she overheard a private telephone conversation Marnie had with her mother, who lives in Baltimore (earlier, Marnie had told Mark that her mother is dead). Mark feigns skepticism and playfully distracts Lil with ideas about her future. Yet as the scene comes to a close, Hitchcock keeps Mark in tight frame, and we watch as the corners of his mouth slowly drop and he stares into the distance—presumably at the woman on horseback in the distance, who eludes him.

This is followed by a fade-to-black that lasts a full three seconds—surely the longest-held fade-to-black in the film, and possibly in all of Hitchcock.[50] No doubt the purpose of the fade-to-black is to allow the viewer to appreciate the full import of Mark's reaction to Lil's information. It is no wonder then that Mark's next move is to regain control by means of the telephone. In the scene that follows, Mark receives a long-distance call he is expecting. He receives the call downstairs, then decides to take the call upstairs in his office. As he heads toward the staircase, he instructs Lil, who is standing nearby, "Hang up as soon as I get it." He then stops halfway up the stairs, turns back to Lil, and commands more than asks, "Uh, Lil, you will hang up, won't you." In his private office and with Lil cut off (he presumes, but can we?), Mark can hold in his hand what Schantz calls the "ideal telephone," which "disappears into the content of the message it transmits. Moreover, it always reaches the person you want, when you want, without exposing you to unwelcome interruption. Its sound is clear."[51] The ideal telephone, Schantz further explains, "is a powerful fantasy that lures women and men alike, but only men find this fantasy sustained for them in the movies."[52] One might consider, here, Marnie's telephone conversation with her mother, in the library, just prior to the scene in which she is reunited with Forio. Marnie's telephone is not ideal; she clasps the transmitter with one hand, with the other hand covering the lower end of the handset. Her fingers are positioned awkwardly. This is how one holds the telephone when conditions are far from normal. The conversation with her mother is clandestine, and it is subject to interruption at any moment despite the fact that she has closed the doors to the library (or because of it). It allows Lil to approach silently the library without detection, to listen in on Marnie's conversation. Lil has the advantage here because, from behind closed doors, she can determine, with considerable accuracy, Marnie's location inside the room. Attached as she is to the telephone, Marnie cannot approach the door without putting her conversation with her mother on hold, and Lil would be aurally alerted to this pause. Hitchcock photographs Marnie from behind, over her left shoulder, her head turned away from us. The framing suggests vulnerability; the shot is overhead, the conversation is overheard.

By contrast, Mark's telephone conversation is photographed from the reverse angle: from the front, over his right shoulder. This overhead shot has Mark turned toward the camera, suggesting face-to-face conversation, the ideal transmission of voices. Mark grips the handset tightly, his fingers aligned perfectly so as to cover it completely. On the other end of the telephone is Mr. Boyle, a private detective we never see but whom Mark has hired. From him, Mark learns that the mother, Bernice Edgar (Louise Latham), had killed a man. Mark then instructs Mr. Boyle to call him when he has more information about "the child . . . the little girl . . . the daughter," and then reminds him to send photostats of all court records. Throughout his conversation with Mr. Boyle, Mark has been taking handwritten notes, documenting every detail. Hitchcock gives us a scenography of information transmission: the telephone connects Mark to the detective, who traces the origins of Marnie's troubles via court documents, photocopies of which are to be sent to Mark, who, all the while, is transcribing by hand. Telephony, typography, photostatography, stenography—these are the canny technologies of telegraphic communication, which, in ideal form (the Photostat Corporation instruction manual tells you that "the Photostat Never Makes a Mistake") and in combination, guarantee the highest reach of control; Mark has at his disposal a whole arsenal of methods for securing information about what is going on inside Marnie's head. But Marnie has no sympathetic affection for Mark, and for this reason her mind is off limits.[53] Mark, however, has no respect for boundaries, for physical or mental space. He forces himself on her in the rape scene and, as Piso writes, "forces his way into the memories of Marnie and her mother."[54] Even after doing so, however, Mark does not know the whole story. As Bernice sternly tells him, "You don't know the whole story and nobody does but me!" Knowing he does not know the whole story has been Mark's frustration all along—a point made explicit in the bizarre trailer for the film.[55] His calls do not go through, no signal is returned—not even a busy signal or a voice message.

This disconnection is established visually in the film whenever Marnie turns her head away from Mark—a repeated gesture—or verbally in Marnie's words, which, though they may be within earshot of Mark, are not spoken to him. Later in the night, well after Mark's phone call from Mr. Boyle, Marnie has a nightmare—the recurring one that involves repeated taps on the window, thunder and lightning, flashes of red, and coldness. After a lengthy back-and-forth in which Mark attempts to convince Marnie to "help" herself, the two play a word association game. Mark hurls the word *red* at her, and Marnie breaks down. He rushes to her bedside and tries to comfort her. But Mark's embrace resembles the drunken sailor's (Bruce Dern); it brings no comfort, only the aching, tear-filled cry "Oh help me! Help me, oh God, somebody help me!" The cry for help goes out to anyone ("Somebody!") who can hear, but the cry does not go out to Mark; he remains, to the end, more foe than friend.[56] In the film's climactic final scene, Marnie goes into a trance when Bernice lunges at Mark. "You let my momma go, you hear?" she pleads in her girlish, southern voice. Mark turns to her and demands, "Who am I, Marnie?" While Marnie may have no idea where she is or who is speaking to her, her answer is spot-on: "You're . . . you're one of them"—one of the men who want in.

Our Old Friend Telepathy

The lure of the fantasy of telepathy in *Marnie* is the lure of recognition without vision, intimacy without touching, a more perfect union. Several feminist critics have focused on Marnie's desire for her mother, for the perfect union that is the fantasy of the pre-Oedipal. And while these critics—and others—have noted Marnie's desire for Forio, few have pursued this desire in any direction other than back to the figure of the mother.[57] And while many of these same critics have rightly understood Marnie's attachment to Forio as an example, among many, of her resistance to heteronormativity, I would like to suggest that this attachment is something like an occult relation. Further, it is the figure of the telepathic woman that destabilizes heteronormativity by expanding the boundaries of a sympathetic community of non-males and, more strikingly, nonhumans. Thinking of Marnie's love for horses as an occult relation furthers our understanding of the film as, in Piso's words, "a nightmare of social exploitation and violation."[58] From this nightmare, Marnie flees to the fantasy of telepathy.

The film's concern with the occult—animal magnetism, hypnotism, telepathy, trances and waking dreams, the auguries of lightning and flashes of red—is in large part what makes it so strange. Indeed, it is remarkable that scholars have ignored the aspects of occultism in the film and in Hitchcock generally.[59] One of the strangest aspects is Marnie's occult relation with horses, a relation that Hitchcock expanded from the source material. At one point in the novel, Marnie describes a long evening she spent with Forio, "rubbing him down and brushing and combing his mane and tail. He loved this sort of thing and almost talked while I did it."[60] While this image of affectionate grooming is reimagined in Hitchcock's film as the scene in which Bernice Edgar brushes Jessie's hair, triggering a longing in Marnie for the intimacy she once shared with her mother, it is the odd embellishment about equine speech that is reimagined and elaborated in the film as Marnie's strange love affair with horses.

In a taped conversation between Hitchcock and Tippi Hedren, dated October 23, 1963, there is mention of lines of dialogue in a draft of the script that ultimately went unused. Early in the film, Mark proposes to take Marnie to the racetrack. She accepts this offer, and the two of them make their way to Atlantic City—an hour's drive from metropolitan Philadelphia. When they arrive at the racetrack, Marnie asks Mark to take her to the paddock. There,

Figure 5.4. *Marnie*: Marnie at table 8

Marnie presses Mark about his dislike of horses.[61] She asks him, "How can you not love horses? I can read their minds," to which Mark responds, no doubt pointing at a horse, "What's he thinking?" Marnie, in a rare moment of lightheartedness (or a typical moment of hostility toward people), tells him, "He's thinking that if he can ease over against the railing, he can pretend to stumble and with a little luck break the jockey's leg."[62] For a line of dialogue not used in the final version of the film, it echoes strongly, reverberating backward and forward in the filmed story. Marnie's telepathic insight takes us to the past, to the traumatic event that is the source of her psychological condition: her mother's struggle with the drunken sailor, which results in the mother's broken leg and the sailor's death at the hands of a frightened young Marnie. We are also taken into the future, for it is Marnie who will be thrown from a horse, her beloved Forio, later in the film during the foxhunt held at Wykwyn Manor. But it will be Forio's leg that is broken, not Marnie's. Here, too, is a scene that ends in death: Marnie's sudden, heartbreaking euthanization of Forio, which is given the same coda that ends the flashback scene: "There, there now." Thus Marnie displays a telepathic prowess that defies space and time (both "there" and "there," "now").

Although these lines did not make it to the final shooting script, the racetrack scene retains its occult significance. Mark has just brushed off a stranger who approached Marnie. As he sits down, we see a cardholder that indicates the two are seated at table 8. We have seen the cardholder earlier in the sequence, when Marnie is confronted by the stranger. In the shot in which we hear him ask, "I said, aren't you Peggy Nicholson?" the cardholder is to the right of the frame, next to a pair of binoculars (figure 5.4). Soon Mark returns and rids Marnie of her pest for the moment. Mark then asks

Figure 5.5. *Marnie*: our old friend telepathy

about the stranger, sarcastically referring to him as her "fan." Marnie reassures Mark that she just seems to have one of those faces, and Mark changes the subject to the next race. In the shot that follows, we see the pair of binoculars, dead center in the frame, next to the cardholder. Marnie asks to go to the paddock, specifically to have a look at Telepathy, a horse Marnie had been watching since he was a two-year-old.[63] As the two approach the horse, Mark tells Marnie he is reluctant to bet on such a "lanky piece of business," but he agrees nonetheless. However, the jockey riding Telepathy, the horse whose name is linked with what Mark calls Marnie's "superior knowledge," is wearing a red-spotted jersey with the number 8. When Marnie sees this, the screen floods with red, and she must look away. She then pleads with Mark not to bet on Telepathy after all.

Now, given the ways in which strange, probing (and probed) prosthetic eyes haunt this scene, as discussed in chapter 2, we can associate the red polka dots that trigger Marnie's flash with optic wounds, sockets bloody and emptied by probing fingers. When Mark asks why he is not to bet on Telepathy, Marnie—with her head turned to one side, leaving only her left eye visible—says, "He's walleyed." But this, of course, is a white lie. The horse's irises are dark brown (walleyed horses have bluish-white irises). Still, there is some truth in her claim that number 8 is walleyed (figure 5.5). The number 8—formed as two red circles with white irises—adorns the jockey's sleeve just below his right shoulder. Like a pair of sockets emptied, the eyes of which are multiplied and splattered across the jersey in a grisly red-on-white pattern, the figure is a violent illustration of hurtful watching.

As noted above, the fantasy of telepathy is the nonocular transmission of thought. This fantasy is no doubt linked with Marnie's fear of prosthetic eyes, which shadow her, call her out, expose her, and threaten to destroy her fantasy of telepathic bliss.[64] Thus the need to look away, to close her eyes, to form a protective wall across them. Marnie's walleyes shield her from her trauma, which Mark incites when he rapes her in their honeymoon suite. As he forces her down into bed we see white spots fill Marnie's irises. Mark's eyes, by contrast, are predatory—large, bulbous, demanding, far more hurtful than the probing prosthetic eyes at the racetrack. Hitchcock has Mark's eye consume the frame—he is in full-on attack, eyes on eyes. George Toles, who has written on the metaphorical scheme of the eye in Poe, Bataille, and Hitchcock, argues that "the 'invader,' whatever his harsh business, always breaks in through the same eye window."[65] *Marnie*'s racetrack scene, surely one of the oddest in a film full of odd scenes, suggests that the link between the fantasy of telepathy and the fear of prosthetic eyes is closer, more intimate than one might think. For is it not built into the logic of telepathy that we are all exposed by it? After all, how did the stranger know Marnie / Miss Nicholson was at the track that day? How did he zero in on her precise location when, by all appearances, she was not to be seen?[66]

The racetrack, as Lisa Zunshine points out, is often the scene of mind reading, both in literature and film. It is one social setting among many "in which unsuspecting spectators are turned into objects of observation."[67] Yet Zunshine has zero interest in the possibility of occult meaning, of "plain old telepathy," choosing instead what she calls the more interesting application of "theory of mind," understood broadly (and often incompletely) as mind reading.[68] In her discussion of what she terms "embodied transparency," the moment in fiction and film when a character's body language becomes legible to keen observers, Zunshine turns to the racetrack scene from *Notorious*, which resembles the racetrack scene in *Marnie*. Alicia and Devlin meet at the Hipódromo da Gávea in Rio de Janeiro. It is the first of their meetings since Alicia reluctantly agreed to infiltrate the Sebastian estate. She has information to pass along to Devlin regarding a dinner party Alex Sebastian hosted the previous evening. As Devlin grows jealous, the two have a spat. Sebastian then approaches them, and Devlin excuses himself. Alicia, with binoculars to hide her crying eyes, does her best to reassure Alex that she detests Devlin, that he doesn't mean anything to her. "I'd like to be convinced," Alex tells her. "Would you maybe care to convince me, Alicia, that Mr. Devlin means nothing to you?" That Alex allows himself to suspend his suspicions about Devlin means he is a poor mind reader. Thus, a racetrack is a place where characters "think they learn some important truths about the people whom they observe, while, in fact, it's where they come up with wrong interpretations that serve to thicken the plot."[69]

But this racetrack scene is far more uncanny than Zunshine allows; it is a scene of mixed signals, narrative interference, and strange linkages of past and present. The scene begins with a shot of Alex, binoculars in front of his eyes, seated next to his mother, who is holding a newspaper. Far below this pair of peepers, close to the track, is Devlin, who finds Alicia waiting for him. "I don't think they can see us, Alex and his mother," she assures Devlin. We know, from chapter 2, just how effective a combination of a newspaper and a pair of binoculars can be. Alex may seem to be watching the race, and Mrs. Sebastian may seem to be reading a newspaper, but the two are discussing Alicia's conspicuous absence. And given the suggestive opening shot of this scene, with the peak of Corcovado Mountain towering high above the São Paulo Jockey Club, it is clear that Alex and his mother are engaged in high-altitude surveillance. And Alicia is not safe.

What begins as an encounter fortified by the promise of telepathic fantasy ("Don't telephone me anymore, just rely on my popping up," Devlin tells her. "Can you hear me?" she replies, her lips barely moving) ends as a conversation gone haywire, no doubt due to interference from above. "Are you betting on this race?" Alicia asks. "No," replies Devlin. "Alex says number 10 is sure to win, he knows the owner," says Alicia. Given the way this scene anticipates the standoff of prosthetic vision from *Marnie*, one wonders if Alicia is now receiving this information telepathically from Alex. "Thanks for the tip," says Devlin (but to whom?). Alicia continues to channel her new playmate: "Alex says they have been holding him back all season but—" and is then interrupted by Devlin, who launches a fierce verbal attack on Alicia. "I can't help recalling some of your remarks. About being a new woman. Daisies and buttercups, wasn't it?"

The last remark is a cutting, hurtful reference to Alicia's daydreamy, mocking self-portrait earlier in the film of "a nice, unspoiled child whose heart is full of daisies and buttercups."[70] This vision of "daisies and buttercups," initially dismissed sarcastically, returns to Devlin here at the racetrack. It once was a vision, however distant, of youth, of sweetness and light, of unspoiled children and their playthings. Now, the phrase is, to Devlin, a cruel joke on him. Alicia cannot abide this notion and, turning to Devlin, spits, "Oh you idiot!" Alicia's contention, which is credible, is that Devlin threw her at Alex. Devlin responds that he threw her at nobody, that "a man doesn't tell a woman what to do, she tells herself." In the end, as Devlin sees things, the answer had to come from Alicia. Now, to Devlin, the miracle girl filled with daisies and buttercups is just "hokey-pokey," and Alicia has failed the love test.

Just then, Alicia puts the binoculars up to her eyes, and we see a pair of horses race by, right to left, in each lens. It is one of the more memorable shots from the film, striking perhaps because the images reflected in Alicia's binocular lenses are too clear, too well-framed. The timing is also key, as Alicia raises the binoculars to her face at the moment she feels the most acute emotional pain. This has led many critics to argue that Alicia uses the binoculars to mask her tears from Devlin—a gesture betraying the deepest shame. While this is a plausible reading of the shot, it doesn't quite account for its strangeness. The shot stands out because it achieves a greater degree of abstraction than any other shot in the sequence. The effect calls attention to itself, to the foregrounding of the optical device. Alicia is abstracted as well—hemmed in by process shots both front and back, surrounded by cinematic artifice. As much a reflection of the race Alicia and Devlin are (not) watching within the diegesis, the image in the binocular lenses gives us a glimpse into their past, the precise moment when, most assuredly and quite unexpectedly, Devlin throws Alicia for Alex to catch. It is the recent past, at the riding club, the place where Prescott (Louis Calhern), Devlin's superior, arranged for Alicia to make contact with Alex. She is riding alongside Devlin as the two approach Alex, riding with an unknown woman, from behind. As Devlin and Alicia overtake Alex and his companion, Alicia turns her head slightly toward Alex. But she hides her eyes beneath her riding hat, as if in hopes of not being recognized—that is, she looks closely enough to confirm it is Alex, but not for him to recognize her. This is both a half-hearted and a full-hearted effort. As she and Devlin ride ahead, Alicia says, with a smile on her face, "I guess I'm the girl nobody remembers." Devlin responds, "We'll stick around, give him another chance." But Devlin doesn't wait for a second chance; instead he frightens Alicia's horse by kicking its side, sending it galloping off. Alex chases after, steadies Alicia's horse, and as we see from a distance—and from Devlin's perspective—the two shake hands.

As magical as the stranger's newspaper in the racetrack scene in *Marnie*, Alicia's binoculars give us a glimpse into the past—or an impression of the past, as Alicia perceives it. What we see in the binocular lenses is not just a reflection but a projection as well, of things before Alicia's eyes. For a moment, we can read Alicia's mind. More than this, a telepathic network is formed linking Alicia, Devlin, and the racing horses. As Marc Raymond Strauss puts it, the "racing horses rush by in a 'reflection' on her binoculars, the animals seeming to speak for her as she tells him, 'I see, some kind of love test.'"[71] If, as Strauss is suggesting here, the racing horses speak of a love test, it is Devlin who has failed it. It is he who fails to answer, in Alicia's intentional failure to make herself recognizable to Alex, a love call. Here at the racetrack, Devlin sees a fallen woman. But Alicia did not fall—she was thrown.[72] Devlin will correct himself later in the film, in Prescott's office at the embassy, when Beardsley (Moroni Olsen) speaks men's minds on the subject of Alicia's virtue: "I don't think any of us have any illusions about her character, have we, Devlin?" Devlin's sarcastic response is, were we to grade it, a perfect ten: "Not at all, not the slightest. Miss Huberman is first, last, and always not a lady. She may be risking her life, but when it comes to being a lady, she doesn't hold a candle to your wife, sir, sitting in Washington playing bridge with three other ladies of great honor and virtue." As Modleski notes, Devlin "perfectly articulates the double bind in which Alicia is placed."[73] Alicia does good work only insofar as she remains "notorious." If, as Devlin says, she is "made over by love," she fails at her job. The choice for Alicia is an impossible one: fail at your job or fail the love test. Devlin expresses the logic of this double bind at the embassy, but he does so in Alicia's absence, in a room full of men. At the crowded racetrack, however, Devlin sounds more like Beardsley: "Dry your eyes, baby. It's out of character. Except, keep on your toes—it's a tough job we're on." Just then, Alex emerges from the crowd and approaches them. In a shot that bridges this scene with the following, in Prescott's office, we see Devlin, seated at a table at an outdoor café, at night, alone.

Devlin remains, until the end of the film, "a fat-headed guy, filled with pain." And while the question of who fills this man with pain and why has been handled persuasively by Modleski, we have yet to consider if Devlin's head, swollen with masochistic urges, prevents him from tuning into Alicia's.[74] Just prior to his cutting remark about daisies and buttercups, Devlin mocks Alicia's well-deserved pride in being eight-days sober. "Practically whitewashed," he tells her. In response, Alicia tells Devlin she is very happy. It is a quiet expression of utter transparency: Alicia at her most honest, most open, and most vulnerable. As she speaks the words, "Why won't you let me be happy?" her eyes scan Devlin's face, flitting softly left and right a dozen times in five seconds.[75] Begging off shame, Alicia scorns Devlin: "Why don't you give that copper's brain a rest? Every time you look at me, I can see it dwelling over its slogans: 'Once a crook always a crook; once a tramp always a tramp.'" Alicia, it seems, has slipped into his head and now reads his thoughts: "Go ahead, you can hold my hand," she tells him, though Devlin speaks not a word. Operating like an unlicensed telepath, Alicia studies the confusion in Devlin's mind, telling him what he knows, what he's thinking to himself, what he will not share openly with her. "And now you're scared of yourself. You're afraid you'll fall in love with me." Devlin is not seeing straight, not thinking straight. His fat copper's brain is fatigued. Thus in *Notorious*, we have a reversal of the telepathic impulses in *Marnie*: while Mark desperately wants to be inside Marnie's head but is refused access, Alicia begs an unwilling Devlin to come into her head, to know what he fails to see: that she is good and her love for him is true. Only later, when it's very nearly too late, will Devlin find the time to give his copper's brain a rest, ignore what he sees before him (what he thinks is a drunk Alicia), read between the lines, make the psychic connection, and "pay a call."

Psycho-Analysis and Telepathy

While it should be noted that telepathy is not the only avenue of shared knowledge and intimacy open to women (there are the more conventional ones, such as letters, telephones, secret meetings, etc.), it is one to which the men in Hitchcock have limited access. For this reason, telepathy—and other forms of occult communication—is a refuge for women from the men who stalk them through a Hitchcock landscape fraught with danger. This is not to say that men are entirely unwelcome in female telepathic networks—as suggested in my discussion of *Notorious*. It is simply a question of letting the right one in, so to speak (Devlin and not Alex, for instance). The problem is that often the men in Hitchcock have both a deep curiosity and great antipathy regarding the female mind. While the balance may shift (toward curiosity, as with L. B. Jefferies, or toward antipathy, as with Detective Tom Doyle, in *Rear Window*), what is constant is ambivalence. Historically, one can trace this ambivalence back to a strange convergence of what Luckhurst calls "the invention of telepathy" and the invention of another method of reading minds: psychoanalysis.[76] What follows is an attempt to understand one of the more memorable sequences in Hitchcock's *Psycho*: Marion's preempted drive to Fairvale. I have yet to encounter any scholarship on the film which considers the possibility that, during this drive, Marion telepathically listens in on actual conversations about her (between Lila and Sam, between her boss and Cassidy). Yet I will show that networks of communication, both canny and uncanny, play an important role in the first forty-eight minutes of the film and help set the stage for a showdown between female minds and the men who want access.

In the summer of 1921, Freud prepared a lecture, later titled "Psycho-Analysis and Telepathy," to be given in September at a meeting of the Central Executive of the International Psycho-Analytical Association.[77] From what we know about the history of this early foray into the topic, Freud seems a little discombobulated. Reading the opening paragraph of the lecture, one might even detect something like panic: "Scarcely have we triumphantly repulsed two attacks . . . when another peril has arisen. And this time it is something tremendous, something elemental, which threatens not us alone but our enemies, perhaps, still more."[78] The enemies to which Freud refers are Alfred Adler and Carl Jung, and their common threat is "occult" phenomena: "Of facts, that is, that profess to speak in favour of the real existence of psychical forces other than the human and animal minds with which we are familiar, or that seem to reveal the possession by those minds of faculties hitherto unrecognized."[79]

Freud proceeded to describe two cases, both of which impressed upon him the possibility that telepathy was "the kernel of truth" around which the entirety of the field of occultism was built.[80] In both cases, the patient learns of a prophecy that, while proving to be false, nevertheless aroused powerful feelings. Was telepathy at work in both cases? "The obvious thing," concluded Freud, "would be to dismiss the question entirely and to consign it to the rubbish heap among so many other meaningless and ostensibly occult messages."[81] Yet Freud is unable to dismiss the question entirely and, in a manner typical of his attitude toward the occult, concedes, "Unluckily I must add that it was possible—and precisely by the help of analysis—to find an explanation."[82] The explanation led Freud to conclude—with not a little bit of apprehension—that thought transference indeed existed:

> I have nothing to say about all the other miracles that are claimed by occultism. My own life, as I have already openly admitted, has been particularly poor in an occult sense. Perhaps the problem of thought-transference may seem very trivial to you in comparison with the great magical world of the occult. But consider what a momentous step beyond what we have hitherto believed would be involved in this hypothesis alone.[83]

Freud was never freed from doubt about the possibility of telepathy. Indeed, as noted by his biographer and friend, Ernest Jones, it is possible to find in Freud's writings both a belief in and a dismissal of telepathy: "The wish to believe fought hard with the warning to disbelieve. They represented two fundamental features of his personality, both indispensible to his achievements. But here he was truly wracked; little wonder he bewailed that the topic 'perplexed him to distraction.' "[84] To be sure, Freud's writings on telepathy can be considered hysterical texts; the possibility that telepathy may indeed exist could only induce anxiety in a man whose profession requires that, through other means besides telepathy, he get inside another's head.[85] To the end, Freud was hounded by his old friend telepathy.

Freud closes his essay on psychoanalysis and telepathy with a story about the custodian of the Basilique Saint-Denis. Freud recalls how the custodian, after telling of the martyrdom of Saint-Denis by beheading, would add that Saint-Denis is said to have picked up his head and carried it under his arm for some distance. Freud continued: "But the custodian used to remark: '*Dans des cas pareils, ce n'est que le premier pas qui coûte.*' The rest is easy."[86] One interpretation of Freud's anecdote is that by believing in the existence of thought transference—in overcoming the resistance to it as possibility—one has taken the first, and most difficult, step. After that, "the rest is easy." But as Nick Totton points out, the anecdote "concerns a primary theme of hysteria—*what one can do without one's head*: what the body can do on its own."[87] The anecdote, Totton further adds, came to Freud during a visit to the Basilique Saint-Denis while he was studying hysteria with Charcot at La Salpêtrière, the medical complex where the French neurologist taught. Totton is largely interested in how the anecdote helps us understand some paradoxes in Wilhelm Reich's thoughts about the mind-body split. What interests me here, however, is the relation between telepathy and hysteria ("How often, we realize, telepathy features in accounts of hysteria!"), a relation that seems fraught with its own paradox.[88]

Presumably, a telepath can do little or nothing without her head. No head, no thoughts. Yet hysteria, as many feminist critics have shown, is also associated with feminist resistance. It is conceived as "a specifically feminine pathology that speaks to and against patriarchy."[89] One might say that *hysteric* is the name given to the woman who struggles to keep men out of her head. Here we may think of Dora, the hysteric patient made famous by Freud who broke off her treatment unexpectedly—a decision that Freud could interpret only as "an unmistakable act of vengeance" against him.[90] For some feminists, the decision is an unmistakable act of resistance. Hélène Cixous, in her treatise "The Laugh of the Medusa," champions Dora as "the indomitable, the poetic body . . . the true mistress of the Signifier."[91] So if we take the anecdote that ends "Psycho-Analysis and Telepathy" to be about Freud's own hysteria about telepathy, it may also be understood as expressing his frustration at being cut off from women's heads, or cut out of their thoughts. While neither the anecdote nor the essay in which it appears bears a direct relation to Freud's experience with the Dora case (which ended two decades prior to the writing of "Psycho-Analysis and Telepathy"), a curious association cannot be ignored. Freud felt that Dora's decision to break off treatment was not just an act of vengeance against him but an act of self-injury as well. Thus hysteria reminds us of the double bind that the prohibitive telepath is in: *I cut off my head so no man can get in.* It is no wonder, then, that many feminists are dubious of the political potential of hysteria. Elaine Showalter traces a line of doubt among feminist critics and artists about the fascination with Dora in particular and hysteria in general.[92] As it was for Saint Denis and Dora both, "rebellion turned back on the self."[93]

But let us not forget the "some distance" that, like Saint Denis, the hysterical woman creates before succumbing at last. What are the small victories purchased at great cost? This is, I argue, precisely the question posed in the first forty-eight minutes of *Psycho*. For reasons that should be clear, we now turn to Marion Crane and the "some distance" she creates from the moment of her crime to the instant of her death. In a more comic tone, the film prepares us for this question just before Cassidy's arrival at Lowery's office. Marion comes to work with a headache, and she asks her coworker Caroline (Patricia Hitchcock) for some aspirin. Caroline doesn't have any aspirin, but she has something stronger: "Mom gave them to me the night of my wedding. Teddy was furious when he found out I'd taken tranquilizers." We can assume, here, that this bit of prescription drug deception—passed on from mother to daughter, a shared secret between women—is a small act of rebellion. Like her mother before her, Caroline divorced her head from her body on the night of her wedding as a way of coping with the stress that comes from bedding down with a man who believes he is entitled to sex. The fury of Teddy was a price Caroline was willing to pay.

Next, there is an exchange between Caroline and Marion about telephonic relays. "Any calls?" asks Marion, to which Caroline reports, "Teddy called—me—my mother called to see if Teddy called. Oh, your sister called to say she's going to Tucson to do some buying and she'll be gone the whole weekend and . . ." Enter Cassidy (Frank Albertson). It's a proper entrance, as it interrupts the transmission of information between women, from Lila (Vera Miles) to Caroline to Marion. After she steals the money, swaps out automobiles, and makes the final stretch to the Bates Motel, Marion will intercept telephone conversations and telephonic messages between her boss, Caroline, and Lila. If there was an instance of telepathy in Hitchcock for Freud to subject to psychoanalysis, this is a good one.

The sequence is well known: almost immediately after she trades in her car for a different one and drives away from California Charlie's dealership, Marion begins to hear voices in her head. First is California Charlie himself, speaking to the officer: "That's the first time I've seen a customer high-pressure the salesman. Somebody chasing her?" Next is the officer: "I better have a look at those papers, Charlie." Thus begins a roughly three-and-a-half-minute sequence, structured by a single-shot/reverse-shot pattern of a close-up of Marion driving, followed by a point-of-view shot, through the windshield, of the road ahead. In succession, we hear the voices of Marion's coworker Caroline and her boss Mr. Lowery (Vaughn Taylor) in two brief exchanges, followed by Mr. Lowery on the telephone with Marion's sister Lila, then Cassidy, the man from whom Marion has stolen $40,000. The purpose of this scene, the reason for the elegant simplicity of its shot/reverse-shot structure, is to focus our attention on Marion, on her interiority and transparency. In this highly privileged moment, we are allowed to read her mind; it is an intimacy guaranteed by Marion's gaze, direct at us, which never shies away. Hitchcock's camera seems to be in a hypnotic standoff of vision; a purer instance of telepathic communication is not to be found in the filmmaker's career.

But is this an instance of telepathy? Or is it simply a somewhat unconventional use of the voice-over—in this case, a series of voice-overs, each speaking words Marion can only imagine are being said about her? If neither option seems quite right, what other possibilities are available to us? Thinking through the options of how film can, in general, represent what a character is thinking, Schantz creates a short list of three possibilities: "textual, oral, and what is sometimes called audiovisual communication." The first, seldom used, consists simply of the inclusion of written text within the frame, placed in a cartoon bubble near the character's head or, like subtitles for a foreign language film, placed along the bottom of the screen. The oral option is what Schantz calls "the much maligned voice over." The third option, perhaps as uncommon as the first, "is simply to *show* us what a character thinks." Schantz's example of this, "the most elegant and 'cinematic' solution, comes from the film *High Fidelity* (dir. Stephen Frears, 2000) in a scene in which Rob Gordon (John Cusack) imagines a series of encounters in his music store with his romantic rival, Ian (Tim Robbins). Schantz concludes that, in all instances, "we still need language." In a sense, then, we can never really get away from the voice-over. Schantz then quotes filmmaker Chris Marker, who claims that the voice-over "is the destiny of cinema: it is soliloquy, it is a telephone system to the inner self."[94]

As we have seen, however, the telephone system suggests ideal communication between relatively stable subjects. What we experience with Marion's "voices over" is far less stable. If Marion is indeed imagining what others are, at that moment (or at other moments?), saying about her, why such perfect impersonation? A more conventionally cinematic approach would have Marion's voice-over (her voice, the voice of Janet Leigh) speaking *for* the others (e.g., "I can hear that awful Cassidy now, he's probably telling Mr. Lowery that I was never to be trusted, that I was . . . that I was *flirting* with him!"). This is the approach Hitchcock takes in the film's final scene. As the camera slowly tracks in on Norman, wrapped in a blanket, we listen to the voice inside his head. He is using his mother's voice to tell us what "they" are probably thinking: "I hope they're watching. They'll see. They'll see, and they'll know . . . and they'll say, 'Why, she wouldn't even harm a fly.'" This latter example of voice-over, with Norman-as-Mother telling us what he thinks others are thinking about him, conforms neatly to Marker's idea of telephonic communication between character and viewer. In the former example, however, Marion goes completely haywire.[95]

Our dilemma thus far has been that the voice-overs sequence in *Psycho* departs from the cinema's familiar methods of communicating a character's thoughts to the viewer, which leaves open the possibility of telepathy. The revised draft of the *Psycho* shooting script, dated December 1, 1959, does little to resolve the dilemma. The voice-overs scene begins intelligibly enough. The screen direction is that the camera is close on Marion's face (the script uses the name from Robert Bloch's novel, Mary), "recording her anxiety, her fears. Her guilt shines bright in her eyes and she is a person unaccustomed to containing this much guilt in this realistic a situation."[96] Then we hear, in this draft of the script, the sound of California Charlie's voice, "as clearly as Mary hears it in her imagination." But here, the script suggests two things at once—that Marion *hears* the voices and that she *imagines* them. The next screen direction is no less confused: "The 'imagined voice' we hear is actually the voice of the Car dealer." Not only does the use of quotation marks suggest indeterminacy about whether or not the voice is imagined (why, indeed, are quotation marks necessary?), but the rest of the screen direction all but wipes away the possibility that the voice is imagined. It is "actually" California Charlie's voice.

A similar equivocation can be detected when the script introduces the voices of Lowery and Caroline. Again, the screen direction begins unremarkably: "Mary looks weary, tired with strain and with hard driving. Her eyes are heavy with worry and deep thought." But then things take an even more bizarre turn:

> We hear the sound of an agitated buzz of an intercom system, a sound emanating from Mary's imagination.
>
> After the second buzz, we hear the voice of Caroline.
>
> CAROLINE'S VOICE
>
> Yes, Mr. Lowery.
>
> LOWERY'S VOICE
>
> Caroline . . . Mary still isn't in?
>
> CAROLINE'S VOICE
>
> No, Mr. Lowery . . . but then she's always a bit late on Monday mornings.
>
> LOWERY'S VOICE
>
> Buzz me the minute she comes in.
>
> Again Mary shakes her head, forces herself to stop hearing these "invented" scenes of her imagination.

Here, the narrative technologies of telephonic and telepathic communication become strangely conflated. The unused screen action—the sound of the buzzing intercom system and Marion's reaction to it—suggests a kind of occult conference call, though Lowery instructs Caroline to buzz him the minute Marion "comes in" when Marion is, in effect, already buzzed in, already privy to the conversation between him and Caroline. Note, again, the curious use of quotation marks around the word "invented"—as if Joseph Stefano, Hitchcock's screenwriter, has no plans to let us off the hook with assurances that Marion is only imagining this conversation.

While the "buzz" is not in the final shooting script, the ambiguity—about whether or not Marion is imagining the conversations—remains in the film. Added is a brief conversation Marion imagines with Sam, which inaugurates the voice-overs sequence in the final version of the film. Marion has driven perhaps no more than mile—she is still in downtown Phoenix—when she hears Sam's voice, speaking from Fairvale: "Marion, what on Earth? What are you doing up here? Of course I'm glad to see you, I always am . . . what is it, Marion?" This is the only conversation in the sequence in which Marion is addressed directly, and it has the odd effect of sounding very much like a telephone conversation. While it would seem to be a face-to-face conversation ("Of course I'm glad to see you"), the absence of Marion's response to Sam's direct question suggests that Sam's signal is being transmitted telephonically to Marion. Stranger still, it is a signal from a future that never arrives—Marion does not make it to Fairvale.

Figure 5.6. *Psycho*: Teletalk

If these conversations seem "scripted by Marion's imagination," as William Rothman understands them, they are scripted with uncanny vividness.[97] The choice to have the "actual voice," as the shooting script describes it, of each character in Marion's head reading her words has the chilling effect of making the "voices over" seem the result of thought transference. Thinking of this phenomenon in his lecture "Dreams and Occultism," Freud describes thought transference as "so close to telepathy" as to be "the same thing. It claims that mental processes in one person—ideas, emotional states, conative impulses—can be transferred to another person through empty space without the familiar methods of communication by means of words and signs."[98] And while "familiar methods of communication" are not at work in thought transference, Freud doesn't hesitate to turn to such methods as a way of effectively illustrating the thought-transference process. His example is of a woman ("mother or daughter or fiancée") intuiting the death of a loved one at the precise moment of the event: "It is as if she had been informed by telephone, though such was not the case; it is a kind of psychical counterpart to wireless telegraphy."[99] Marion's mind, then, does indeed seem wired for sound, wired for what might be called "teletalk"—which it so happens is the name of the intercom device that sits on Marion's desk at Lowery's office, the very device Lowery asks Caroline to use to alert him of Marion's arrival, the very device that buzzes in Mary's ear. It is visible in the left of the frame, in front of Caroline, who watches as Marion places Cassidy's $40,000 into an envelope (figure 5.6). While it may seem to be an innocuous thing, it is, I argue, linked to the question of Marion's "better sense."

Designed by the Webster Electric Company, the Teletalk was one among many intercom systems used by small and large businesses alike—a staple of thousands of offices throughout the country and one of the principal means for women like Marion of professional communication with their male superiors. The model on Marion's desk, designed by industrial designer Brooks Stevens, was advertised as "the first high powered intercommunication system."[100] Interestingly, Marion appears to have full control of the intercom system, for it is a "Master Station" that is on her desk (as opposed to a "Speaker Station," or simple call-in terminal). A "Master Station," according to a Teletalk instruction manual, "can originate calls with other Master Stations or Speaker Stations." Master Stations operate on a dual circuit system, the "S" circuit and the "M" circuit. This may seem like a dry, technical detail, but it leads to a rather striking feature of the intercom system: "The 'M' circuit *is not* secretive—any Master unit can monitor a Speaker unit or another Master Station. Any Master can listen in on conversations between any other two units."[101] Thus Marion is associated with both high-powered intercommunication and the threat of telepathic invasion. No wonder, then, that Marion's lonely drive from Phoenix to Fairvale is accompanied by substantial signal interference and crosstalk. "Even when Marion is alone," writes Rothman, "she has no privacy."[102]

Marion does not make it to Fairvale, although she is close (Norman will tell her that it is only fifteen miles away). Instead, she settles down for a night's rest at the Bates Motel. Scholars frequently remark that it is during her prolonged exchange with Norman over dinner that Marion regrets her actions and decides she must return the money and face the consequences. As Rothman puts it, and I take it he speaks for many, "She has come to understand that going through with the project she initiated by stealing the $40,000 would be madness. When she adds, 'Thank you,' she is thanking Norman for more than his food and company. She is also expressing gratitude for the lesson she feels she has learned."[103] Following this logic, we might retroactively interpret the voice-overs sequence as highly suggestive of Marion's growing doubt about her actions. Hardly telepathic, Marion is simply expressing shame, concern for her worried sister, the fear of retribution, and so on. But if Marion is developing a good conscience during this sequence, all is spoiled by the voice of Cassidy—the man who (like Strutt for Marnie) fills Marion with disgust. As I hear Cassidy's voice and see the look on Marion's face (which rhymes, in an eerie way, with "Mother's" final smile at the camera), I cannot help suspecting that Marion is now hell-bent on going through with the madness.

And I don't want Marion to return the money, or to return to Sam for that matter. What fascinates me—and I wager it fascinates many a spectator of *Psycho*—is Marion's mobility. But the film will countermobilize a host of hurtful watchers to check her speed and disrupt her course—a course she is not allowed even to begin to chart. Marion is under surveillance, and no fantasy of speed and telepathy will keep her safe. For all her mobility, Marion's path leads her to the Bates Motel, where there is only stasis. There is a dreadful logic here, one that Freud would say is suggestive of Marion's powerful death drive. Indeed, if Freud were to do some *Psycho*-analysis, he would doubtless conclude that Marion's telepathic experience is the expression of "unconscious psychical reality," the wish for her own death. Freud felt strongly that telepathy was connected with death, and stated as much in his essay "Dreams and Telepathy":

> By far the greater number of all telepathic intimations relate to death or the possibility of death; when patients under analysis keep telling us of the frequency and infallibility of their gloomy forebodings, we can with equal regularity show them that they are fostering particularly strong death-wishes in their unconscious against their nearest relations and have long been thus suppressing them.[104]

Of course, Marion does not wish for Lila's nor her mother's death. If she suppresses any death wish against anyone, it is against Sam's ex-wife—or, perhaps because she does harbor this unspeakable desire, against herself. Why Marion has a death wish will remain unclear. But the gloom is palpable from the outset in the hotel room she shares with Sam at the beginning of the film. The scene is heavy with dark, ironic statements such as "Check out time is 3:00" and "Oh Sam, this is the last time." These "gloomy forebodings" persist throughout the first part of the film and culminate in Marion's drive from Arizona to California, particularly when she hears Cassidy's voice: "Well I ain't about to kiss off forty thousand dollars! I'll get it back and if any of it's missin' I'll replace it with her fine, soft flesh!" This, the gloomiest of forebodings, is borne out when Norman, knife in hand, slashes and tears Marion's fine, soft flesh.

For Laura Mulvey, *Psycho* is the literalization of the death drive, the compulsion to return to what Freud refers to as an "old state of things," which is stasis. Marion's desperate journey may have been motivated by the desire for marriage, for a happy ending to that sad story played out in the hotel room. But her desire for marriage is conflated with her desire—and the film's need—for an end, for stillness, for death. Writes Mulvey,

> Although Hitchcock's "killing off" of Marion does, indeed, contravene the conventions of Hollywood and the traditions of story-telling, the conflation between marriage and death makes a radical, but formal, point about narrative structure. Desire for marriage, and for the happy ending, are not simply dispersed through a naturalistic device but violently truncated and superimposed. The interchangeability of death and marriage, functioning as figures of ending, is dramatized, ironically, and tragically.[105]

For Mulvey, *Psycho* brings to the surface what much of Hollywood cinema represses, which is the stillness that is film's own "old state of things"—the celluloid strip, unprojected, its frames frozen, not yet come to life on the screen as glorious (but illusory) movement. *Pyscho* is, above all, about "The End." By this logic, Marion's death, forty-eight minutes into the film, is far from surprising: it is foretold.

Psycho may indeed be Hitchcock's occult masterpiece, the ultimate horror mystery story. "I still can't believe. . . . It must be some kind of mystery," says Lowery in one of his voice-overs—or as I argue, as Marion overhears him telepathically. It is no wonder, then, that the voices echoing the humdrum Teletalk intercommunications that made up Marion's day-to-day life should accompany Marion's literal death drive from Arizona to California. Marion is haunted by voices already expressing awareness of her nonpresence, of something gone wrong, of her stasis; as Sam worriedly tells Lila, "She may be, well, unable to answer the phone." This is the nightmare of the telepathic fantasy: that you can tune in to the news of your own death.

Conclusion: Cool Medium

It is fitting that *Family Plot* should bring to a close the career of the master of occult storytelling.[106] The film centers around Blanche Tyler (Barbara Harris), a con artist posing as a psychic who operates, with the assistance of her boyfriend George Lumley (Bruce Dern), a séance service.[107] The film begins with Blanche, mid-séance, channeling her spiritual spokesman, "Henry." Blanche's client, Julia Rainbird (Cathleen Nesbitt), is a wealthy spinster whose sleep of late has been troubled by visitations from her long-dead sister Harriet. The sister, it seems, had a child out of wedlock, and Julia forced her to give up the child to avoid scandal. Now, Harriet has returned to play upon the guilty conscience of her older sister. Blanche, through "Henry," then channels Harriet herself. Cooing, Blanche-as-Henry-as-Harriet tells Julia, "I've waited so long to hear from you, Julia. I've been so unhappy without you." Needing no further prompting, Julia makes a promise to her sister Harriet that she will find her son, if he's still alive, and take him in her arms and love him. "I'll make him one of us," she promises her dead sister, "and, and, and give him everything. . . . Everything!"

Blanche, now emptied of her spiritual proxies, collapses in her chair, exhausted. "What in the world's been going on here? I feel as though I've been properly done over," says Blanche. Julia then asks if Blanche remembers anything. "Only the gist," replies Blanche, who then asks for a sip of sherry to clear her throat ("Henry" speaks in a low, gravelly voice). "In a nutshell," says Blanche, "about forty years ago you arranged to have your sister Harriet's baby given away without a trace. And now, your bad dreams and troubled conscience tell you to find the grown-up person, take him into the family and bestow your wealth on him." Julia evaluates Blanche's nutshell as "excellent." Further, Julia promises to pay Blanche $10,000 if she, through

"Henry," can learn from Harriet of the lost son's whereabouts. This, in a nutshell, is the family plot.

Though it gets complicated: the plot of Blanche and George trying to track down the lost Rainbird heir crosses with another plot, that of the Rainbird heir himself, who, as a young boy, took the name of his foster parents, Shoebridge, but now goes by the name of Arthur Adamson (William Devane). He spends his time plotting kidnappings with his coconspirator Fran (Karen Black). Arthur has an appetite for precious diamonds, which he collects as ransoms for the kidnap victims he hides in the high-security cellar of his home. Eventually, the plots converge when the well-meaning Blanche, thinking she has successfully tracked down the lost Rainbird heir ("Through psychic means," she proudly adds), realizes she has also found the man who kidnapped Bishop Wood, Adamson's latest victim. Drugged by Arthur, Blanche is dragged to the cellar and locked up. Eventually, George arrives at the Adamson home, discovers Blanche, and together they lock Fran and Arthur in the cellar. As the two begin to leave Arthur's house, Blanche suddenly goes into a trance. She walks halfway up a long staircase and, arm extended out over the railing, points to the large chandelier that hangs from the ceiling, her finger inches from one of the large diamonds Arthur has hidden. "Blanche, you did it! You are psychic! You're not a fake!" cries an elated George. Blanche slowly emerges from her trance, and in the final shot of Hitchcock's final film, she smiles, looks into the camera, and winks.

As scholars have suggested (and there seem to be precious few scholars who have written about Hitchcock's final film), *Family Plot* is about the double meaning of the word *plot*—"the conspiracy and the cemetery," as Michael Wood puts it. It is also about the plotting of plots, a meditation on narration itself. Hitchcock said he was drawn to the material (the 1972 novel *The Rainbird Pattern*, by Victor Fanning) because of the "structural image of those two separate plots and separate characters coming gradually, inevitably together."[108] In this way, we can think of Hitchcock's last film as the culmination of his fascination with the design that is the plot of *Strangers on a Train* and so many other Hitchcock films ("It's a fascinating design, one could study it forever," he told Truffaut).[109]

Yet *Family Plot* is also the culmination of Hitchcock's interest in secret female knowledge, in magical thinking, in occult forms of communication. Rightly, critics note another pun that we should associate with the film: *medium*—both an intermediate figure through whom the living speak with the dead (Blanche) and the cinema itself, the dominant medium of the twentieth century (with Hitchcock considered one of its masters). Typically, critics attend to the latter as a means of reflecting on how the film offers us a compendium of Hitchcockian tricks. It is the auteur's tongue-in-cheek (or winking) farewell to his audience. As Murray Pomerance notes, Hitchcock has become by this point "intensely reflective and self-referential, in a way that is deeply satisfying for the admirer who cherishes moments of recognition and reprise."[110] Similarly, William Rothman sees the film "as a curtain call: light, assured, intended for pleasure, it is an acknowledgment that the body of the concert is over."[111] While it is Blanche who has the last laugh (looking in the camera and winking in the final shot), for Rothman, the truly cool medium of the film is Hitchcock himself. Rothman, in a rhetorical trompe l'œil, effortlessly changes Blanche's wink into Hitchcock's: "With this wink, Hitchcock returns us to his guiding intuition that the 'art of pure cinema' overcomes or transcends our distinction between the real and the unreal, between the real and the possible, between reality and fantasy." For Rothman, *Family Plot* is "a medium's salute to a medium."[112]

I confess I see something attractive in forging in *Family Plot* an alliance between one medium (Blanche) and another (Hitchcock's cinema), but in doing so I'd like to set for this alliance rather different terms than those set by Rothman and others. To begin with, I'd like to devote some much-needed thought to that *other* medium—that is to say, to Blanche and her magical thinking. While it is common, and somewhat warranted, to refer to Blanche as a fraud (we get a lot of help from George, who makes such cutting remarks as "You're about as psychic as a dry salami!"), the film evokes both doubt *and* faith in Blanche's occult powers. During the séance that opens the film, while Julia bemoans her sister's nocturnal visitations, her "whining, complaining," Blanche lifts her left hand to her face, her fingers covering her eyes—a performative gesture meant, one presumes, to convey a humbled medium's exquisite embarrassment. Yet Hitchcock's camera lingers on this gesture just long enough for us to see Blanche lift her head slightly, to have a quick peek at her client as she divulges more and more about this very private affair: "I've been wanting to do it for a year. But it is I, Julia Rainbird, who has made the decision. I don't need her to goad me on." We then get an extreme close-up of Blanche's face, now with both hands covering her eyes. Then, the index and middle fingers of her left hand separate, exposing her left eye so it may secretly look. Hitchcock's camera is resolved to show us Blanche's tell—just as it had sought out the drummer's twitching eye during the elaborate crane shot in *Young and Innocent* (1937). Peeking, the way Blanche does, is cinema's stock-in-trade for conveying hokum and guile. We see what Julia doesn't: Blanche is a phony.

After the séance, Blanche climbs into the backseat of George's taxi. When he asks how the séance went, Blanche says, "She's hooked, waiting to be pulled in." So our medium, while clever, is no more psychic than George is. In fact, the two are con artists—small time, for sure (George asks if Blanche has caught another one of her "twenty-five-dollar sardines"), but capable. George then asks for details, and Blanche tells him, "Henry came to me from the Upper Brightness, whispered to me, 'This woman's been having sleep problems.' From there on, things followed." George takes offense at this—not because it's completely bogus, but because *he* is the one who furnished Blanche with information about Julia's troubled sleep. He reminds her that it was the local druggist who told him about Julia, that she was trying to get sleeping pills without a prescription. Yet Blanche denies that George gave her this information. "That would have been very, very useful to me!" she says to George, who then insists to Blanche that he *did* tell her. Blanche responds, "No, you always *think* to tell me things and you *forget* to. I have to go through heaven and hell, the great beyond with Henry!" The bickering continues for a few more moments, but the issue is left unresolved. Instead, Blanche suggests to George that he's jealous of Henry. Here, screenwriter Ernest Lehman leaves the issue behind completely with a nifty little detour: "I like your jealousy," says Blanche. "It's your driving that stinks."

So we are left to wonder just how Blanche knew of Julia's troubled sleep. And this is not a matter of "he said, she said." Rather, it's a matter of "he said, he said." Either Henry told Blanche about Julia's troubled sleep or George did. Further, Blanche seems to have a case when she says that George always *thinks* he tells her but *forgets* to. In other words, Blanche has learned not to rely on George, to trust that Henry will come through for her. Of course, there are several other possibilities before us. One is that it is Blanche who always forgets that George tells her things. This seems unlikely, however, given that it is George's job to play private eye. If information comes from anywhere, it comes from George. Both of them know that; it's part of their con. Another possibility is that Blanche is teasing George, that she is playfully boasting about her "psychic" abilities to goad him. She is, after all, in a rather playful mood. But this possibility isn't entirely convincing either. Blanche seems genuinely surprised—even a little ticked off—when George tells her that he had spoken to the druggist. A third possibility: George did tell Blanche about the druggist, but Blanche was not paying attention at the time. The information nevertheless was "planted" in Blanche's head; she heard George, but only subconsciously. This possibility has the advantage that here, Blanche and George are both being honest. The only problem, of course, is that it suggests a somewhat ridiculous standard practice: George does tell Blanche things but only when she is not paying attention to him.

A fourth possibility, one the film doesn't dismiss entirely, is that Blanche is indeed psychic. George may have visited the druggist and gleaned from him the information Blanche needed, but what if he *did* forget to tell Blanche? What if we believe Blanche when she says, exasperatedly, that George always forgets to tell her things? That she must rely instead on Henry? What if George knows this and is feigning incredulity? He too is a con artist, a deceiver. He is, in fact, an actor. Why should we trust him any more than Blanche? Why should we believe him when he says, "It was me! It's always me. Without my research, you're about as psychic as a dry salami." Is this playacting? And—since we are, after all, dealing with a comedy—who says dry salamis aren't psychic?[113] And what is it with George, who, as Pomerance observes, persists in using phallic references?[114] Apart from his dry salami, George refers to his "crystal balls," then tells Blanche she doesn't need to worry about his "performance" that evening in bed, that she's going to see "a standing ovation." Is George compensating for some . . . inadequacy? (Blanche had just told him not to fret "or our waterbed will be no fun at all tonight"). Does George sometimes fail to . . . *please* Blanche? Does George fear there are other pleasures Henry brings Blanche, besides information? *Is* George jealous of Henry? What are we to make of George's outburst, "Henry, my ass!"?

Given its comic register, one wonders if *Family Plot* is making light of the male subject, specifically the male subject who is positioned outside an uncanny female network. As much as George may insist on his indispensability ("It's me! It's always me"), his information, purchased from another man, is redundant. The séance inside the Rainbird home is exclusive; George must wait outside in the taxi. And the women require no tips from an outsider. Indeed, what is exchanged inside the Rainbird home is private female knowledge: the secret of the lost Rainbird heir, Harriet's illegitimate son. And while one might question Julia Rainbird's decision to force her sister to give up her child ("In a family like ours," she tells Blanche, "a scandal had to be covered up at all costs"), the decision also made necessary the creation of private discursive space between Julia and Harriet, where knowledge of the boy could be safely hidden. Forty years later, Julia makes use of this same private network, which now includes Blanche (as well as that spirit in drag, Henry). Julia then tells Blanche that she is "sufficiently old-fashioned and sufficiently protective of the Rainbird name to want to seek some missing heir in a private and secret fashion, rather than go to detective agencies and put notices in the newspapers." Thus the opening scene in *Family Plot* establishes that female voices, passing from and through one another, will not fall on unsympathetic male ears.

Compare this scene with the one in the Constantine home, which follows our introduction to Fran and Arthur, who have pulled off another successful kidnapping, of Victor Constantine (Nicholas Colasanto). We are now in Constantine's office—a space reminiscent of the office of Gavin Elster in *Vertigo*, with its opulent furnishings, portraits of ships on the wall, and a model ship encased in glass in front of a large window behind Constantine's massive desk.[115] It is a place of men: Constantine, at his desk, and three federal agents investigating the kidnapping. Whereas the story of the lost Rainbird boy is a secret kept between women, the story of Constantine's kidnapping is brought to experts on surveillance and detection, men in the field who are familiar with technologies of crime and punishment. Asked to narrate, once again, the events of his kidnapping—as he can best remember them—Constantine says he was in an underground parking garage when he heard voices and felt a prick in his shoulder. The next thing he remembered was waking up in a room, the cellar in Arthur's home. He then recalls hearing "a disembodied" voice. But this is no séance he is describing; it is Adamson's voice Constantine heard, electronically altered, being transmitted through a loudspeaker.

Thus a delightful opposition is established early in the film, in part to soften up the criminal pair of Blanche and George, but also to restore some of our faith in the occult. Both Arthur and Blanche bring into their homes the victims off whom they profit. As Pomerance playfully puts it, Bishop Wood "is spirited away by Arthur and Fran," and "Blanche is 'spirited' away in everything she does."[116] Both communicate with their victims using voices seemingly not of this world (Constantine describes the voice he hears as "unrecognizable"). Blanche exerts her powers though self-induced "trances"; Arthur exerts his through a hypodermic needle, sending his victims into a ketamine-induced slumber. Blanche and George are trying to restore a family by reuniting an estranged son with his aunt; Fran and Arthur routinely restore families, for a hefty price, only after first tearing them apart. Blanche and George's criminal activities are harmless, even comically so. Fran and Arthur's criminal activities, by contrast, are very serious. The former pair trade in the private, female discourse of secrets, sympathetic intimacy, and the shared knowledge of "too many memories . . . too much pain . . . too much sorrow," as Henry puts it. Arthur and Fran are agents of antipathy; they maintain the cold isolation between people. In his lavish home Arthur plays bad host to his kidnapping victims, serving up a cruel mockery of hospitality in the cellar chamber. Everything about Arthur is dislocation and detachment, inhuman and synthetic—like the chemical toilet he forces his victims to use, a thing with no connection to any network, just cold isolation. And Arthur is not just an agent of *cold* isolation; the young Shoebridge locked his foster parents in their bedroom while his greasy grind Maloney lit the house on fire, killing them both. In doing so, Shoebridge orphaned himself. And he remains, with Fran, radically uncongregated.

What makes Blanche and George so touching is that they think they are bringing good news to the lost Rainbird heir. Yes, they are in it for the money, but they take the famous line from Sam Peckinpah's *The Wild Bunch* (1969), "$10,000 cuts an awful lot of family ties," and turn it on its head. When Blanche finally meets Adamson and gives him the news that in finding him she can finally reunite him with his family and its fortune, she says, "It's a happy moment for us all, isn't it?" At this moment, Blanche believes—or perhaps fantasizes—that she has fully realized her powers of the occult. This is the promise of reunion that the séance offers. And has Blanche ever doubted her potential? Even here, she insists that her psychic powers enabled her to find Arthur. But is this just a pretense? Is the film playing us for a sucker, like Ida? When is a trance a trance?

Blanche, after being doped up by Arthur's handy syringe, lies unconscious in the cellar, awaiting her fate—a "suicide" staged by Arthur. George manages to sneak into the house unnoticed and find Blanche in bed, apparently out cold. He tries to wake her, and she quickly and quietly shushes him. Her "trance" is feigned—after all, Blanche is, like Judy in *Vertigo*, a pro when it comes to those "beautiful, phony trances." Arthur and Fran return to the cellar to retrieve what they think is Blanche's unconscious body, but Blanche leaps out of bed like a woman possessed and, screaming her head off, runs out of the cellar. George bolts the door shut with Fran and Arthur inside, locks it, and takes the key. "Blanche," he tells her, "you faked that one beautifully. You are still the champ." Then Blanche begins to swoon. Is it the lingering effect of the ketamine? The soundtrack swells with John Williams's score, and a choir of heavenly voices calls to her, leading her up the cellar stairs. A baffled George follows behind her. In a lovely tracking shot—Hitchcock's last—the camera follows her as she emerges from the cellar, walks through the grand foyer of the Adamson home, and climbs halfway up the stairs. After the camera zooms in on the diamond hidden in the chandelier, Hitchcock cuts to a close up of George. In a reaction shot, he has a look of genuine delight. "Blanche, you did it!!! You are psychic! You're not a fake!" George goes to phone the police. The camera rests at the bottom of the stairs, tilted up, looking proudly at Blanche.

We return, now, to Blanche's eyes. During the séance that opened the film, Blanche peeked. The gesture betrays her—as the gesture often does in the cinema—as a counterfeit, a cheat. "No peeking!" is the saying every child knows. With both eyes closed, Blanche had the appearance of a genuine medium; she was all modesty when in congress with the spirit world. But when the fingers that shielded her face split, revealing her left eye, she exposed herself to us as a fraud (figure 5.7). Now, at the end of the film, Blanch winks her right eye (figure 5.8). And the wink is the inverse of the peek. While the latter is used to steal signals, the wink itself is a signal. It is a sign of control, and we take it at face value.[117] As in the beginning of the film, here now, at the end of the film, Blanche's left eye is open and her right is closed. What do we make of this symmetry? Is this late wink a reminder of the earlier peek? Is Blanche signaling to us that, after all, she's about as psychic as a dry salami? Or is she winking at us as if to say, "George may have doubted me until now, but you—you knew all along, right? We both knew."

In his essay on Hitchcock's adaptation of *The Rainbird Pattern*, Lesley Brill, echoing a chorus of male critics, writes, "Blanche anchors *Family Plot*. It begins and ends with her, and she functions as something like the director's proxy. Hitchcock thus ends his career, as he began it, with a plucky, resourceful heroine. . . . Blanche's wink is also Hitchcock's closing wink. Through Blanche, Hitchcock both acknowledges a reciprocity of goals with the audience and retains some control."[118] If, however, we do not take Blanche's wink at face value, we are left to wonder how, exactly, Hitchcock ends his career. What, in the end, is Hitchcock saying about his heroines' resources? Brill all too easily dismisses any question of danger and threat, of duplicity and betrayal. Brill thinks that Blanche's wink gets Hitchcock off the hook for good, that this meeting of minds—Hitchcock's and Blanche's—signals that we should put the question of Hitchcock's misogyny to rest. "The notion of Hitchcock as a torturer of females," he writes, "is overdue for composting."[119]

Figure 5.7. *Family Plot*: Blanche peeks

Figure 5.8. *Family Plot*: Blanche winks

But Brill's use of the adjective *resourceful* should stop us. It calls to mind Mark Rutland's description of the girl going by the name of Marion Holland. Mark walks into Strutt's office at the beginning of *Marnie* to find the latter filing a police report. A girl has stolen from the Strutt safe a total of $9,967. "The little witch," Strutt spits. "I'll have her put away for years! I knew she was too good to be true. Always so eager to work overtime, never made a mistake. Always pulling her skirt down over her knees as though they were a . . . national treasure. She seemed so nice, so efficient, so . . ." Mark finishes Strutt's sentence with "resourceful?" He speaks the word with an upward inflection, changing Strutt's statement into a question. Here in *Family Plot*, at the end of Hitchcock's career, the resourcefulness of his female heroines remains in question. Let us consider that Blanche's wink is her own, that it signals to us the ambivalence of resourcefulness, the enigmatic "pluck" of the Hitchcock female heroine. What, after all, is the Hitchcock female a heroine of? She is a heroine of her own story, of course, and she uses her resourcefulness to avoid, as best she can, ending up as compost.

Hitchcock never did know the whole story.

Afterword

✦

How to Keep Hitchcock Flat

> Although social scientists are proud of having added volume to flat interactions, it turns out that they have gone too fast. By taking for granted this third dimension—even if it's to criticize its existence—they have withdrawn from inquiry the main phenomenon of social science: the very production of place, size, and scale. Against such a three-dimensional shape, we have to try to keep the social domain completely *flat*.
>
> —Bruno Latour, *Reassembling the Social*

Giving expressive significance to Hitchcock's sense of place, to the way people in affectively charged relationships move within and between places, and to how people and objects within places interact in transformative ways, has been the aim of this book. I have tried to show in the preceding chapters how a critical approach to Hitchcock's films that stresses the *relational* gives us the best traction in our exploration of the Hitchcock landscape. Tracing the relations among people, places, and things in Hitchcock allows us to engage with his films in a more intimate way. When engaging with a Hitchcock film, however, one should remember to keep its landscape flat, to resist the temptation to add volume or scale to people, places, and things. Which is to say, perhaps, that to navigate the Hitchcock landscape is to follow traces wherever they may lead, guided by the assumption that one is "inside a 2-D world only made up of lines," as Latour says.[1]

But what does it mean to keep Hitchcock flat? What I hope I have shown in this book is that it means attending carefully to connections not just between people but between people, places, and things—because places and things have just as much to say in determining the course of events in a film as people do. For example, we could consider Father Benoit's bicycle in *I Confess*, which, for whatever reason, likes to fall down on its own. It would be easy—and certainly not wrong—to read the bicycle symbolically, as Murray Pomerance does when he links it with Father Benoit's myopia: "He doesn't have the eyes to take proper care of his equipment. But the broken equipment is a pair of wheels, like eyes: his eyes are so bad he can't see whether or not he's got bad 'eyes.' Ultimately he's a person who isn't looking."[2] It also would be easy to understand this collapsing bicycle as an example of Hitchcock's predilection for offbeat humor, even in this, one of Hitchcock's most solemn films. And it would be easy—and, again, not wrong—to understand the bicycle as representing Hitchcock's own fear of falling over, a fear he had harbored since childhood. But to turn from the bicycle toward some larger context, to some "elsewhere" (Hitchcock's humorous tone, Hitchcock's psyche) is to allow the possible associations between the bicycle and other actants in the film to remain invisible, to deny the bicycle its rightful place among social interactions (or, as I have been suggesting here, in the Hitchcock landscape). So what if we thought of the bicycle as a real player in the show while not denying that it is also the other things? Let's follow the bicycle and listen to what it says about the course of events in the film.

The first time we see the bicycle is not the first time it makes itself known. We hear it crash to the floor offscreen just before Father Benoit (Gilles Pelletier) enters the dining room to join Father Logan and Father Millars (Charles Andre) for breakfast, which is being served to them by Otto Keller's wife, Alma (Dolly Haas). The sound of the falling bicycle punctuates, like a cymbal crash, Millars's kind but ironic words about Otto that "one can learn a great deal from him." Millars then asks Benoit why he keeps his bicycle inside, and Benoit replies that it doesn't always fall, and he wouldn't know where else to put it. This prompts a joking reply from Logan, who says it's a good thing that Benoit doesn't ride a horse. Benoit then asks Alma if her husband could repair his bicycle's flat tire. Mrs. Keller reminds him that it is Wednesday, the day Otto tends to the garden of Villette, the man her husband has murdered. Her words, however, betray her growing concern that Logan—to whom Villette confessed his sin—might turn her husband in to the police, now gathered at Villette's home. She too, moments earlier, was reminded by Otto that it is Wednesday, and therefore he must go to Villette's home to tend his garden. Now, as Mrs. Keller reminds Benoit that it is Wednesday, Hitchcock's camera tracks in on Logan, who nervously looks at his watch. We hear, offscreen, Millars tell Benoit that he should know how to patch a tire himself: "One should be able to take care of one's possessions. One has a face, one would shave it." Just as his words take this curious turn, from things to people, Logan jumps out of his chair unexpectedly and leaves.

The bicycle is visible for the first time just after the scene in which Ruth Grandfort goes to meet her husband in parliament. He tells her she looked depressed (deflated?) earlier that morning, to which she responds, "I don't seem depressed now, do I?" The scene fades to the next, and we see Benoit carrying his bicycle down the stairs of the church rectory, where he encounters Otto and says to him, "The tire wasn't flat after all." When Otto confronts Logan, who is atop a ladder painting a wall in the rectory, he begs for help. "I can't give myself up. You must tell me some other way." As his desperation deepens, Otto becomes a threat—to Logan certainly but also to himself.

That is why Alma interrupts this confrontation by reminding her husband to mend the tire of Benoit's bicycle. "But the tire wasn't flat at all, Alma," Otto tells her.

One might protest here and say that it's not about the bicycle, it's about the game of keeping secrets (Alma doesn't want Otto to mend the tire; she wants to keep him away from Logan). Yet the bicycle is a player in this game. That is, rather than see the bicycle simply as crossing paths with the plot of *I Confess*, one might see it as part of a series of actions and reactions that *is* the plot of *I Confess*. More than pressing itself forward into the story here and there, the bicycle is *used*, it becomes functional—despite its seeming disutility. That it crashes to the floor and feigns deflation belies its significance. When Robertson lightly presses Larrue by telling him, "Here you have a case in which there are no clues, no motives, no suspects," we should remember that the bicycle coconspires with Alma to ensure this.

I stop here, though not because the movement of associations has stopped. One might continue to follow the bicycle and consider its next appearance. It is carried through the hall of the rectory past Logan, who is being led by Murphy to an interview with Larrue, further stoking Otto's fear. Millars says to Benoit, "Oh, now you're bringing your bicycle into the study. How much further into the rectory are you going to push it?" It is a question Otto might be asking himself about Larrue's investigation. One might also continue to pursue the movement of associations by following Logan, who does not ride a bicycle (or a horse) but instead walks. The point I am making is that when navigating a flattened Hitchcock landscape, one has to move very slowly. I trust that, at times, I have tried the patience of my reader by moving too slowly, or by taking unexpected turns. But I also trust I have shown that in doing both I have traced connections that have, until now, remained invisible to us. Perhaps I have also inspired in my readers a desire to engage more intimately with Hitchcock's films.

To be sure, it goes without saying that this desire to engage intimately with a Hitchcock film isn't mine alone.[3] On multiple platforms and a variety of media, one can find the creative work of those who share a similar desire to engage more intimately and creatively with it. I'd like to consider three such examples, each of which can help Hitchcock critics keep their explanations flat. The first is Jeff Desom's extraordinary video project *Rear Window Timelapse* (2012), which reedits footage from the film to create a single view of the courtyard and apartment complex seen from Jeff's window, with all the film's events unfolding simultaneously, rather than sequentially, in just three minutes. However, this compression of *Rear Window*, the subtraction of time rather than volume (the fourth dimension, rather than the third), has the odd effect of disengaging the viewer altogether from the plot of *Rear Window*. The viewer sees people darting around a place among other things, not a story sped up. By visually compressing *Rear Window* this way, Desom's video allows us to see more clearly the *relational* nature of the neighborhood—an idea that the characters in the film struggle not to forget. In *Rear Window Timelapse*, the newlyweds, the artist, Thorwald, and the composer seem more like cohabitants and less like isolated monads.

This is why I think the real star of *Rear Window Timelapse* is not the time lapse but the courtyard itself, a place that seems like a living, breathing thing with its diurnal rhythms, its ceaseless activity, its flickering lights, its puffs of steam and plumes of chimney smoke.[4] The result is a symphony of people, place, and things (the inclusion of Johannes Brahms's *Hungarian Dance No. 5*, performed by Hugo Winterhalter and His Orchestra, certainly helps heighten this result). And while this view is visually stunning, *Rear Window Timelapse* betrays the true logic of the panorama. As Latour has argued, "The Greek word *pan*, which means 'everything,' does not signify that those pictures survey 'the whole' but that, on the contrary, they paper over a wall in a blind room on which a *completely* coherent scenery is being projected."[5] We think we get the whole, but we don't. After all, someone unfamiliar with *Rear Window* will not be able to say much about it by watching *Rear Window Timelapse*. But someone very familiar with *Rear Window* and its *multiplicity* of views might benefit from *adding* the single, coherent panorama that is *Rear Window Timelapse* to her understanding of the former. This is why Latour says that, while not to be taken too seriously, panoramas are useful:

> Far from being the place where everything happens, as in their director's dreams, [panoramas] are local sites to be added as so many new places dotting the flattened landscape we try to map. But even after such a downsizing, their role may become central since they allow spectators, listeners, and readers to be *equipped with a desire for wholeness and centrality*. It is from those powerful stories that we get our metaphors for what "binds us together," the passions we are supposed to share, the general outline of society's architecture, the master narratives with which we are disciplined.[6]

Rear Window Timelapse, then, fulfills a desire that spectators of *Rear Window* surely have, which is to see the whole picture, the single panorama that is the courtyard. But it also reminds us that it *isn't* the whole picture, it reminds us that what "binds us together" is to be found by tracing, ever so slowly, the multiplicity of views that the film affords us. As Lisa Fremont says, "Let's start from the beginning again, Jeff. Tell me everything you saw—and what you think it means."

My next example is the 1000 Frames of Hitchcock project, found on the website known as the *Alfred Hitchcock Wiki*, established in 2003 and run by Dave Pattern.[7] Every (available) film directed by Hitchcock has been "reduced" to one thousand frames, creating a "library of images which can be used for blog posts, web articles and reviews, etc."[8] A user can visit any one of the fifty-two Hitchcock films included on the site and see it flattened

Figure 6.1. 1000 Frames of Hitchcock: One thousand frames of *Downhill* (extract)

out before her as a vertical scroll. As with *Rear Window Timelapse*, the 1000 Frames of Hitchcock project removes time and in doing so disengages the viewer from plot. The complex of people, places, and things now becomes ever more visible, as it does in the above extract from the "1000 Frames of *Downhill*" (figure 6.1). We see, in a single view, people seated in the boarding school's crowded dining hall, then a pocket watch, now a tower clock, then a handwritten note, a shop sign, and the shop itself (Ye Olde Bunne Shoppe), as well as various passersby. By flattening Hitchcock this way, we ascribe equal agency to people, places, and things, and see more clearly how they relate to and fold into one another. As well as I could ever hope to in these pages, the 1000 Frames of Hitchcock project illustrates how one might flatten out the Hitchcock landscape, map it so as to better navigate it and trace the associations within it, wherever they may lead us.

My third example is the oldest, though not necessarily the best known: *Phoenix Tapes*, a video by German artists Christoph Girardet and Matthias Müller that was commissioned for the Museum of Modern Art, Oxford's 1999 exhibit, *Notorious: Alfred Hitchcock and Contemporary Art*. In its original form, the video comprised six individual segments, each featuring a montage of short clips edited together from VHS cassette copies of Hitchcock's films. The first, "Rutland," focuses on places in Hitchcock; the second, "Burden of Proof," is a compendium of things, mostly in close-up; the third, "Derailed," features clips of trains in Hitchcock; the fourth, "Why Don't You Love Me?," deals with Hitchcock's mothers; the fifth, "Bedroom," is a collage of sequences of violence against Hitchcock's women. These segments could be viewed on television monitors located in five separate sites in the exhibit, while the sixth part, "Necrologue," a close-up of Ingrid Bergman's face, was viewed as a screen projection.

"Burden of Proof" catalogs no less than fifty things—purses, pins, briefcases, lighters, letters, telephones, and steering wheels, to name but a few. Not a single thing is untouched by people. Indeed, for a segment ostensibly about *things* in Hitchcock, it is also about the *people* with whom they interact. Nearly every single clip shows a hand reaching for or grasping some thing; things never get their own close-up. Some of the things even bear the name or initials of the user, such as "Rebecca," "Margaret Edgar," "R.O.T.," and "A to G." Thus the things in Hitchcock tell stories of fluid identity, of deception and intrigue. In one clip we see the initials J.J. on a large piece of luggage being painted over with a new set of initials, H.H. (as American newspaper reporter Johnny Jones becomes Huntley Haverstock in *Foreign Correspondent*). In this way, "Burden of Proof" demonstrates not only the intimacy people and things share, but also their complex relations. As Christine Sprengler notes, "*Burden of Proof* offers a meditation on the relationship between object and action, the transformation of everyday objects into props, and how gestures activate the inanimate. Through doing so, *Burden of Proof* appears to ask the question, what generates the narrative charge, the object or the action?"[9] Such a question turns on its head Spengler's assertion that "gestures activate the inanimate," making us consider how the inanimate activate people (just as the bread knife may be said to activate Winnie Verloc in *Sabotage*, or the windmill may be said to activate Johnny Jones in *Foreign Correspondent*). Thus we experience a flattening of differences between people, places, and things—an absence of hierarchical scale.

On the whole, the segmented format of *Phoenix Tapes* paradoxically belies the ways people, places, and things are indiscrete categories in the flattened Hitchcock landscape, something I've tried to demonstrate in this book. Marc Raymond Strauss, in a recently published book called *Hitchcock's Objects as Subjects: The Significance of Things on Screen*, also emphasizes the relational nature of the Hitchcock landscape, and stresses its "flatness" in part by quoting the director himself: "'You see,' Hitchcock told Peter Bogdanovich, 'the point is you are, first of all, in a two-dimensional medium. Mustn't forget that. You have a rectangle to fill. Fill it. Compose it. . . . I follow the geography of the screen.'"[10] What Strauss omits from this quotation is Hitchcock's statement that he *doesn't* follow "the geography of the set"—that three-dimensional space, sometimes referred to as the "pro-filmic event," with which the spectator can never engage.[11] The Hitchcock landscape, one might say, is a Euclidean plane.

Throughout his six-decade-long career, Hitchcock's weight "would fluctuate drastically and often," as Casey McKittrick recently noted, "dipping down to 189 pounds at its lowest, usually registering over 250, and creeping up to what was medically considered a dangerous 300 pounds."[12] Hitchcock's struggle to maintain a healthy figure, McKittrick argues, managed to find its expression in his cinema (this is also Jan Olsson's view, which guides *his* recent book, *Hitchcock à la Carte*). One of Hitchcock's most inventive cameos, for his 1944 film *Lifeboat*, plays on this struggle. We see him on a page of the newspaper that circulates among the lifeboat passengers hawking the "obesity slayer" Reduco. As I noted in chapter 2, there are two images of the director: one (the "before" image) of his fatter, happy self, and another (the "after" image) of his thinner but less happy self. American publicity was, it seems, as obsessed with Hitchcock's figure as he was, and seldom did a trade magazine miss an opportunity to make a fat joke. Hitchcock critics, too, are obsessed with this "fat man," this "cumbersome figure," this "portly master of the involuntary scream."[13] It's as if we were determined to keep Hitchcock fat. But as noted above, Hitchcock wasn't always fat. He was, however, always flat.

NOTES

Introduction

1. François Truffaut. *Hitchcock* (New York: Simon & Schuster, 1983), 138.

2. Bruno Latour, *Reassembling the Social: An Introduction to Actor-Network-Theory* (New York: Oxford University Press, 2005), 5.

3. "This is not a sociology," Latour quips, "but a *slow*ciology." *Reassembling the Social*, 122.

4. Bruno Latour, "Foreword: The Flat Earthers of Social Theory," in Michael Power, *Accounting and Science: Natural Inquiry and Commercial Reason* (New York: Cambridge University Press, 1994), xii.

5. D. A. Miller, *Hidden Hitchcock* (Chicago: University of Chicago Press, 2016), 50.

6. Latour, *Reassembling the Social*, 6.

7. George Toles does just this, in his essay on Hitchcock's 1951 film, "Occasions of Sin: The Forgotten Cigarette Lighter and Other Moral Accidents in Hitchcock," in *A Companion to Alfred Hitchcock*, ed. Thomas Leitch and Leland Poague (New York: Wiley Blackwell, 2013), 529–52.

8. Informed by the work of Charles Sanders Peirce, Deleuze categorizes the images of cinema into a triadic system: the affection image (Firstness), the action image (Secondness), and the relation image or mental image (Thirdness).

9. Gilles Deleuze, *Cinema 1: The Movement Image*, trans. Hugh Tomlinson and Barbara Habberjam. (New York: Continuum, 1986), 201.

10. Deleuze, *Cinema 1*, 202.

11. Deleuze, *Cinema 1*, 203.

12. I borrow this term from Tyler Curtain's helpful review of Ned Schantz's *Gossip, Letters, Phones: The Scandal of Female Networks* (a book that continues to shape my thinking). Seeing Schantz's book as a potential alternative to the standard monograph, Curtain suggests that the "critical field book would allow us to cut through a field of many different grains or, to use a metaphor more up to the task, to work a garden where one row bears many different fruits." "Toward a Cultural Critical Field Book," *Novel: A Forum on Fiction* 44, no. 1 (2011): 151.

13. Barney Warf and Santa Arias, "Introduction: The Reinsertion of Space into the Social Sciences and Humanities," in *The Spatial Turn: Interdisciplinary Perspectives*, ed. Barney Warf and Santa Arias (New York: Routledge, 2008): 1.

14. Rosenbaum, Jonathan. "Trailer for Godard's Histoire(s) du Cinema," *Trafic* 21 (1997), online at http://www.jonathanrosenbaum.com/?p=15760.

15. Smith, Murray. *Trainspotting* (London: BFI, 2002), 89–90n18.

16. Speaking of his audience, Hitchcock told Truffaut, "They're going to sit there and say 'show me' and they expect to anticipate, 'I know what's coming next.' I have to say 'Do you?' " *Hitchcock/Truffaut*, directed by Kent Jones (2015; Universal City, CA: Universal Pictures Home Entertainment, 2016), DVD.

17. Alfred Hitchcock. "Close Your Eyes and Visualize!" in *Hitchcock on Hitchcock*: Vol. 2, *Selected Writings and Interviews*, ed. Sidney Gottlieb (Berkeley: University of California Press, 1995), 249.

18. Other terms have been used, specifically in reference to Hitchcock. Slavoj Žižek's term, the "Hitchcockian blot," refers to an arresting moment in a Hitchcock film when the normal, everyday is shattered. The blot, writes Žižek, "emerges as a foreign body, a counter-natural element in a natural pattern. It estranges and perverts its orderly background, which suddenly becomes filled with uncanny possibilities." Žižek's examples are the windmill spinning against the wind in *Foreign Correspondent* and Thorwald's cigarette glowing in his darkened apartment room in *Rear Window*. "Hitchcockian *Sinthoms*," in *Everything You Always Wanted to Know about Hitchcock, but Were Afraid to Ask Lacan*, ed. Slavoj Žižek (New York: Verso, 1992), 133.

19. Miller, *Hidden Hitchcock*, 4.

20. Deleuze, *Cinema 1*, 204.

21. During the opening credits, we get our only glimpse of the occupants (or their guests). Two women appear, and one begins brushing her hair. Then the camera tracks in through Jeff's open window, pushing them out of frame.

22. Peter Wollen, "An Alphabet of Cinema," in *Paris Hollywood: Writings on Film* (New York: Verso, 2002), 20. In addition to Wollen, I should acknowledge Rashna Wadia Richards, whose *Cinematic Flashes: Cinephilia and Classical Hollywood* (Bloomington: Indiana University Press, 2013) guided me to think of arresting moments in Hitchcock as cinematic flashes. The latter's approach to rethinking the history of the classical Hollywood system bears some similarity to my approach to navigating the Hitchcock landscape. She calls for a "reinvigorated film analysis" (17) by turning to the work of Benjamin among others. Her articulation of a critical contemporary cinephilia is what she believes can reinvigorate it. Referring to Laura Mulvey's argument about the role new technologies play in the spectatorial experience, Richards privileges the interruptions of narrative flow made possible by digital media playback. Quoting Mulvey, Richards argues that "these interruptions break down the relentless onward drive of narrative events, providing access to 'key moments and meanings . . . that could not have been perceived when hidden under the narrative flow and movement of film'" (17). Edwards combines a historical materialist approach with a critical cinephilia to seek out "stunning distractions"—distractions that offer the kind of "fortuitous exhilaration" (23) Benjamin articulated in his *Arcades* project—in order to write an alternative history of classical Hollywood.

23. Eugenie Brinkema, *The Forms of the Affects* (Durham, N.C.: Duke University Press, 2014), 18.

24. Brinkema, *The Forms of the Affects*, 19.

25. Brinkema, *The Forms of the Affects*, 22.

26. Hitchcock used a similar conceit in the theatrical trailer for *North by Northwest*, titled "A Guided Tour with Alfred Hitchcock." The *North by Northwest* trailer, running half as long as the theatrical trailer for *Psycho*, uses actual scenes from the film to plot a leisure tour of "say, about 2,000 miles." The tour begins in New York, with stops in Chicago, the Great Plains, and Mount Rushmore. Hitchcock teases the audience by alluding—however obliquely—to the fantasy of inhabiting a film: "Now for the best news of all: you can enjoy this

wonderful vacation while seated comfortably in this theater"—a fantasy no doubt nourished by VistaVision and Technicolor.

27. Murray Pomerance, *An Eye for Hitchcock* (New Brunswick, N.J.: Rutgers University Press, 2004), 241.

28. Pomerance, *An Eye for Hitchcock*, 241.

29. Pomerance, *An Eye for Hitchcock*, 242.

30. One wonders, too, if this moment (in the theatrical trailer and in the scene from *Psycho* to which it alludes) mocks the ideal of the peephole, which is meant to provide motel guests with a feeling of security: the ability to see who has come knocking before opening the door, the assurance that places (inside the motel room, outside the motel room) are not permeable.

31. This gesture differs from the cameo appearance, insofar as Hitchcock here enters a completed film.

32. I borrow this term from Tom Cohen, who uses it in a passage from *Hitchcock's Cryptonomies*, vol. 1, *Secret Agents* ([Minneapolis: University of Minnesota Press, 2005], 70), in which he closely reads the sequence in *Psycho* when Lila investigates the Bates mansion.

33. The trailer ends with scrolling text addressed to its potential audience members: "The picture you MUST see from the beginning. . . . Or not at all! . . . for no one will be seated after the start of . . . Alfred Hitchcock's greatest shocker, *Psycho*." This tag was part of a larger publicity campaign aimed at what was called "the care and handling of *Psycho*." As Linda Williams notes, a "film 'press book' " was distributed by Universal to theater exhibitors instructing them 'how properly to exhibit the film and police the audience.' " "Discipline and Fun: *Psycho* and Postmodern Cinema," in *Alfred Hitchcock's* Psycho*: A Casebook*, ed. Robert Kolker (New York: Oxford University Press, 2004), 186.

34. Murray Pomerance, "Some Hitchcockian Shots," in *A Companion to Alfred Hitchcock*, ed. Thomas Leitch and Leland Poague (Malden, Mass: Wiley-Blackwell, 2011), 238. While the work of Murray Pomerance, D. A. Miller, and Tom Cohen differ sharply in style and tone, I think each critic is drawn to Hitchcock's images (for Miller, his "hidden pictures," for Cohen, his "cryptonomies"), and drawn *close* (for Miller, he is drawn "too close") in this way.

35. D. A. Miller, *Hidden Hitchcock*, 4.

36. Alfred Hitchcock, "Film Production," in *Hitchcock on Hitchcock: Selected Writings and Interviews*, ed. Sidney Gottlieb (Berkeley: University of California Press, 1995), 214.

37. Hitchcock, "Film Production," 214.

38. William Rothman, *Hitchcock: The Murderous Gaze* (Albany: State University of New York Press, 2012), 53.

39. Lesley Brill, *Crowds, Power, and Transformation in the Cinema* (Detroit, Mich.: Wayne State University Press, 2006), 1.

40. Brill, *Crowds, Power, and Transformation in the Cinema*, 10.

41. In *The Wrong Man* (1956), the right man, Daniel, has, at best, only a passing resemblance to Manny Balestrero. And of course in *Vertigo* (1958), Judy is twice made to look like Madeleine Elster, though how closely she resembles the real Madeleine Elster the film does not disclose.

42. Pamela Wojcik, *The Apartment Plot: Urban Living in American Film and Popular Culture, 1945 to 1975* (Raleigh, N.C.: Duke University Press, 2010), 67.

43. *Vertigo* is perhaps Hitchcock's most sustained examination of spatial dislocation. For useful resources on the subject, see Douglas A. Cunningham's excellent edited collection, *The San Francisco of Alfred Hitchcock's Vertigo: Place, Pilgrimage, and Commemoration* (Lanham, Md.: Scarecrow, 2012); Murray Pomerance's chapter on the film in *An Eye for Hitchcock*; and part 2 of Barbara Straumann's *Figurations of Exile in Hitchcock and Nabokov* (Edinburgh: Edinburgh University Press, 2008), to name a few.

44. See Pomerance's chapter on *I Confess* in *An Eye for Hitchcock*, 170–213.

Chapter 1

1. See especially Sidney Gottlieb, "Early Hitchcock: The German Influence," in *Framing Hitchcock: Selected Essays from the Hitchcock Annual*, ed. Sidney Gottlieb and Christopher Brookhouse (Detroit: Wayne State University Press, 2002), 35–58.

2. Charles Eidsvik, *Cineliteracy: Film among the Arts* (New York: Horizon Press, 1978), 126. See, too, Lesley Brill's *Crowds, Power, and Transformation in Cinema*. "The twentieth century," writes Brill, "by many accounts the century of the crowd, was also a century of motion pictures, encompassing virtually all the history of cinema and its growth into a dominant global medium. Movies are so full of crowds that one is tempted to suppose that cinema is suited by its very materials to their representation" (2).

3. Siegfried Kracauer, *Theory of Film: The Redemption of Physical Reality* (New York: Oxford University Press, 1960), 31. In a section of this same text titled "The Small and the Big," Kracauer notes the cinema's affinity for the small in examples from D. W. Griffith, whose close-ups reveal cinema's scientific aspirations: "Like science, [the cinema] breaks down material phenomena into tiny particles, thereby sensitizing us to the tremendous energies accumulated in the microscopic configurations of matter" (50). As for the cinema's affinity for the big, Kracauer singles out the crowd. Whereas photography could easily succeed in rendering the crowd when other established arts failed, only film could capture the crowd in motion. "In this case," writes Kracauer, "the instrument of reproduction came into being almost simultaneously with one of its main subjects. Hence the attraction which masses exerted on still and motion picture cameras from the outset. It is certainly more than sheer coincidence that the very first Lumière films featured a crowd of workers and the confusion of arrival and departure at a railway station" (50–51). Kracauer here overstates the confusion of passengers at the railway station in the famed Lumière short. As with the workers in *Sortie des usines Lumière à Lyon*, many of the passengers in *L'arrivée d'un train en gare de La Ciotat* respond to their being photographed with bemused interest—thus suggesting a mutual affection between crowds and cinema. It is perhaps worth noting here that another important force came into being during this period: Alfred Hitchcock himself (born August 13, 1899).

4. Beginning, quite possibly, with *The Lodger: A Story of the London Fog*. While it has long been confirmed (by Hitchcock himself) that he appears early in the film seated at a desk in the *Evening Standard* office, some critics suggest that Hitchcock also appears later in the film in the crowd that chases and apprehends the lodger.

5. Brill, *Crowds, Power, and Transformation in the Cinema*, 128.

6. Paula Marantz Cohen, *Alfred Hitchcock*, 42.

7. McGilligan, *Alfred Hitchcock*, 22

8. Michael Walker, *Hitchcock's Motifs* (Amsterdam: Amsterdam University Press, 2005), 343.

9. Walker, *Hitchcock's Motifs*.

10. John Plotz, *The Crowd: British Literature and Public Politics* (Berkeley: University of California Press, 2000), 6.

11. Plotz, *The Crowd*, 12. I understand my use of the term *crowd* and all of its various meanings and contexts is similar to that of Ian Munro, who suggests "that the uncategorizable connotations of the word 'crowd' are an important aspect of its cultural character. The crowd is an inherently polymorphous concept, always evading definition; although it is possible to examine the cultural meanings of the crowd . . . a manifested crowd is a kind of blank—meaningless without a context to frame it and a discourse to fill it" (*The Figure of the Crowd in Early Modern London: The City and Its Double* (New York: Palgrave, 2005), 2.

12. Take, for example, a somewhat unusual invocation of the crowd in a scene from *Marnie* (1964). Shortly after she robs the Rutland bank, Marnie (Tippi Hedren) retreats to the Red Fox Tavern, where she is confronted by a livid Mark Rutland (Sean Connery). Marnie shields herself with yet another phony story about her past, but Mark is fed up with the lies and, with a promise of violence, demands the real story: "Don't crowd me, lady. I'm fighting a powerful urge to beat the hell out of you." The "gray space" here is not simply the suggestion that the minimum number of people who "crowd" is one. After all, the phrase "don't crowd me" is commonly used in the most sparsely populated of situations. More than this, the phrase suggests a toughness one has, a toughness that matches or betters that of the crowding party. Evan Hunter, who adapted Daphne du Maurier's short story for *The Birds* (and Winston Graham's novel, before being fired by Hitchcock), was not only the author of the respected novel *The Blackboard Jungle* (1954) but also the author of crime thriller novels such as *Don't Crowd Me* (1953). It's no wonder, then, that Mark's response to being "crowded" by Marnie is to threaten unrestrained violence—the very thing we associate with crowds. And anyone familiar with the film knows that it is Mark who crowds Marnie, not the other way around.

13. See Rothman's reading of the opening sequence of *The Lodger* in *Hitchcock: The Murderous Gaze*, 2d ed. (New York: SUNY Press, 2012). See also Leslie Abramson's discussion of both *The Ring* and *The Birds* in *Hitchcock and the Anxiety of Authorship* (New York: Palgrave Macmillan, 2015).

14. Even before his first film as a director, Hitchcock had staged a crowd scene for *The Blackguard* (1925), a film credited to Graham Cutts. Hitchcock worked on the film as art director, and as noted by Patrick McGilligan, he borrowed a trick he learned from Murnau and "hired dwarves to stand far from the camera . . . creating an artificial perspective for a crowd scene." *Alfred Hitchcock*, 63.

15. "The baiting crowd," writes Elias Canetti, "forms with reference to a quickly attainable goal. The goal is known and clearly marked, and it is also near. This crowd is out for killing and it knows whom it wants to kill. It heads for this goal with unique determination and cannot be cheated of it. The proclaiming of the goal, the spreading about of who it is that is to perish, is enough to make the crowd form. This concentration on killing is of a special kind and of an unsurpassed intensity. Everyone wants to participate; everyone strikes a blow." *Crowds*

and Power (New York: Farrar, Straus and Giroux, 1960), 49. Everyone, including Hitchcock himself.

16. It is often said that Hitchcock, in the second of two cameos in the film, can be seen in the crowd, throwing punches at the innocent man who hangs suspended by handcuffs from a fence. Hitchcock's first cameo from the film is in the editor's office of the *Evening Standard*. He is seated, with his back turned to us. In the "second cameo," one can see Hitchcock (if it is indeed him, and very likely it is not) just to the right of the Lodger, as detective Joe (Malcom Keen) makes his way along the wall in an effort to free him. As the result of an unusual jump cut, Hitchcock seems to disappear from his position in the crowd, about two persons away from the Lodger, and reappear in another position, this time directly above the Lodger, appearing to assist Joe by hoisting the Lodger safely up from the angry crowd below.

17. Truffaut, *Hitchcock*, 52.

18. Hitchcock says, in his interview with Truffaut, "I remember that at the premiere an elaborate montage got a round of applause. It was the first time that ever happened to me." Truffaut, *Hitchcock*, 52. Though Hitchcock does not specify which montage sequence was lauded, it is very likely the opening sequence, which is, by far, the most stunning in the film.

19. In the highly influential *Crowds and Power* by Elias Canetti, one finds a brief essay titled "The Crowd as a Ring." In it, Canetti directly links the crowd of the ring, or arena, with the crowds of the surrounding city: "The arena is well demarcated from the outside world. It is usually visible from far off and its situation in the city—the space which it occupies—is well known. People always feel where it is, even if they are not thinking of it. Shouts from the arena carry far and, when it is open at the top, something of the life which goes on inside communicates itself to the surrounding city" (28).

20. Marilyn Fabe, *Closely Watched Films: An Introduction to the Art of Narrative Film Technique*, Tenth Anniversary Edition (Berkeley: University of California Press, 2014), 136–37.

21. McGilligan, *Alfred Hitchcock*, 129.

22. See McGilligan, *Alfred Hitchcock*, 129. In a note to the text, McGilligan writes, "A publicity photo in the *Picturegoer* showed the director tending bar, though sadly the cameo was dropped from the final film, when Hitchcock had second thoughts about intruding on the famous play."

23. Gene D. Phillips says that this sequence is a clear allusion to Vidor's *The Crowd*, of which Hitchcock was quite fond. *Alfred Hitchcock* (Woodbridge, Conn.: Twayne, 1984), 56. Yet its choreography is nearly Busby Berkeleyesque. More telling, however, is the way the sequence illustrates what Gabriel Tarde says about the social in *The Laws of Imitation*. As Jonathan Crary notes, Tarde's work offered a scheme for understanding social cohesion: "At the heart of his work was the notion that 'society could not exist or change or advance a single step unless it possessed an untold store of blind routine and slavish imitation which was constantly being added to by successive generations.' 'Social self-organization' was propagated, according to Tarde, not by laws or civic institutions but by a process of imitative repetition: 'society may be defined as a group of beings who are apt to imitate one another.' " *Suspensions of Perception: Attention, Spectacle, and Modern Culture* (Cambridge, Mass.: MIT Press, 1999), 241–42.

24. See Truffaut, *Hitchcock*, 95–96.

25. Ned Schantz, "Hospitality and the Unsettled Viewer: Hitchcock's Shadow Scenes," *Camera Obscura* 25, no. 1 (2010): 12.

26. The avalanche itself is a potent "crowd symbol." According to Elias Canetti, the "crowd symbol" is a collective unit that, although it does not consist of human beings, nevertheless feels like a crowd. In his essay on crowd symbols in *Crowds and Power*, Canetti describes in detail eleven crowd symbols, the first of which is fire (the others are the sea, rain, rivers, forest, corn, wind, sand, the heap, stone heaps, and treasure). In his brief description of fire, Canetti could very well be speaking of the birds in Hitchcock's film: "Fire spreads; it is contagious and insatiable. The violence with which it seizes whole forests and steppes and cities is one of the most impressive things about it. . . . No one is ever surprised when fire breaks out; here, there, or somewhere, it is always expected. Its very suddenness is impressive and people invariably search for a cause. The fact that often none can be found adds to the awe inherent in the idea of fire. It has a mysterious ubiquity; it can appear anywhere and at any time (76).

27. D. A. Miller, "Anal *Rope*," *Representations* 32 (Autumn 1990): 124.

28. Something suggests that Brandon is not meant to be in this shot: his hands are not moving. Two fingers rest along a forged carving fork at the bottom left of the frame. Supposedly busying himself with the chicken, Brandon seems temporarily frozen. One could argue that this is an error; perhaps the camera operator did not notice that John Dall's fingers were in frame. Yet upon closer examination, one can see the camera actually panning slightly to the left, as if to find those fingers.

29. It is an image borrowed from Fritz Lang's *Der müde Tod* (1921), the shot of a young woman (Lil Dagover) walking through a wall and ascending a stairway to Death's lair in search of her dead husband. Hitchcock had said that this film, one of the finest examples of German Expressionism, had an enormous influence on him, and he frequently cited it as his favorite film. Interestingly, the young woman is drawn to the lair because she had seen a crowd of dead people (in which she sees her husband) walking through the same wall.

30. Leslie Abramson has suggested that Hitchcock loses interest during this period in "the surveilling forces of crowds, mobs, gatherings, and assemblages of seated attendees drawn to visual attractions" (*Hitchcock and the Anxiety of Authorship*, 224). But what do we make of the large gathering of people outside of the Villette house in *I Confess*? Are these people not "densely congregated beholders"? I agree with Abramson that *The Birds* provides a grim and dark vision of audiences, of "constant paranoid watching." But I believe Hitchcock's interest was never on the wane.

31. For a brief but fascinating discussion of the link between Hitchcock's cameo in this film and the motif of crowds and doubles, see Michael Walker's *Hitchcock's Motifs*, 94–95.

32. Abramson, *Hitchcock and the Anxiety of Authorship*, 224.

33. Abramson, *Hitchcock and the Anxiety of Authorship*, 226–27.

34. Almost a century ago, Justice Oliver Wendell Holmes argued that "the most stringent protection of free speech would not protect a man falsely shouting fire in a theatre and causing a panic" (qtd. in Flemming Rose, *The Tyranny of Silence* [Washington, D.C.: Cato Institute, 2011], 124). Holmes's statement was

not without precedent. In fact, there had been recent instances in which people were killed trying to escape from a theater in which someone had shouted fire. Robert M. Hazen and Margaret Hindle Hazen describe an incident in which more than one hundred people were trampled to death when a cry of "Fire!" rang out in the crowded Shiloh Baptist Church in Birmingham, Alabama, on the night of September 19, 1902. There had been no fire. *Keepers of the Flame: The Role of Fire in American Culture, 1775–1925* (Princeton, N.J.: Princeton University Press, 1992), 65

35. Canetti, *Crowds and Power*, 27.

36. Brigitte Peucker, "Blood, Paint, or Red? The Color Bleed in Hitchcock," in *The Cambridge Companion to Alfred Hitchcock*, ed. Jonathan Freedman (New York: Cambridge University Press, 2015), 196.

37. David Freeman, *The Last Days of Alfred Hitchcock* (New York: Overlook Press, 1984), 235–36.

38. Antonia Lant, "The Film Crowd," in *Moving Pictures: American Art and Early Film*, ed. Nancy Mowll Matthews, Charles Musser, and Marta Braun (Manchester, Vt.: Hudson Hills Press, 2005), 159.

39. Lant, "The Film Crowd," 159.

40. Lant, "The Film Crowd," 160. Lesley Brill similarly finds a negative attitude toward crowds pervading the discipline of film studies: "Insofar as film studies has thought about crowds, its conception generally fits Lenelis Kruse's description: 'What is common to the progenitors of crowd psychology in the late 19th century, but not much less common to many contemporary theorists[,] is their "description" of mass behavior in dramatic and highly negative terms, such as extraordinary, exaggerated, bizarre, chaotic, evil, and disgusting'—and, above all, suggestible and easily manipulated. Film studies generally continues, in short, to view crowds as Le Bon, Tarde, and their followers have done" (*Crowds, Power, and Transformation in the Cinema*, 4). For an example of the scholarship Brill may have in mind, see William Luhr and Peter Lehman, "*Experiment in Terror*: Dystopian Modernism, the Police Procedural, and the Space of Anxiety," in *Cinema and Modernity*, ed. Murray Pomerance (New Brunswick, N.J.: Rutgers University Press, 2006), 175–93. Rebecca Solnit offers a counterbalance with her commentary on the weaknesses of Le Bon's work and the positive outcomes of modern crowd behavior in *A Paradise Built in Hell: The Extraordinary Communities That Arise in Disaster* (New York: Viking Penguin, 2009).

41. The exact origin of the term *flickers*—referring to motion pictures—is unknown, although the OED lists an article dated 1899 that refers to the irritation caused to the eye by "flicker on the screen." It's clear, however, that the abbreviated version, *flick*, was in widespread use by the 1920s and is still commonly used today.

42. Brill, *Crowds, Power, and Transformation in the Cinema*, 1.

43. Brill, *Crowds, Power, and Transformation in the Cinema*, 15.

44. Brill, *Crowds, Power, and Transformation in the Cinema*, 15.

45. Tom Cohen, *Hitchcock's Cryptonomies*, 147–48.

46. This utterance, so reminiscent of Ted's gibberish about acts of providence ("An act is defined as any activity actuated by actual action"), bracketed on either side by crowd laughter, further highlights the crowd's movie-making ability.

47. Brill, *Crowds, Power, and Transformation in the Cinema*, 128.

48. Brill, *Crowds, Power, and Transformation in the Cinema*, 128.

49. Brill, *Crowds, Power, and Transformation in the Cinema*, 130–31.

50. See Georg Simmel, "The Metropolis and Mental Life," in *The Blackwell City Reader*, ed. Gary Bridge and Sophie Watson (Malden, Mass.: Blackwell, 2002): "There is perhaps no psychic phenomenon which is so unconditionally reserved to the city as the blasé outlook. It is at first the consequence of those rapidly shifting stimulations of the nerves which are thrown together in all their contrasts and from which it seems to us the intensification of metropolitan intellectuality seems to be derived. . . . The essence of the blasé metropolitan attitude is an indifference toward the distinctions between things. Not in the sense that they are not perceived, as is the case of mental dullness, but rather that the meaning and the value of the distinctions between things, and therewith of the things themselves, are experienced as meaningless" (14).

51. Bruno Latour, *We Have Never Been Modern* (Cambridge, Mass.: Harvard University Press, 1993), 2.

52. David M. Henkin, *City Reading: Written Words and Public Spaces in Antebellum New York* (New York: Columbia University Press, 1998), 125.

53. Henkin, *City Reading*, 126.

54. Lesley Brill thinks Thornhill's fate is sealed when he separates himself from the crowd by stealing the taxi: "When Roger Thornihill cuts ahead of a woman to commandeer her cab, he implicitly violates the principle of equality upon which the crowds depend. Most of what threatens him thereafter occurs because of his removing himself from the protection of the crowd" (*Crowds, Power, and Transformation in the Cinema*, 8). Leaving aside Brill's minor error that Thornhill steals the taxi from a man, not a woman (he is obviously confusing this scene with a shot in the film's opening sequence of two older women fighting over a taxi), one could insist that it is not until Thornhill leaves the taxi and joins the crowd once more that he becomes endangered. The difference now is that Thornhill is without his newspaper. But even if we concede that Thornhill is safe when in numbers and in danger when removed from them (which is, I think, a consistent pattern in the film), here, early in the film, he has the protection of his newspaper, his link to the crowd.

55. Brill, *Crowds, Power, and Transformation in the Cinema*, 130.

56. Andrew Uroskie, "Far above the Madding Crowd: The Spatial Rhetoric of Mass Representation," in *Crowds*, ed. Jeffrey T. Schapp and Matthew Tiews (Stanford, Calif.: Stanford University Press, 2006), 323.

57. Uroskie, "Far above the Madding Crowd," 323.

58. The figure of the downward spiral is found throughout Hitchcock, from beginning to end. Like multiple opposing vortices, the chain of downward spiral travels through the Hitchcock universe, from the earliest films to the two masterpieces of his last, great period: *Vertigo* and *Psycho*.

59. As Hugh Kenner first noted, with the poetry of T. S. Eliot in mind, "'Pumped' and 'sucked' are appropriate metaphors; Eliot's most famous crowd *flows* across London bridge like a viscid liquid." *The Mechanic Muse* (New York: Oxford University Press, 1987), 28.

60. Tom Cohen, in his formidable two-volume study, *Hitchcock's Cryptonomies*, suggests that "the 'eternal recurrence' would have been Zarathustra's MacGuffin. It is purely cinematic, and Hitchcock inherited in cinema the banal

literalization of the eternal recurrence as a questioning of the structure of mnemonic repetition, the priority of inscriptive programs (celluloid) over phenomenality (projection)" (186).

61. Sara Blair, "Hitchcock on Location: America, Icons, and the Place of Illusion," in Freedman, *The Cambridge Companion to Alfred Hitchcock*,, 74n22.

62. Blair, "Hitchcock on Location," 77n22.

63. Kracauer, *Theory of Film*, xlix.

64. Kracauer, *Theory of Film*, 50.

65. Kracauer, *Theory of Film*, 73.

66. These are the various meanings of *affinity* to be found in the *Oxford English Dictionary*. Each takes us closer to what I take to be Kracauer's point about the relationship between life in big cities and the medium of photography.

67. Graeme Gilloch, *Siegfried Kracauer: Our Companion in Misfortune* (Malden, Mass: Polity, 2015), 131.

68. Specifically, Kracauer's study of Jacques Offenbach and an essay entitled "Motion Picture Treatment." Gilloch, *Siegfried Kracauer*, 191.

69. In addition to Sarah Street's essay on the woman's handbag noted above, see George Toles's "Occasions of Sin."

70. Bruno Latour, *Politics of Nature: How to Bring the Sciences into Democracy*, trans. Catherine Porter (Cambridge, Mass.: Harvard University Press, 2004), 22.

Chapter 2

1. Ink with graphite under drawing. Signed b.r. "Phil May 96." 26.7 × 15.5 cm., 10–7/16 × 6–1/8" sheet. Lent Courtesy of Private Collection. Rpt. in Catherine Carter Goebel, ed., *Origins of Modernity* (Rock Island, Ill.: Augustana College, 2005), 155.

2. Philip Fisher, *Still the New World: American Literature in a Culture of Creative Destruction* (Cambridge, Mass.: Harvard University Press, 1999), 251. This idea is echoed by David M. Henkin, who draws an equally explicit link between the newspaper format and the crowd: "Discrete news stories, tendentious political commentaries, competitive commercial claims, and ostensibly unrelated bits of information blended together in the print columns of the metropolitan press in a characteristically urban juxtaposition of unlikely neighbors that also imbued all of the texts with the appearance of sharing a single, impersonal authority." *City Reading*, 119.

3. It is worth noting that out of all of Hitchcock's cameos, four of them involve newspapers: in one cameo, Hitchcock appears as a newspaper editor (*The Lodger* [1926]); he appears reading a newspaper in two cameos (*Foreign Correspondent* [1940] and *Stage Fright* [1950]); in a fourth, he is pictured in a newspaper (*Lifeboat* [1944]). One may further speculate that in his cameo in *Young and Innocent* (1937), Hitchcock appears as a photographer who works for a newspaper, which would bring the total number of newspaper-related cameos to five.

4. Hitchcock was known to lend his image to picture stories, such as "The Murder of Monty Woolley," which appeared in the June 15, 1943, issue of *Look* magazine (56–57, 77.)

5. There are objects of significance that appear in more than one Hitchcock film, such as the key in both *Notorious* and *Dial M for Murder* and the ring in both *Shadow of a Doubt* and *Rear Window*. Yet neither of these objects

has the busy itinerary of Hitchcock's newspaper. Sarah Street's insightful essay, "Hitchcockian Haberdashery" (in Gottlieb and Brookhouse, *Framing Hitchcock*, 147–58) draws our attention to another busy Hitchcockian object: the woman's handbag. Like the newspaper, the handbag is given "consistent, obtrusive visual attention" in several films (147). What makes the newspaper a more prominent object is not that it appears in far more films (Street sees the handbag as essential only in films made during the years 1954–64) but that its meaning, its function, its very shape is always changing. To be sure, the Hitchcock handbag is a focal enough object to be worthy of study, but it is an unchanging visual symbol of "the threat of secrets or independent female identity" (151). For a fuller inventory of significant objects in Hitchcock's films, see Walker, *Hitchcock's Motifs*.

6. Ina Rae Hark, "'We Might Even Get in the Newsreels': The Press and Democracy in Hitchcock's World War II Anti-Fascist Films," in *Alfred Hitchcock: Centenary Essays*, ed. Richard Allen and S. Ishii Gonzalès (London: BFI, 1999), 335.

7. Hark, "'We Might Even Get in the Newsreels,'" 334.

8. For a discussion of "matters of fact" and "matters of concern," see Bruno Latour, *What Is the Style of Matters of Concern? Two Lectures on Empirical Philosophy* (Assen, Netherlands: Van Gorkum, 2005), 39.

9. Ned Schantz, *Gossip, Letters, Phones: The Scandal of Female Networks in Film and Literature* (New York: Oxford University Press, 2008), 56.

10. Rothman, *Hitchcock*. Mel Brooks, in his parody of Hitchcock's films, *High Anxiety* (1977), takes the idea of the murderous newspaper literally. The psychiatrist Richard H. Thorndyke (Brooks) is waiting impatiently for a newspaper, which he had requested several times from a hotel bellboy. In a hilarious take on the shower scene from *Psycho*, the newspaper is finally delivered. Shrieking hysterically, the bellboy stabs Thorndyke repeatedly with the rolled-up newspaper. Stunned, Thorndyke collapses in the tub as the newspaper ink washes down the drain.

11. In Hitchcock, the newspaper is all eyes. Is it any wonder, then, that the film's final confrontation is staged in a way that clearly suggests a media celebrity being hounded by the paparazzi? The full force of the idea of Hitchcock's newspaper as "all eyes" is felt if one recalls a pivotal moment in the film: when Thorwald leaves his apartment with a strange woman—a woman Jeff could confirm is decidedly not Mrs. Anna Thorwald had he not taken his eyes off Thorwald and fallen asleep. Later in the film, in a shot that further ties the newspaper to Thorwald's guilt, we see Detective Doyle through the alleyway adjacent to Thorwald's apartment—a space that affords us our only glimpses of the Greenwich Villagers who crowd the streets. Doyle has just left Jeff's apartment, unconvinced by Jeff's reasoning, and, further, provides "proof" that Anna Thorwald is safe and sound, and very much alive, in Merritsville. Once outside of Jeff's apartment and on the street, Doyle is approached by a newsie selling papers; he refuses to buy a copy, and the scene ends with a fade to black. If Jeff misses his chance to see what the newspaper has known all along, Doyle refuses to see. A similar connection with the newspaper and eyes comes in *The 39 Steps*, on the train when Hannay spots the news story of Annabella's murder in the newspaper he is reading. In a clever reverse shot, Hannay lowers his newspaper just enough to reveal the suspicious eyes of the passenger seated across from him.

12. The films in which the newspaper can be considered a prominent and recurrent object are *The Lodger*, *Champagne* (1928), *Blackmail* (1929), *Rich and Strange* (1931), *The 39 Steps* (1935), *The Lady Vanishes* (1939), *Foreign Correspondent* (1940), *Shadow of a Doubt* (1943), *Lifeboat*, *North by Northwest* (1959), *Psycho* (1960), and *Marnie* (1964). But the newspaper is an important object in other films, frequently tied to a character's presumed (if sometimes mistakenly so) guilt. In *Strangers on a Train*, it is not clear if Bruno recognizes Guy because he's seen him in the sports section of the newspaper or its society pages—given Bruno's polymorphous perversity, it is most likely both. After the opening sequence of *To Catch a Thief* (1955), in which a woman's scream is followed by a shot of a black cat prowling the rooftops, we find ourselves in the estate of John Robie. We see a cleaning woman tidying up, and then the camera cuts to a shot of a black cat, lying on top of a newspaper. A close-up of the paper shows a story, "The Cat Prowls Again?" written by Art Buchwald. Robert A. Harris and Michael S. Lasky note that there are claw marks slashed through this story (*The Complete Films of Alfred Hitchcock* [New York: Citadel Press, 2002], 171). But the claw marks are in the column to the right (both columns fall under the heading "Europe's Lighter Side"). The story recalls the film's title shot of a window of a travel agency—a shot that will be virtually repeated early in the title sequence of *North by Northwest*. In *The Wrong Man* (1956), we see that Manny Ballesrtero likes to read the racing pages of the newspaper and pick the winning horses—a hobby that, as Paula Marantz Cohen rightly claims, marks Manny as a potential criminal from the start (see *Alfred Hitchcock*, 127). In *Vertigo*, Scottie is twice seen reading a newspaper while nervously waiting for Madeleine to appear. In *Frenzy*, a newspaper is pushed underneath the door of Babs's apartment, as Blaney sleeps in her bed. On the front page is a story about yet another necktie murder. In the following shot, we see Babs's landlord reading the same story, in which a perfect description of Blaney is given. This sequence is perhaps the culmination of a whole career devoted to putting heroes wrongly accused on the front page.

13. Even with only two James Bond films released to date, audiences of *Marnie* would no doubt be reminded of the opening of a James Bond film, in which Secret Service agent 007 is spied through a gun barrel. Here, as Mark Rutland, Connery is equally disarming, as he will twice dismiss the man advancing on Marnie (whom he recognizes, rightly, as Peggy Nicholson). But for an instant, with his back turned and his binoculars following the race, Connery seems vulnerable.

14. Quoted in Henkin, *City Reading*, 109.

15. Frederick Knight Hunt, *The Fourth Estate: Contributions Towards a History of Newspapers, and of the Liberties of the Press*, vol. 1 (London: David Bogue, 1850), 2.

16. Gerald Stanley Lee, *Crowds: A Moving-Picture of Democracy* (New York: Doubleday, Page, 1913), 28.

17. If the stroking inside the hole of the newspaper does not sufficiently suggest that rape is on the minds of the men in *Marnie*, it is important to recall that Hitchcock insisted on including the scene from Winston Graham's novel in which Mark rapes Marnie, despite the objections of the second of his three screenwriters on the project, Evan Hunter. Although the film itself is full of suggestive references to rape (the red suffusions, the drops of red ink on Marnie's shirt, and

so on), the trailer for Hitchcock's film makes an explicit connection between sexual violence and investigative probing. Over the scene in Mark's office when the thunderstorm hits, Hitchcock delivers a campy voice-over characteristic of his introductions and send-offs from *Alfred Hitchcock Presents*. As we see the shot of a tree trunk bursting through the window, Hitchcock says, "Marnie's trouble goes deeper than that . . . far deeper." Over a subsequent shot of Mark kissing Marnie, Hitchcock continues: "And this is the problem that Mark must probe."

18. Nor is Roger Thornhill really looking through the binoculars at Mount Rushmore. This bit of deception may account for his odd statement, "I don't like the way Teddy Roosevelt is looking at me." As Stanley Cavell has observed, Roosevelt isn't looking at Roger Thornhill. But then again, Thornhill isn't looking at Roosevelt either. See "*North by Northwest*," in *A Hitchcock Reader*, ed. (Malden, Mass.: Wiley-Blackwell, 2011), 250–63. In the first scene from *Vertigo*, in which we see Scottie shadowing Madeleine, he is waiting in his car outside the Brocklebank Apartments, looking distracted as he pretends to read a newspaper.

19. Robin Wood. *Hitchcock's Films Revisited*, rev. ed. (New York: Columbia University Press, 2002), 45.

20. As my students familiar with the East Coast have told me, the opening shot of *Shadow of a Doubt* is actually of the Pulaski Skyway in New Jersey. Uncle Charlie does get around, doesn't he?

21. Elsie B. Michie, "Unveiling Maternal Desires: Hitchcock and American Domesticity," in *Hitchcock's America*, ed. Jonathan Freedman and Richard Millington (New York: Oxford University Press, 1999), 45–46.

22. Michie, "Unveiling Maternal Desires," 46.

23. Michie, "Unveiling Maternal Desires," 37.

24. Michie makes the same observation, though she mistakenly claims that Uncle Charlie now refers to the house as "a farm." This change, argues Michie, is due to Uncle Charlie's "belief in the domestic values of the past. Uncle Charlie is relentlessly interested in enforcing traditional conceptions of gender difference" ("Unveiling Maternal Desires," 53n50). To Ann, the newspaper is a home. To Roger, a farm.

25. Rothman *Hitchcock*, 40.

26. Rothman, *Hitchcock*, 9–10.

27. Tom Ryall, citing the work of Alan Lovell, refers to the "the *News of the World* culture" that is portrayed in *The Lodger*, a tabloid newspaper culture from which Hitchcock's cinematic identity derived: "The '*News of the World* culture' with its emphasis on sexuality and violence is a central component of the 'strong under-life' of British cinema which runs counter to the 'cinema of good taste, characterized by restraint, understatement and sophistication' preferred by the orthodox film culture and it is to the subversive counter-current that Hitchcock's British films relate." See *Alfred Hitchcock and the British Cinema* (London: Athlone Press, 1996), 179.

28. Rothman, *Hitchcock*, 9–10

29. Gustav Le Bon, *The Crowd: A Study of the Popular Mind*, 2nd ed. (New York: Macmillan, 1897), 22.

30. See Jeffrey T. Schnapp and Matthew Tiews, "Introduction: A Book of Crowds," in Schnapp and Tiews, *Crowds*, ix.

Chapter 3

1. Edgar Allan Poe, "William Wilson," in *Thirty-two Stories*, ed. Stuart Levine and Susan F. Levine (Indianapolis, Ind.: Hackett Publishing, 2000), 117.

2. In fact, as Michael Walker has pointed out, the double has never appeared in a Hitchcock film—whether in an apartment or not. Strictly speaking, "the double looks exactly like the hero but has an independent identity" (*Hitchcock's Motifs*, 147). Charlie and her uncle, Bruno and Guy, Roger Thornhill and George Kaplan—these are not sets of doubles except in the broader, larger sense of the word (recall that Charlie says to her uncle, "We're *sort of like* twins"). In Hitchcock, the double is more of a formal pattern, a structuring principle, with *Strangers on a Train* being perhaps the finest example. Even *The Wrong Man* might be disqualified as a film about the double, since Daniel knows nothing about Manny Balestrero, and his resemblance to Manny is only passing.

3. See especially Brad Stevens, "Troubled Bodies: Notes on Hitchcock's Television Work," *Hitchcock Annual* 19 (2014): 82–130; and Jan Olsson, *Hitchcock à la Carte* (Durham, N.C.: Duke University Press, 2015).

4. Thomas Leitch, "The Outer Circle: Hitchcock on Television," in Allen and Ishii Gonzalès, *Alfred Hitchcock*, 65.

5. For an excellent example of this critical approach, see Jan Olsson's *Hitchcock à la Carte*, in particular the chapter titled "Smaller Screen, Bigger Brand: Hosting 'Hitchcock.' "

6. Olsson, *Hitchcock à la Carte*, 68–69.

7. Alfred Hitchcock, "After-Dinner Speech at the Screen Producers Guild Dinner," in Gottlieb, *Hitchcock on Hitchcock*, 58.

8. Qtd. in James Naremore, "Hitchcock and Humor," *Hitchcock: Past and Future*, ed. Richard Allen and Sam Ishii-Gonzalès (New York: Routledge, 2004), 31.

9. Only just. *The Trouble with Harry* premiered October 3, 1955. The first episode of *Alfred Hitchcock Presents*, "Revenge," premiered the night before, on October 2.

10. Wojcik, *The Apartment Plot*, 3.

11. Wojcik, *The Apartment Plot*, 87.

12. Wojcik, *The Apartment Plot*.

13. Wojcik, *The Apartment Plot*, 51.

14. Wojcik, *The Apartment Plot*, 133.

15. George Toles, "Hitchcock's Female Gaze," in *A House Made of Light: Essays on the Art of Film* (Detroit, Mich.: Wayne State University Press, 2001), 221.

16. Ned Schantz, "Hitchcock and the Unsettled Viewer," 13.

17. Of course, the entire film is about the "public privacy" of the modern, urban apartment. I regularly teach a course on Hitchcock, and I recall one semester, during a discussion of *Rear Window*, one young man raised his hand and asked, "Doesn't anyone in this film ever knock?"

18. Of the seventeen episodes of *Alfred Hitchcock Presents* that Hitchcock directed, ten take place—either partly or entirely—in a house. Excluding "The Case of Mr. Pelham," the remaining six episodes take place in a mobile home ("Revenge"), a car ("Breakdown" and "One More Mile to Go"), a cruise ship ("A Dip in the Pool"), a mountain ("The Crystal Trench"), and a church ("The Horse Player").

19. Port was considered to be the fortified wine of choice among British drinking men in the nineteenth century. To "soften their rough masculinity," however,

men turned to sherry. In *The Politics of Wine in Britain: A New Cultural History* (New York: Palgrave Macmillan, 2013), Charles Ludington says that sherry was considered "fortified but not French, feminine but not effeminizing. In the post-war era, it was a magical elixir. British middle-class men turned to sherry to express their respectability, which like politeness required taming aggressive masculinity with a dose of gentle refinement." Thus sherry became the drink of choice among "respectable women" (117). In *Domesticating Drink: Women, Men, and Alcohol in America, 1870–1940* (Baltimore, Md.: Johns Hopkins University Press, 2001), Catherine Gilbert Murdock finds that the decanter (which "stored wine, sherry, and cordials in a limited, and thus more respectable amount") was, in nineteenth-century America, often associated with the female drinker (67–68).

20. "Until recently, homosexuality offered not just the prominent, it offered the only subject matter whose representation in American mass culture appertained exclusively to the shadow kingdom of connotation, where insinuations could be at once developed and denied where . . . one couldn't be sure whether homosexuality was being meant at all" (D. A. Miller, "Anal *Rope*," 119).

21. D. A. Miller, "Anal *Rope*," 150.

22. The well-known TV actor Raymond Bailey appeared on *Alfred Hitchcock Presents* ten times, and on four occasions (including "The Case of Mr. Pelham") played a doctor. He also played a doctor in *Vertigo* (1958), diagnosing Scottie's condition as "acute melancholia coupled with a guilt complex."

23. In this way, the painting has a function similar to the painting of the jester in *Blackmail* (1929), which, as Maurice Yacowar writes, "works as a test of the people it meets. It is the very spirit of irony, seeming innocent but a tricky test of its viewer's alertness." *Hitchcock's British Films* (Hamden, Conn.: Archon, 1977). 86.

24. D. A. Miller, "Anal *Rope*," 118.

25. *Carom* is a billiards term. While *carom billiards* refers generally to any game of billiards, a carom occurs when the cue ball strikes two object balls.

26. Wojcik, *The Apartment Plot*, 111.

27. Wojcik, *The Apartment Plot*, 112.

28. Wojcik, *The Apartment Plot*, 112.

29. Justin Weir, *Leo Tolstoy and the Alibi of Narrative* (New Haven, Conn.: Yale University Press, 2001), 1.

30. D. A. Miller, "Anal *Rope*," 122.

31. Roland Barthes, "Myth Today," in *A Barthes Reader*, ed. Susan Sontag (New York: Hill and Wang, 1982), 109.

32. D. A. Miller, "Anal *Rope*," 122.

33. Robert J. Corber, "Hitchcock's Washington: Spectatorship, Ideology, and the 'Homosexual Menace' in *Strangers on a Train*," in Freedman and Millington, *Hitchcock's America*, 99–122.

34. There is a third occasion: when Guy encounters a priest who repeats Bruno's line, "I beg your pardon, but aren't you Guy Haines?" And while one could argue that Guy is not alone with the man since Anne is present, the sequence suggests nothing less than the paranoia to which I refer. Seemingly "safe" in the presence of a woman who can ward off any unwanted advances, Guy grabs Anne by the arm, and the two hastily leave the compartment. Better safe than sorry.

35. This refrain is taken from the children's song "The Billy Goat," also known as (among other titles) "Bill Grogan's Goat" and "The Tale of a Shirt."

36. Collins certainly fits the profile of a gay man cruising: the direct eye contact, the suggestive sing-song, and even the handkerchief, which gay men used to advertise their sexual preferences to other gay men. According to Florence Tamange, a wide, folded handkerchief in a jacket pocket signaled passive. A handkerchief divided in two meant passive or active. Bruno divides his in two (naturally). Collins's handkerchief is wide and folded. *A History of Homosexuality in Europe*, vols. 1–2, *Berlin, London, Paris 1919–1939* (New York: Algora Publishing, 2006), 346.

37. This line, spoken by Guy, makes his brief encounter with Collins seem all the more queer. What might be shameful to Collins is not only that he may, in fact, have come on to Guy, but that Guy can and will give the details of this come-on—including the most shameful detail that, due to the ingestion of copious amounts of bourbon, Collins could not perform.

38. Just after his meeting with Collins, and the night before his appearance before Captain Turley, Guy is waylaid by Bruno, who has been waiting across the street from Guy's apartment. The scene is reminiscent—not vaguely so—of cruising. Answering the call, Guy joins Bruno in the darkness and, when the police arrive at his apartment, hides with him in the shadows.

39. It is interesting to consider how frequently in Hitchcock the private, intimate encounters between men are associated with criminality—Tony and Swann in *Dial M for Murder*; Thorwald and Jeff in *Rear Window*; Guy and Bruno in *Strangers on a Train*; Father Logan and Otto in *I Confess,* to name but a few.

40. I borrow this term from Eve Kosofsky Sedgwick, *Epistemology of the Closet* (Berkeley: University of California Press, 1990), 164.

41. Walker, *Hitchcock's Motifs*, 270.

42. It's possible the network objected to the line, as the idea of two male characters laying claim to the same man would have seemed too suggestive. But the change from "My man!" to "Peterson!" doesn't entirely unhinge the notion that there's competition over who has rights to him.

Chapter 4

1. Tom Conley, *Cartographic Cinema* (Minneapolis: University of Minnesota Press, 2007), 2.

2. I refer to this movie review in an essay of mine entitled "The Map Is Not the Country: Cartography in Joel and Ethan Coen's *No Country for Old Men*." *Film Criticism* 36, no. 2 (Winter 2001): 2–21.

3. David Denby, "Dream On: *Hairspray* and *Ratatouille*," *New Yorker*, July 23, 2007.

4. Tom Conley, "Locations of Film Noir," *Cartographic Journal* 46, no. 1 (2009): 16.

5. See especially John Orr, *Hitchcock and Twentieth Century Cinema* (New York: Wallflower Press, 2005); James Naremore, "Hitchcock at the Margins of Noir," in Allen and Ishii Gonzalès, *Alfred Hitchcock*.

6. Tom Conley, "Locations of Film Noir," 143.

7. Tom Conley, "Locations of Film Noir," 144.

8. Ana Salzberg, "VistaVision and the Cinematic Landscape of *Vertigo*," in Cunningham, *The San Francisco of Alfred Hitchcock's* Vertigo, 75.

9. Truffaut, *Hitchcock*, 347.

10. André Bazin, *The Cinema of Cruelty: From Buñuel to Hitchcock*, ed. François Truffaut (New York: Arcade, 1982), 154.

11. Truffaut, *Hitchcock*, 347.

12. In fact, Hitchcock was at his trimmest during the making of *To Catch a Thief* (1955), when Bazin spoke with him. For a full and fascinating study of the connections between Hitchcock's style, his genius for self-promotion, and his lifelong struggle with weight, see Olsson, *Hitchcock à la Carte*.

13. Daphne du Maurier, "The Birds," in *Don't Look Now*, compiled by Patrick McGrath (New York: New York Review of Books, 2008), 99–100.

14. Du Maurier, "The Birds," 100.

15. Truffaut, *Hitchcock*, 17

16. Qtd. in Charles L. P. Silet, "An Interview with Evan Hunter," in Gottlieb and Brookhouse, *Framing Hitchcock*, 201.

17. Richard Allen, "Daphne du Maurier and Alfred Hitchcock," in *A Companion to Literature to Film*, ed. Robert Stam and Alessandro Raengo (Malden, Mass: Blackwell, 2004), 322.

18. Truffaut, *Hitchcock*, 285.

19. Walter Raubicheck and Walter Srebnick. *Scripting Hitchcock*: Psycho, The Birds, *and* Marnie (Urbana: University of Illinois Press, 2011), 18.

20. "Transcripts of a story conference between Alfred Hitchcock and 'Tippi' Hedren, February 24, 1962, 17 pp., 18 pp. and 10 pp.," Alfred Hitchcock Papers, Margaret Herrick Library, Academy of Motion Picture Arts and Sciences, Beverly Hills, California (my emphasis).

21. Du Maurier, "The Birds," 60.

22. See Robin Wood, *Hitchcock's Films Revisited*, 151–53.

23. Du Maurier, "The Birds," 59.

24. Norbert Wiener, *Cybernetics or Control and Communication in Animals and Machines* (Cambridge, Mass: MIT Press, 1961), 7–8

25. Thomas Goetz, in a recent article for *Wired* magazine, gives us a fine, commonplace example of a "feedback loop": the use of "dynamic speed displays, or driver feedback signs: a speed limit posting coupled with a radar sensor attached to a huge digital readout announcing 'Your Speed.'" The feedback loop, writes Goetz, is "a profoundly effective tool for changing behavior. The basic premise is simple. Provide people with information about their actions in real time (or something close to it), then give them an opportunity to change those actions, pushing them toward better behaviors. Action, information, reaction." "Harnessing the Power of Feedback Loops." *Wired*, July 2011.

26. Wiener, *Cybernetics*, 181.

27. Qtd. in Wiener, *Cybernetics*, 170.

28. In the revised screenplay, dated November 13, 1961, there is a scene where Charlie gives Melanie the address: "1000 Chestnut Street, right here in San Francisco." "Where is that, Charlie?" Melanie asks. Charlie replies, "Not too far. Just a few blocks off."

29. From the November 13, 1961, draft of the screenplay: as she is driving into Bodega Bay, Melanie asks the caged lovebirds, "Where do you suppose the post office is?"

30. Critics also fail to note that Melanie spends her Thursdays raising money to send a Korean boy to school. After telling Mitch of her philanthropic interest,

she mentions Rome: "That entire summer, I did nothing but . . . well, it was very easy to get lost there." In one of many instances in the film (also present in the du Maurier story), Melanie links directionlessness with avian chaos: she sometimes visits bird shops on Fridays.

31. See Raubicheck and Srebnick, *Scripting Hitchcock*, 92–94. Clearly, it is the witty banter between the warring Mitch and Melanie that brings Hitchcock's film close to the screwball tradition. However, the comic touches in the film are also related to directionlessness. The scene in the post office, for instance, is played for laughs.

32. Vivian Sobchack, *Carnal Thoughts: Embodiment and Moving Image Culture* (Berkeley: University of California Press, 2004), 23–27.

33. Sobchack, *Carnal Thoughts*, 23.

34. Sobchack, *Carnal Thoughts*, 25.

35. Sobchack, *Carnal Thoughts*, 27–28, emphasis in original.

36. In an interesting, and somewhat obscene, moment in the 2006 film *The Pervert's Guide to Cinema*, Slavoj Žižek reenacts Melanie's boat ride in *The Birds* and confesses that he has lost his way: "What am I doing? [fussing with the steerage on the outboard engine] I'm sorry, I'm sorry, now I've got it. . . . My God, I'm thinking like Melanie. Do you know what I'm thinking now? I want to fuck Mitch—that's what she was thinking! Oh sorry, sorry, sorry! Oh my God, I got this spontaneous confusion of directions."

37. Du Maurier, "The Birds," 55.

38. Murray Pomerance, "Thirteen Ways of Looking at *The Birds*," in *Hitchcock at the Source: The Auteur as Adapter*, ed. R. Barton Palmer and David Boyd (Albany: State University of New York Press, 2011), 285.

39. Du Maurier, "The Birds," 63.

40. Du Maurier, "The Birds," 63.

41. Du Maurier, "The Birds," 63.

42. Du Maurier's story contains a scene in which dozens of birds travel down the chimney into the kitchen range. Although the location was changed to the Brenners' living room, the birds' attack via the chimney is similar to du Maurier's version. In the second revised draft of Hunter's script, dated March 2, 1962, the similarities are even stronger. Both Nat and Mitch light a fire, which forces some of the birds back up the chimney and sends others around the room and out the open windows. However, rather than showing Mitch lighting a fire in the fireplace, Hitchcock dissolves, midway, into the subsequent scene with Sheriff Malone, so that the viewer does not see the result of the attack.

43. Lee Edelman comes the closest in *No Future: Queer Theory and the Death Drive* (Durham, N.C.: Duke University Press, 2004). He rightly points out that this attack is "the first all-out assault," the first in the film that is "fully choreographed," and from this observation concludes that the attack "suggests the extent to which the birds take aim at the social structures of meaning that observances like the birthday party serve to secure and enact: take aim, that is, not only at children and the sacralization of childhood, but also at the very organization of meaning around structures of subjectivity that celebrate, along with the day of one's birth, the ideology of reproductive futurity" (121). One should emphasize, in regard to his claim that the birthday party is the target of the birds' attack, that the attack occurs at the moment that seems farthest removed from

the party's ostensible social function: to celebrate Cathy's birth (and her, and the other children's, future reproductive ambitions). That is, the attack comes at a moment during the party when the children are playing *this* game—a game that, after all, could be played at *any* children's party, and at any time of the year—not just on a birthday. If there is a target, it is indeed the children—no question—but the children are targeted precisely when they are playing a game in which success depends on cybernetic mechanisms of maintaining orientation while blinded.

44. William Leon Dawson and John Hooper Bowles, *The Birds of Washington: A Complete Scientific and Popular Account of the 372 Species of Birds Found in the State*, vol. 1 (Seattle, Wash.: Occidental, 1909), 276.

45. While it is true that, as Mitch observes, the pattern of the bird attacks is on-again/off-again, my point is simply that, in the film's final moments, we expect the bird attack to be on-again.

46. "Story memo. October 12, 1961. 26 pages," Alfred Hitchcock Papers, Margaret Herrick Library, Academy of Motion Picture Arts and Sciences, Beverly Hills, California.

47. William Rothman, "The Universal Hitchcock," in Leitch and Poague, *A Companion to Alfred Hitchcock*, 348.

48. Conley, *Cartographic Cinema*, 3, emphasis in original.

49. Sobchack, *Carnal Thoughts*, 22n17.

50. Wood, *Hitchcock's Films Revisited*, 198.

51. Alexander Welsh, *George Eliot and Blackmail* (Cambridge, Mass: Harvard University Press, 1985), 23.

52. Robert J. Belton, *Alfred Hitchcock's* Vertigo *and the Hermeneutic Spiral* (Cham, Switzerland: Springer, 2017), 118.

53. Belton, *Alfred Hitchcock's* Vertigo, 118.

54. I suspect I am not alone in wondering why Scottie is not overcome with vertigo here, as the staircase takes him to a considerable height. One might suggest that reason steadies him, that the confidence and authority expressed by his badge give him equilibrium. Regardless, one can't help but sense, while watching this scene, a foreshadowing of events. Here, in the McKittrick Hotel, we see Scottie climbing tall stairs only to discover that he has lost his Madeleine—a scene that is repeated later in the film, at Mission San Juan Bautista.

55. For more on "Hardheaded Scot" and the scientific method he represents, see Dan Flory, "*Vertigo*: Scientific Method, Obsession, and Human Minds," in *Hitchcock and Philosophy: Dial M for Metaphysics*, ed. David Baggett and William A. Drumin, 115–28 (Chicago: Open Court, 2007).

56. Pomerance, *An Eye for Hitchcock*, 253.

57. A similar moment of "now you see me, now you don't" occurs later in *Shadow of a Doubt*, when Charlie insists to Detective Jack Graham that her uncle is in her room. This time the detective is right.

58. Michel de Certeau, *The Practice of Everyday Life*, vol. 1 (Berkeley: University of California Press, 1984), 93.

59. De Certeau, *The Practice of Everyday Life, 93.*

60. "Six weeks and two days of intensive filming were required to complete the location sequences. A few interior sequences, involving considerable dialogue but settings which could duplicate in exact detail the Quebec originals, were filmed on Warner Bros. sound stages after the company returned from location."

"Production Notes," Box 1 of 2, Folder 653 (Folder 13), courtesy of the Margaret Herrick Library.

61. Like other French cities in North America, Quebec City was built on a grid—but only partly. As John William Reps has shown, while the upper city is linear, with many of its streets intersecting at right angles, the lower city was nonlinear and irregular. *The Making of Urban America: A History of City Planning in the United States* (Princeton, N.J.: Princeton University Press, 1969), 65. *Montreal and Quebec for Dummies* warns that "the city was not built on a grid, so it can be disorienting, but don't worry—sooner or later, you'll arrive at a wall, a cliff, or a gate, and you'll be able to figure out where you are on a map." Austin MacDonald, *Montreal and Quebec for Dummies*, 2nd ed. (Hoboken, N.J.: Wiley, 2006), 209.

62. According to the OED, the noun *lure* is the oldest form of the word: "Loss, either the action or process of losing, or what is lost; destruction, perdition." Thus Inspector Larrue's name links him also with Father Logan, the subject of his investigation, whose city wanderings are of great interest.

63. V. F. Perkins is one of the earliest critics to single out the one-way signs. He sees in them a strong association with Hitchcock's cameo, which "displayed himself in his independence as the director. "*I Confess*: Photographs of People Speaking," *CineAction* 52 (July 2000): 43. When not connecting the street signs to the director himself, critics turn to metaphor. For example, Homer B. Pettey says they "serve as apocalyptic omens for the spatial separation that portends Father Logan's ordeal with upper-class authorities." "Hitchcock, Class, and Noir," in Freedman, *The Cambridge Companion to Alfred Hitchcock*. 83.

64. Pomerance, *An Eye for Hitchcock*, 183.

65. Amy Lawrence, "Constructing a Priest, Silencing a Saint: The PCA and *I Confess*," *Film History* 19 (2007), 61.

66. My discovery of this hesitant pedestrian would likely qualify as what D. A. Miller calls a "hidden picture." According to Miller, what is intelligible to the casual viewer of Hitchcock is the director's "manifest style," surface details of (only) narrative interest. But a "too-close viewer" suspects, rightly, there is more to Hitchcock, more to his manifest style, than meets the eye. The "too-close viewer" finds herself lured into the excessive nooks and crannies of Hitchcock's "understyle," where directorial touches—"hidden pictures"—never before seen or felt abound. Hitchcock's hidden pictures are "microstructures recessed deep in the film text where, visible but inconspicuous, they have never been seen, or at least never been remarked, by Hitchcock critics. These microstructures are too coherent *as* structures to be unplanned, but so deviously concealed that, once they *are* observed, the ostensible story is completely lost to view. Minimal, meager, without narrative interest or utility, the hidden pictures are exercises of pure style, of style devoid of uncaring substance." "Hitchcock's Understyle: A Too-Close View of *Rope*," *Representations* 121, no. 1 (Winter 2013): 12.

67. The theme of the lured child can be found in numerous folktales and children's stories, including "Hansel and Gretel," *Alice in Wonderland*, and "Granny Tucker," to name a few. It is usually to "some awfulness" that the child is lured.

68. Deborah L. Parsons, *Streetwalking the Metropolis: Women, the City and Modernity* (New York, N.Y.: Oxford University Press, 2000), 73.

69. Qtd. in Parsons, *Streetwalking the Metropolis*, 7.

70. On April 2, 1952, Barbara Keon, who coauthored an early version of the script of *I Confess*, placed a request for "pictorial material on Quebec—churches, waterfront, Map of Quebec, showing location of prison, courts, imp. Points of interest." Box 1 of 2, Folder 1013 (1/34). Courtesy of the Warner Bros. Archives, School of Cinematic Arts, University of Southern California.

71. Welsh, *George Eliot and Blackmail*, 17.

72. Walker, *Hitchcock's Motifs*, 140.

73. Gerald Bruns, "Cain, or The Metaphorical Construction of Cities," *Salmagundi*, 74/75 (1987): 70.

74. Bruns, "Cain," 73.

75. Bruns, "Cain," 70.

76. Bruns, "Cain," 74.

77. Here I am alluding to Nicholas Christopher's account of film noir, *Somewhere in the Night: Noir and the American City* (New York: Simon and Schuster, 1997), specifically the book's first chapter, "Into the Labyrinth."

78. Smith, *Trainspotting*, 89–90n18.

79. These are precisely the themes of Robert Lepage's 1995 film *Le confessionnal*. The film takes place in Quebec City at two different points in time and switches back and forth, sometimes fluidly, sometimes with unexpected cuts. The first is the period following the Quiet Revolution, roughly 1988 or 1989. Here we find Pierre (Lothaire Bluteau) returning from Japan, where he was an art student, to Quebec City to search for his estranged half-brother, Marc. The second setting is Quebec City of the Duplessis era—specifically, the few weeks in 1953 when Alfred Hitchcock was in town shooting *I Confess*. The film opens with the Quebec City premiere, which Hitchcock (Ron Burrage) attends.

Chapter 5

1. Schantz, *Gossip, Letters, Phones*, 80.

2. Robert Heinlein, *Time for the Stars* (New York: Tor Books, 2010), 22–23.

3. It should be noted that the term *telepathy*, first defined by the Society for Psychical Research (SPR) in a meeting in London in December 1882, was meant to cover a wide variety of unexplained phenomena, not simply mind-to-mind communication. Roger Luckhurst writes that "the SPR collated strange mesmeric effects, Spiritualist mediumship, apparitions and ghostly manifestations, Crooke's 'psychic force,' and Cox's psychism, and reconceived them through its principal organizing term: telepathy." *The Invention of Telepathy* (New York: Oxford University Press, 2002), 59. See, too, Nicholas Royle, *Telepathy and Literature: Essays on the Reading Mind* (Cambridge, Mass.: Blackwell, 1991), 6.

4. One could include Mr. Memory from *The 39 Steps*, but having a head full of information is not supernatural. He is no fortune-teller, no mind reader, just a vessel of facts. Of the men in Hitchcock's films, Bruno Antony (Robert Walker) from *Strangers on a Train* (1951) is a potential candidate for a genuine telepath. During the scene in Bruno's private train compartment, early in the film, Bruno shows off his mind-reading skills. Referring to his father, Bruno asks Guy, "Now what do think of a character like that?" Guy begins to respond, "Well I think, possibly . . ." But Bruno cuts him off and says, "Yes, I hate him too." And, as Ned Schantz has reminded me in one of our many conversations about telepathy in Hitchcock, there is Chief Inspector Hubbard, who, in the closing moments of *Dial M for Murder* (1954), reads the mind

of Tony (Ray Milland). As he watches Tony through the window, he gives us a play-by-play: "He's trying to remember when he put the key back in there. Now he's given up. I'm afraid we've had it this time. He's going way down the street. Hold it. He's stopped again. He's turning round. He's staring at the key. Of course, that's Swann's key, isn't it? Now he's got it! He's coming back fast. He's remembered."

5. Schantz, *Gossip, Letters, Phones*, 3.

6. Schantz, *Gossip, Letters, Phones*, 7.

7. This is how Jerrold E. Hogle describes the literary genre, as playing with and oscillating between "the earthly laws of conventional reality and the possibilities of the supernatural. "Introduction: The Gothic in Western Culture," in *The Cambridge Companion to Gothic Fiction*, ed. Jerrold E. Hogle (Cambridge, Mass.: Cambridge University Press, 2002), 2.

8. Tania Modleski, *The Women Who Knew Too Much: Hitchcock and Feminist Theory*, 3rd ed. (New York, N.Y.: Routledge, 2015), 98.

9. Modleski, *The Women Who Knew Too Much*, 25.

10. Schantz, *Gossip, Letters, Phones*, 91.

11. Schantz, *Gossip, Letters, Phones*, 94.

12. Schantz, *Gossip, Letters, Phones*, 95.

13. Schantz, *Gossip, Letters, Phones*, 95.

14. I wish to be clear that I do not disagree with Schantz's reading of *Shadow of a Doubt*. Indeed, I think it is perhaps the finest piece of scholarship on this film. To be perfectly honest, I wish to hijack it—to use it as a rocket booster, if you will, into the farther reaches of what might be called "film future."

15. Think of Mrs. Henderson's confusing the word *telepathy* with *telegraphy*. Her response to Charlie's question, "Do you believe in telepathy?" is, "Well I ought to, it's my business!" For a fuller discussion of the relationship between the invention of the telephone and the occult, see Luckhurst, *The Invention of Telepathy*, esp. 135. See also Royle, *Telepathy and Literature*, esp. 5.

16. "There is, then, every reason to think that [Ann's] reading has prepared her well. Indeed *Dracula* is the other novel we know Anne [*sic*] has read, and when held up with *Ivanhoe* it captures the great ambivalence generated by Uncle Charlie as an outsider. Anne knows better than to assume every man of mystery is Richard the Lionhearted, returning to save the country, and not a vampire." Schantz, *Gossip, Letters, Phones*, 88.

17. James McLaughlin, "All in the Family: Alfred Hitchcock's *Shadow of a Doubt*," in Deutelbaum and Poague, *A Hitchcock Reader*,, 147.

18. Bram Stoker, *Dracula* (New York: Oxford University Press, 2011), 206.

19. Stoker, *Dracula*, 37.

20. Jim Collins, *Uncommon Cultures: Popular Culture and Post-Modernism* (New York: Routledge, 1989), 88.

21. Uncle Charlie seems at his most confident when around other men. In the opening Philadelphia sequence (or is it Jersey City?), when Mrs. Martin tells Uncle Charlie that two *men* have asked about him, he boldly says, "I'll have to meet them. I may even go out and meet them." Moments later, after he deliberately walks past the two detectives and then eludes them, we hear his voice-over: "What do you know? You're bluffing, you've nothing on me." Of course, Uncle Charlie is no fool. While he may not fear the two detectives, it makes better sense to hide in Santa Rosa, California, than in plain sight.

22. Thus it is possible to reverse the inscription to read, more accurately, as "T.S. to B.M." (i.e., from Thelma Schenley to Mrs. Bruce Matthewson). See Michie's marvelous essay, "Unveiling Maternal Desires."

23. Patrick Crogan, "Between Heads: Thoughts on the Merry Widow Tune in *Shadow of a Doubt*," *Senses of Cinema*, no. 6. (May 2000), http://sensesofcinema.com/2000/conference-for-the-love-of-fear/heads/.

24. Schantz, *Gossip, Letters, Phones*, 94.

25. Schantz, *Gossip, Letters, Phones*, 95.

26. Without the "strategic support of a female network," argues Schantz, "Charlie will continue to bear the work of reading—and the pain of knowing—alone." *Gossip, Letters, Phones*, 88.

27. Stanley Cavell, *Contesting Tears: The Melodrama of the Unknown Woman* (Chicago: University of Chicago Press, 1997), 6.

28. Cavell, *Contesting Tears*, 14.

29. Cavell, *Contesting Tears*, 6.

30. She has also made her feelings about marriage known to her uncle, and possibly to a boy named Bill Forest, who, we learn, is asking about Charlie.

31. Tania Modleski notes that Patricia Collinge, who plays Emma, rewrote the proposal scene in the garage so that Charlie does not agree to marriage. Modleski writes, "Given the discontent she has expressed regarding family life, and in particular her disapproval of her hard working mother's subordinate role in the family at the beginning of the film, and given the appalling reprisal (in the person of Uncle Charlie) that this discontent elicits, it certainly seems fitting that she would not want to rush into marriage." "Suspicion: Collusion and Resistance in the Work of Hitchcock's Female Collaborators," in Leitch and Poague, *A Companion to Alfred Hitchcock*, 176.

32. Cavell, *Contesting Tears*, 172.

33. Cavell, *Contesting Tears*, 37.

34. Cavell, *Contesting Tears*, 7.

35. I owe the phrase "mental jump cut" to Ned Schantz, who used the phrase in one of our email correspondences. And it is a description that bears an uncanny resemblance to Nicholas Royle's in his book *Telepathy and Literature*, where he defines telepathy, among various other ways, as "the site of a certain fold, of a cutting or interruption" (7).

36. Modleski, *The Women Who Knew Too Much*, 12.

37. "In some ways the historical appearance of 'telepathy' could be viewed as the inevitable outcome, or hyperbolization, of the importance accorded to 'sympathy' in Romanticism. In the later nineteenth century there is a kind of sliding, whereby the term 'telepathy' comes to stand in for what a few years earlier had been designated as 'sympathetic clairvoyance.' " Royle, *Telepathy and Literature*, 4–5.

38. J. Hillis Miller, "Hardy," in *The J. Hillis Miller Reader*, ed. Julian Wolfreys (Stanford, Calif.: Stanford University Press, 2005), 154.

39. Luckhurst, *The Invention of Telepathy*, 135.

40. Royle, *Telepathy and Literature*, 5.

41. Byron Williams, "Holding the Line," *Telephony: The American Telephone Journal* 60, no. 21 (1911), 645. This echoes the language used by the SPR in their official definition of *telesthesia* and *telepathy*, words meant "to cover all cases of

impression received at a distance without the normal operation of the recognized sense organs." Qtd. in Royle, *Telepathy and Literature*, 2.

42. Williams, "Holding the Line."

43. Williams, "Holding the Line."

44. Unlike Charlie, however, Marnie does not have the privilege of refusing a marriage proposal.

45. Winston Graham, *Marnie* (London: Pan Books, 2013), 194.

46. Several critics have made this claim, although I have yet to find any definitive proof. See Maria del Carmen Garrido Hornos, "Hitchcock and the Hollywood Production Code: Censorship and Critical Acceptance in the 1960s," in *Peeping through the Holes: Twenty First Century Essays on* Psycho, ed. Eugenio M. Olivares-Merino and Julio A. Olivares-Merino (Newcastle on Tyne: Cambridge Scholars Publishing, 2013), 16.

47. Michele Piso, "Mark's Marnie," in Deutelbaum and Poague, *A Hitchcock Reader*, 284.

48. Piso, "Mark's Marnie," 284.

49. Graham, *Marnie*, 333.

50. This is the first of two fades-to-black that bookend the following scene, of Mark in his office speaking with Mr. Boyle. The second fade-to-black is only slightly shorter than the first, and it closes a point-of-view shot of the closed door that connects Mark's office with Marnie's bedroom. At the end of his conversation with Mr. Boyle, Mark, seated at a desk, turns his head to the right as the camera pans up. We hear a muffled sound, a door closing, coming from Marnie's bedroom, and we can presume she is inside. The camera holds just long enough for us to see hanging on Mark's office wall, just to the right of the door that connects to Marnie's bedroom, a Vermeer painting. It is "The Music Lesson" (ca. 1662–64). There is increasing scholarly interest in Hitchcock's use of real art, and with this instance it is easy to understand why. "The Music Lesson" depicts a young girl standing before a keyboard instrument, looking straight ahead, while her teacher, an older man, stands to her right. Above the girl is a mirror, and in it we see her reflection. The reflection, however, has the girl turning her head slightly to her right, toward her teacher, suggesting a kind of doubling, or a hidden sexual desire (or any number of things). Of more interest is the keyboard instrument, known as a virginal, so named because it was played mostly by young girls. It is noted in the blog "Essential Vermeer" that the exterior of the lid of a typical Flemish virginal was plain. When closed, the virginal resembled "an elongated linen closet." When opened, however, the virginal revealed, on the underside of the lid and around the keyboard itself, "decorative block papers," arabesques, and other colorful ornamentation.

51. Schantz, *Gossip, Letters, Phones*, 56–57.

52. Schantz, *Gossip, Letters, Phones*, 58.

53. Of course, anyone who wants to listen to Marnie's thoughts can read Winston Graham's novel, which is written in the first person.

54. Piso, "Mark's Marnie," 291.

55. "Mark is a complex man, dark and forbidding. He can also be kind and considerate. And he is also a troubled man. Troubled because he cannot seem to unravel the mystery of the girl called Marnie."

56. It's not that I haven't felt, at times, during my repeated viewings of this film, that Marnie *might* have positive feelings for Mark. Yet the film seems to go out of its way to thwart efforts on the part of the viewer to secure any conclusive evidence of this. Take, for example, the scene in which Mark and Marnie are driving from the Red Fox Tavern back to Wyckwyn Manor. At one point, Marnie explains to Mark why she stole the $10,000 from Mr. Strutt. "I don't know why. I just kind of went crazy, I guess, but . . . old Mr. Strutt was so . . . I hated him!" To which Mark asks, "Like you hate me?" Marnie pauses briefly, turns to Mark, and says, "Oh no, not you." And while I hear in her response the possibility that Marnie is telling Mark she does not hate him (which is a far cry from a confession of love), her syntax conflates this possibility with two others: "Oh no, not [like I hate] you" and "Oh no, not [as much as I hate] you." Even if one concedes that Marnie is saying she likes Mark, one must remember that at this moment the car is full of her lies. Who is to say this isn't another?

57. See Piso, "Mark's Marnie," 280–94; Paul Gordon, *Dial "M" for Mother: A Freudian Hitchcock* (Teaneck, N.J.: Fairleigh Dickinson University, 2008); Elisabeth Bronfen, *The Knotted Subject: Hysteria and Its Discontents* (Princeton, N.J.: Princeton University Press, 1998); and Florence Jacobowitz, "Hitchcock and Feminist Criticism: From *Rebecca* to *Marnie*," in Deutelbaum and Poague, *A Hitchcock Reader*, 452–73. There is every reason to see Marnie's love for Forio in psychoanalytic terms, and it is not my purpose here to discredit such an approach.

58. Piso, "Mark's Marnie," 281.

59. Of course, anyone who writes about *Rebecca*, *Vertigo*, *Psycho*, or any number of Hitchcock's gothic thrillers, inevitably touches on aspects of the occult, if only implicitly. But Jean Douchet is the only critic I know of who has made explicit the connection between Hitchcock and the occult: "If I believe that the occult is at the basis of Hitchcock's universe, it is not that I am impassioned with the esoteric nor even that I think that it is fundamental for the director. But, simply, it is a way of understanding which permits the artist's imagination the greatest possibilities of revery." "Hitch and His Public," in *A Hitchcock Reader*, 24.

60. Graham, *Marnie*, 109.

61. It is curious that Mark, who professes (and demonstrates) a love for and a scholarly knowledge of zoology, should dislike horses. Indeed, this curiosity is not unlikely the reason that the line of dialogue was cut—and with it, Marnie's words about reading horses' minds. And while Mark's father has a real fondness for horses, his fondness in no way matches Marnie's—in depth or in occultishness. Rutland Sr. says, borrowing from Will Rogers, "The best thing in the world for the inside of a man or a woman is the outside of a horse." Marnie, of course, would never exclude the importance of the "inside" of a horse.

62. Alfred Hitchcock, "Transcript of discussions between Ms. Hedren and Alfred Hitchcock regarding the character of Marnie," Box 40f.—458, Taped 10/23/1963, page 1, tape 4.

63. This is the first of two occasions in which Marnie's syntax conflates two possible meanings. Her actual words are, "I've been watching him ever since I saw him work out as a two-year-old." The slippage here is from the horse being the two-year-old to Marnie being the two-year-old. The former, we assume, is the only logical reading. As a two-year-old, Marnie could not have watched Telepathy

work out, as the horse would not have yet been born. The latter reading, then, can take on only an occult meaning and, further, can withstand any challenge by logic. The second moment comes when Marnie is on the telephone with her mother. As Kelly Oliver has noted, Marnie is "explaining her absence by telling her that she had the flu and couldn't visit or call, saying, 'I'm still a little hoarse,' a homophone of 'I'm still a little horse' " ("Alfred Hitchcock: Fowl Play and the Domestication of Horror," in *Cinematic Thinking: Philosophical Approaches to the New Cinema*, ed. James Phillips [Stanford, Calif: Stanford University Press, 2008], 24). Murray Pomerance picks up on this second moment as well (*Marnie* [New York: Palgrave MacMillan, 2014], 45). In these two instances of syntactical indeterminacy, we experience confusion as to who is little and who is a horse.

64. Marnie imagines herself a horse whisperer. And her desire for physical intimacy with horses is one of the stranger aspects of this film ("Forio, if you want to bite somebody, bite me," she bubbles). It is people, and people only, that repulse Marnie. And although it appears she desires physical intimacy with her mother, Bernice (Louise Latham), Marnie is unable to reach for, and herself give, anything but counterfeit affection. When the stole (an apt gift from a kleptomaniac!) fails to buy Marnie some affection from her mother, she steals a hug. It is an awkward gesture—impulsive, selfish, not at all genuine or generous.

65. George Toles, " 'If Thine Eye Offend Thee . . .': *Psycho* and the Art of Infection," in *A House Made of Light: Essays on the Art of Film* (Detroit, Mich.: Wayne State University Press, 2001), 138.

66. One might argue that the stranger has not zeroed in on Marnie, that their encounter is a coincidence, not stalking. But chance encounters do not typically unfold like this in film. The scene opens with Marnie already in the stranger's sights, which is more suggestive of deliberation than of chance.

67. Lisa Zunshine, *Getting inside Your Head: What Cognitive Science Can Tell Us about Popular Culture* (Baltimore, Md.: Johns Hopkins University Press, 2012), 63.

68. Zunshine, *Getting inside Your Head*, 5.

69. Zunshine, *Getting inside Your Head*, 72.

70. The phrase comes from the 1883 novel of the same name by Charlotte Eliza L. Riddell. In it, a middle-aged clerk by the name of Reuben Cheverley inherits a fortune from his uncle. He meets a writer named John Smith, who warns Cheverley to be careful with his money and not give it to a charismatic lecturer, Thomas William Allan, with whom Cheverley works at the Home and Foreign Insurance Company. Cheverley assures the writer that he plans to use the money to buy a place in the country. Smith responds, "You will like that, I am sure. . . . Among the daisies and buttercups all the women are virtuous, and all the men honest." *Daisies and Buttercups: A Novel of the Upper Thames* (London: Sampson Low, Martson, Searle & Livingston, 1883), 40. The phrase sticks in Cheverley's head:

> For still the vision of daisies and buttercups was perpetually recurring to me. Moreover, the phrase, as thus rendered by Mr. John Smith, stuck to my memory, for the simple reason, I suppose, that it reversed the reading of my boyhood. "Buttercups and daisies"—that was it. I had not heard the three words joined together for over forty years, until he said, "daisies and buttercups."

> Well-a-day, there is to some minds a delight in daisies and buttercups unintelligible to the comprehension even of those who dwell amongst them! (41)

The reading from Cheverley's boyhood is no doubt Mary Botham Howitt's children's poem, "Buttercups and Daisies," published in the 1839 collection *Birds and Flowers, and Other Country Things* (Boston: Weeks, Jordan, 1839). The poem is an ode to childhood innocence, and its last stanza reads, "Welcome, yellow Buttercups, / Welcome, Daisies white, / Ye are in my spirit/Visioned, a delight! / Coming ere the spring-time / Of sunny hours to tell— / Speaking to our hearts of Him / Who doeth *all things well*" (120). That the writer Smith reverses the reading is hardly remarkable. What is remarkable is that this reversal is what sticks in Cheverley's head, and what his story takes as its title. In the same way, Alicia misreads the child's poem (or, if she's aware of the Riddell novel, reads correctly Cleverley's willing misreading of Smith), and her misreading is repeated by Devlin.

71. Mark Raymond Strauss, *Hitchcock's Objects as Subjects: The Significance of Things on Screen* (Jefferson, N.C.: McFarland, 2016), 117.

72. Interestingly, the problem of determining whether a woman falls or is thrown haunts the Hitchcock landscape, most importantly in *Vertigo* (1958). For an interesting discussion of this problem, see Sianne Ngai's chapter, "Anxiety," in *Ugly Feelings* (Cambridge, Mass: Harvard University Press, 2005), 209–47.

73. Modleski, *The Women Who Knew Too Much*, 62–63.

74. See Modleski's reading of *Notorious* in *The Women Who Knew Too Much*, esp. 66–68.

75. It is unusual for an actor's eyes to dart around in this way—or at any rate, busy eyes are considered to be bad form. Michael Caine recounts a story in which he met Marlene Dietrich at a Hollywood party and was told by the legendary actress that he should not move his eyes around so much. "She said she had seen me in a film of mine and my eyes were going all over the place. She told me to pick out something behind the actor you're looking at and just stare at it" (qtd. in Dylan Jones, "2007: Michael Caine," *GQ*, March 29, 2012, https://www.gq-magazine.co.uk/article/michael-caine-2007-lifetime-achievement.

76. Luckhurst, *The Invention of Telepathy*.

77. This is the first of four essays Freud wrote on the subject of telepathy. It was followed by "Dreams and Telepathy" (1922), "The Occult Significance of Dreams" (1925), and "Dreams and Occultism" (1933).

78. Sigmund Freud, "Psycho-Analysis and Telepathy," in *The Standard Edition of the Complete Psychological Works of Sigmund Freud*, ed. and trans. James Strachey, vol. 18 (London: Hogarth, 1955), 177.

79. Freud, "Psycho-Analysis and Telepathy," 177.

80. Ernest Jones, *The Life and Work of Sigmund Freud*, vol. 3 (New York: Basic Books, 1953), 405. The first case involved a young man who came to Freud to be analyzed. His complaint was that of "having forgotten his past life and having lost all interest" (Freud, "Psycho-Analysis and Telepathy," 181). After some time, the young man told Freud of his intense love for his sister, who had married a young engineer of whom their parents disapproved. Although the brother managed to reassure their parents of the engineer's character and, in doing so,

enabled the marriage to take place, he nevertheless harbored deep-rooted feelings of jealousy for his future brother-in-law. Several months passed before the young man returned to Freud again, this time with an exciting story: a fortune-teller had predicted his brother-in-law's death, that summer, of crayfish or oyster poisoning. Since it was now October, and the brother-in-law was very much alive, Freud asked the young man why the fortune-teller's prophecy excited him so. As it happened, the young man told Freud, his brother-in-law *did* nearly die of crayfish poisoning the summer *prior*. The second case also involved a prediction that did not come true: it concerned a woman with depression and obsessional neurosis brought on by her failed marriage. From childhood, the woman expressed an intense desire to have children. Her husband, however, had discovered that due to an illness he was unable to father children. After several years in a mental institution, the woman, now forty, returned to Freud for further analysis. She then told Freud a story of her encounter with a famous fortune-teller, Monsieur le Professeur. While traveling with her husband on business, she spotted le Professeur in the lobby of their hotel. She approached him, and taking her hand, the fortune-teller told the woman, who was then twenty-seven, that she would have two children by the time she was thirty-two. As in the first case, Freud pressed the woman as to why the prediction, which had not come true (the woman was still childless), should have aroused in her such powerful feelings. The woman told Freud that her mother had two children when she was thirty-two.

81. Freud, "Psycho-Analysis and Telepathy," 188–89.

82. Freud, "Psycho-Analysis and Telepathy," 189.

83. Freud, "Psycho-Analysis and Telepathy," 193.

84. Jones, *The Life and Work of Sigmund Freud*, 406.

85. This is Totton's attitude toward Freud's writings on telepathy. He calls "Dreams and Telepathy" "one of Freud's most clearly hysterical works, in two senses: it communicates an excitement indistinguishable from anxiety, and it systematically subverts its own authority and the authority of others." Nicholas Totton. *Psychoanalysis and the Paranormal* (New York: Karnac Books, 2003), 195. Totton trances Freud's hysteria back to what he elsewhere calls "the intrinsic relationship between telepathy and psychoanalysis" (196). Both the therapist and the telepath seek "transparency between subjects" (192).

86. Freud, "Psycho-Analysis and Telepathy," 193.

87. Totton, *Psychoanalysis and the Paranormal*, 198.

88. Totton, *Psychoanalysis and the Paranormal*, 198.

89. Elaine Showalter, "Hysteria, Feminism, and Gender," in *Hysteria beyond Freud*, ed. Sander L. Gilman et al. (Berkeley: University of California Press, 1993), 286.

90. Sigmund Freud, "Fragment of an Analysis of a Case of Hysteria (Dora)," in *The Standard Edition of the Complete Psychological Works of Sigmund Freud*, ed. James Strachey, vol. 7 (New York, Hogarth, 1953), 109.

91. Hélène Cixous, "The Laugh of the Medusa," *Signs* 1, no. 4 (Summer 1976), 886.

92. See Showalter, "Hysteria, Feminism, and Gender," esp. 316–19, 331–33.

93. Showalter, "Hysteria, Feminism, and Gender," 333.

94. Schantz, *Gossip, Letters, Phones*, 81

95. Then again, why not interpret Norman's voice-over as similarly telepathic? That is, what if the unconventional use of the "voices over" in Marion's drive from Arizona to California prepares us for the final scene in Norman's cell? A spoken "thank you" is followed by a voice-over, beginning with the line, "It's sad when a mother has to speak the words that condemn her own son." But who is speaking? Must we submit to "face value," so to speak? That this is Norman's face we see, and therefore his voice we hear?

96. Joseph Stefano, *Psycho* (screenplay, December 1, 1959), https://the.hitchcock.zone/files/scripts/Psycho.pdf.

97. Rothman, *Hitchcock*, 273.

98. Sigmund Freud, "Dreams and Occultism," in *The Standard Edition of the Complete Psychological Works of Sigmund Freud*, ed. James Strachey, vol. 12 (New York: Hogarth, 1958), 39.

99. Freud, "Dreams and Occultism," 36.

100. *Milwaukee Sentinel*, June 5, 1957, section 2, page 8.

101. "Installation Series 700 Teletalk. Bulletin M7D1," Webster Electric, Racine, Wisconsin, 1957.

102. Rothman, *Hitchcock*, 282.

103. Rothman, *Hitchcock*, 293.

104. Freud, *The Standard Edition of the Complete Psychological Works of Sigmund Freud*, vol. 18, ed. James Strachey (New York: Hogarth, 1955), 218.

105. Laura Mulvey, *Death 24x a Second: Stillness and the Moving Image* (London: Reaktion Books, 2006), 92.

106. Hitchcock died on April 29, 1980, almost exactly four years after the release of *Family Plot*, his final film.

107. It is tempting to link *Family Plot*'s heroine with Blanche Wittmann, a well-known patient of Charcot's at the Salpêtrière, where many female patients diagnosed with acute hysteria were treated. Blanche, who arrived at the Salpêtrière in 1877, was thought to have occult powers (or to have feigned having them). Asti Hustvedt writes that at Salpêtrière, "experiments in telepathy, clairvoyance, and what was called '*sommeil à distance*,' or 'telepathic communication,' were conducted to demonstrate the veracity of these 'occult' phenomena. Once again Blanche proved incredibly gifted. . . . However, as the always-suspicious doctors realized, the possibilities of being hoodwinked in these particular instances were great." *Medical Medusas: Hysteria in Nineteenth-Century Paris* (New York: W. W. Norton, 2011), 117.

108. Qtd. in Michael Wood, "Fearful Cemetery," in Freedman and Millington, *Hitchcock's America*, 175.

109. Qtd. in Truffaut, *Hitchcock*, 185.

110. Murray Pomerance, *Alfred Hitchcock's America* (Malden, Mass.: Polity, 2013), 279.

111. Rothman, *Hitchcock*, 354.

112. Rothman, *Hitchcock*, 355. Leland Poague sees Blanche "as Hitchcock's homage to his wife," citing the resemblance between Barbara Harris and Alma Hitchcock. While it is worth applauding his gesture of giving credit (at long last) where credit is due (Alma was Hitchcock's "most loyal of collaborators"), it is a little disappointing that Poague, like Rothman, steals the female's wink and gives it to Hitchcock himself: "Blanche's closing wink to the camera [is] Hitchcock's

valedictory acknowledgment of his audience and of the artfulness of the bond that his camera establishes between his stories and his viewers" ("'Tell Me the Story So Far': Hitchcock and His Writers," in Leitch and Poague, *A Companion to Alfred Hitchcock*, 158). One could argue that the publicity for *Family Plot* contributes greatly to this need to give ownership of Blanche's wink over to Hitchcock. In several variations on the film's poster, we see in Blanche's crystal ball Hitchcock's head, and he is winking at us (with the same eye Blanche uses, the right). For both Poague and Rothman, it seems, Hitchcock is Blanche's "Henry," to whom Blanche asks, "What's the trouble?"—a subtle reference to *The Trouble with Harry* (1955). It is also worth noting that Blanche channels Julia Rainbird's dead sister, Harriet, the feminine equivalent of Harry.

113. Kidding aside, there is within the field of psychical research a considerable amount of literature on nonsentient psychic vibrations.

114. Pomerance, *Alfred Hitchcock's America*, 274.

115. Pomerance lists several self-referential moments in *Family Plot* (to *Marnie*, to the remake of *The Man Who Knew Too Much*, and to *North by Northwest*), but he neglects to mention this reference to *Vertigo*. Once given the prompt by Pomerance, a viewer hopes there may be dozens of other references awaiting detection. A few come to my eye: the address of Blanche's house where she conducts her occult business is number 17, the title of Hitchcock's film from 1932. Even more curious is that the actual address of Blanche's house is 4254 Lexington Avenue in Los Angeles, adjacent to a small street that is marked as 10 W in the film but is actually Bates Avenue. In *Psycho*, the freeway Marion takes only as far as the Bates Motel is the 10 W.

116. Pomerance, *Alfred Hitchcock's America*, 278.

117. This is how Geoffrey Beattie describes the wink in *Visible Thought: The New Psychology of Body Language* (New York: Routledge, 2004), 14.

118. Lesley Brill, "A Brief Anatomy of *Family Plot*," in Palmer and Boyd, *Hitchcock at the Source*, 299.

119. Brill, "A Brief Anatomy of *Family Plot*," 299.

Afterword

1. Latour, *Reassembling the Social*, 172. While *Dial M for Murder* was shot using the 3-D process, Hitchcock never thought of the format as anything more than a fad. Of Hitchcock's attitude toward 3-D and other gimmicks, Sid Gottlieb neatly puts it: "Hitchcock calmly keeps such devices in their proper place. . . . The essence of film remains what it has always been—cutting, character, and story." "Introduction," 211.

2. Pomerance, *An Eye for Hitchcock*, 187.

3. Consider these lines from a review of Steven Jacobs's *The Wrong House: The Architecture of Alfred Hitchcock*: "Who hasn't wanted to investigate the rest of that midtown Manhattan penthouse, the west wing of that castle beneath the fog, or (admit it) the underbelly of that creepy motel and mansion just off the highway?" Greg Chan, "Location, Location, Location: Behind Alfred Hitchcock's Fascination with Domestic Real Estate and Cinematic Architecture," review of *The Wrong House: The Architecture of Alfred Hitchcock* by Steven Jacobs, *Interdisciplinary Humanities* 32, no. 1 (2015): 120.

4. Anyone can do a *Rear Window* time lapse. All one needs to do is fast-forward through a media file or a BluRay disc. What is far more difficult is creating the panorama, as Dessom does.

5. Latour, *Reassembling the Social*, 187.

6. Latour, *Reassembling the Social*, 189.

7. *The Alfred Hitchcock Wiki* is part of an even larger collection of Hitchcock-related sites and blogs, known as the Hitchcock Zone.

8. "1000 Frames of Hitchcock," the Hitchcock Zone, www.the.hitchcock.zone/wiki/1000_Frames_of_Hitchcock (accessed September 18, 2017).

9. Christine Sprengler, *Hitchcock and Contemporary Art* (New York: Palgrave Macmillan, 2014), 59.

10. Marc Raymond Strauss, *Hitchcock's Objects as Subjects: The Significance of Things on Screen* (Jefferson, N.C.: McFarland, 2016), 5.

11. Qtd. in Peter Bogdanovich, *The Cinema of Alfred Hitchcock* (New York: Museum of Modern Art Film Library, 1963), 4.

12. Casey McKittrick, *Hitchcock's Appetites: The Corpulent Plots of Desire and Dread* (New York: Bloomsbury, 2016), 4.

13. Miller, *Hidden Hitchcock*, 24; Tom Cohen, *Hitchcock's Cryptonomies*, 244; Robert A. Harris and Michael S. Lasky, *The Complete Films of Alfred Hitchcock* (New York: Citadel Press, 2002), 16.

BIBLIOGRAPHY

Abramson, Leslie. *Hitchcock and the Anxiety of Authorship*. New York: Palgrave Macmillan, 2015.

Allen, Richard. "Daphne du Maurier and Alfred Hitchcock." In *A Companion to Literature and Film*, edited by Robert Stam and Alessandro Raengo, 298–325. Malden, Mass.: Blackwell, 2004.

Allen, Richard, and S. Ishii Gonzalès, eds.. *Alfred Hitchcock: Centenary Essays*. London: BFI, 1999.

Barthes, Roland. "Myth Today." In *A Barthes Reader*, edited by Susan Sontag, 93–149. New York: Hill and Wang, 1982.

Baudelaire, Charles. *The Flowers of Evil and Paris Spleen*. Rochester, N.Y.: BOA Editions, 1991.

Bazin, André. *The Cinema of Cruelty, from Buñuel to Hitchcock*. Edited by François Truffaut, translated by Sabine d'Estrée and Tiffany Fliss. New York: Arcade, 1982.

Beattie, Geoffrey. *Visible Thought: The New Psychology of Body Language*. New York: Routledge, 2004.

Belton, Robert J. *Alfred Hitchcock's* Vertigo *and the Hermeneutic Spiral*. Cham, Switzerland: Springer, 2017.

Blair, Sara. "Hitchcock on Location: America, Icons, and the Place of Illusion." In Freedman, *The Cambridge Companion to Alfred Hitchcock*, 57–75.

Bogdanovich, Peter. *The Cinema of Alfred Hitchcock*. New York: Museum of Modern Art Film Library, 1963.

Brill, Lesley. "A Brief Anatomy of *Family Plot*." In Palmer and Boyd, *Hitchcock at the Source*, 295–308.

Brill, Lesley. *Crowds, Power, and Transformation in the Cinema*. Detroit, Mich.: Wayne State University Press, 2006.

Brinkema, Eugenie. *The Forms of the Affects*. Durham, N.C.: Duke University Press, 2014.

Bronfen, Elisabeth. *The Knotted Subject: Hysteria and Its Discontents*. Princeton, N.J.: Princeton University Press, 1998.

Bruns, Gerald. "Cain, or The Metaphorical Construction of Cities." *Salmagundi* 74/75 (1987): 70–85.

Bruns, John. "The Map Is Not the Country: Cartography in Joel and Ethan Coen's *No Country for Old Men*." *Film Criticism* 36, no. 2 (Winter 2001): 2–21

Canetti, Elias. *Crowds and Power*. New York: Farrar, Straus and Giroux, 1960.

Cavell, Stanley. *Contesting Tears: The Melodrama of the Unknown Woman*. Chicago: University of Chicago Press, 1997.

———. "*North by Northwest*." In Deutelbaum and Poague, *A Hitchcock Reader*, 250–63.

Chan, Greg. "Location, Location, Location: Behind Alfred Hitchcock's Fascination with Domestic Real Estate and Cinematic Architecture." Review of *The Wrong House: The Architecture of Alfred Hitchcock* by Steven Jacobs. *Interdisciplinary Humanities* 32, no. 1 (2015): 120.

Christopher, Nicholas. *Somewhere in the Night: Noir and the American City*. New York: Simon & Schuster, 1997.

Cixous, Hélène. "The Laugh of the Medusa." *Signs* 1, no. 4 (Summer 1976), 875–93.

Cohen, Paula Marantz. *Alfred Hitchcock: The Legacy of Victorianism*. Lexington: University of Kentucky Press, 1995.

Cohen, Tom. *Hitchcock's Cryptonomies*. Vol. 1, *Secret Agents*. Minneapolis: University of Minnesota Press, 2005.

Collins, Jim. *Uncommon Cultures: Popular Culture and Post-Modernism*. New York: Routledge, 1989.

Conley, Tom. *Cartographic Cinema*. Minneapolis: University of Minnesota Press, 2007.

———. "Locations of Film Noir." *Cartographic Journal* 46, no. 1 (2009): 16–23.

Corber, Robert J. "Hitchcock's Washington: Spectatorship, Ideology, and the 'Homosexual Menace' in *Strangers on a Train*." In Freedman and Millington, *Hitchcock's America*, 99–122.

———. *In the Name of National Security: Hitchcock, Homophobia, and the Political Construction of Gender in Postwar America*. Durham, N.C.: Duke University Press, 1993.

Crary, Jonathan. *Suspensions of Perception: Attention, Spectacle, and Modern Culture*. Cambridge, Mass.: MIT Press, 1999.

Crogan, Patrick. "Between Heads: Thoughts on the Merry Widow Tune in *Shadow of a Doubt*." *Senses of Cinema*, no. 6 (May 2000).

Cunningham, Douglas, ed. *The San Francisco of Alfred Hitchcock's Vertigo: Place, Pilgrimage, and Commemoration*. Lanham, Md.: Scarecrow Press, 2012.

Curtain, Tyler. "Toward a Cultural Critical Field Book." *Novel: A Forum on Fiction* 44, no. 1 (2011): 149–52.

Dawson, William Leon, and John Hooper Bowles. *The Birds of Washington: A Complete Scientific and Popular Account of the 372 Species of Birds Found in the State*. Vol. 1. Seattle, Wash.: Occidental, 1909.

de Certeau, Michel. *The Practice of Everyday Life*. Vol. 1. Berkeley: University of California Press, 1984.

Denby, David. "Dream On: *Hairspray* and *Ratatouille*." *New Yorker*, July 23, 2007.

Denkin, David. *City Reading: Written Words and Public Spaces in Antebellum New York*. New York: Columbia University Press, 1998.

Deleuze, Gilles. *Cinema I: The Movement-Image*. Translated by Hugh Tomlinson and Barbara Habberjam. New York: Continuum, 1986.

Deutelbaum, Marshall, and Leland Poague, eds. *A Hitchcock Reader*. 2nd ed. Malden, Mass.: Wiley-Blackwell, 2011.

Douchet, Jean. "Hitch and His Public." In Deutelbaum and Poague, *A Hitchcock Reader*.

du Maurier, Daphne. "The Birds." In *Don't Look Now*, compiled by Patrick McGrath, 59–100. New York: New York Review of Books, 2008.

Edelman, Lee. *No Future: Queer Theory and the Death Drive*. Durham, N.C.: Duke University Press, 2004.

Eidsvik, Charles. *Cineliteracy: Film among the Arts*. New York: Horizon Press, 1978.

Fabe, Marilyn. *Closely Watched Films: An Introduction to the Art of Narrative Film Technique*. Tenth Anniversary Edition. Berkeley: University of California Press, 2014.

Fisher, Philip. *Still the New World: American Literature in a Culture of Creative Destruction*. Cambridge, Mass.: Harvard University Press, 1999.

Flory, Dan. "*Vertigo*: Scientific Method, Obsession, and Human Minds." In *Hitchcock and Philosophy: Dial M for Metaphysics*, edited by David Baggett and William A. Drumin, 115–28. Chicago: Open Court, 2007.

Freedman, Jonathan, ed. *The Cambridge Companion to Alfred Hitchcock*. New York: Cambridge University Press, 2015.

Freedman, Jonathan, and Richard Millington, eds. *Hitchcock's America*. New York: Oxford University Press, 1999.

Freeman, David. *The Last Days of Alfred Hitchcock*. New York: Overlook Press, 1984.

Freud, Sigmund. *Beyond the Pleasure Principle, Group Psychology, and Other Works*. In *The Standard Edition of the Complete Psychological Works of Sigmund Freud*, translated and edited by James Strachey, vol. 18. London: Hogarth Press, 1955.

———. "Dreams and Occultism." In *The Standard Edition of the Complete Psychological Works of Sigmund Freud*, edited by James Strachey, vol. 12. New York, Hogarth, 1958.

———. "Fragment of an Analysis of a Case of Hysteria (Dora)." In *The Standard Edition of the Complete Psychological Works of Sigmund Freud*, edited by James Strachey, vol. 7. New York, Hogarth, 1953.

———. *New Introductory Lectures on Psychoanalysis and Other Works*. In *The Standard Edition of the Complete Psychological Works of Sigmund Freud*, translated and edited by James Strachey, vol. 22. London: Hogarth Press, 1955.

———. "Psycho-Analysis and Telepathy." In *The Standard Edition of the Complete Psychological Works of Sigmund Freud*, edited and translated by James Strachey, vol. 18. London: Hogarth, 1955.

Garrido Hornos, Maria del Carmen. "Hitchcock and the Hollywood Production Code: Censorship and Critical Acceptance in the 1960s." In *Peeping through the Holes: Twenty First Century Essays on* Psycho, edited by Eugenio M. Olivares-Merino and Julio A. Olivares-Merino, 1–24. Newcastle on Tyne: Cambridge Scholars Publishing, 2013.

Gilloch, Graeme. *Siegfried Kracauer: Our Companion in Misfortune*. Malden, Mass.: Polity, 2015.

Goebel, Catherine Carter, ed. *Origins of Modernity*. Rock Island, Ill.: Augustana College, 2005.

Goetz, Thomas. "Harnessing the Power of Feedback Loops." *Wired*, July 2011.

Gordon, Paul. *Dial "M" for Mother: A Freudian Hitchcock*. Teaneck, N.J.: Fairleigh Dickinson University, 2008.

Gottlieb, Sidney, ed. *Hitchcock on Hitchcock*. Vol. 2, *Selected Writings and Interviews*. Berkeley: University of California Press, 1995.

Gottlieb, Sidney. "Introduction: Hitchcock Speaks." In Gottlieb, *Hitchcock on Hitchcock*, 211–21.

Gottlieb, Sidney, and Christopher Brookhouse, eds. *Framing Hitchcock: Selected Essays from the Hitchcock Annual*. Detroit: Wayne State University Press, 2002.

Graham, Winston. *Marnie*. London: Pan Books, 2013.

Hark, Ina Rae. "'We Might Even Get in the Newsreels': The Press and Democracy in Hitchcock's World War II Anti-Fascist Films." In Allen and Ishii Gonzalès, *Alfred Hitchcock: Centenary Essays*, 333–47.

Harrington, Harry Franklin. *Typical Newspaper Stories*. Boston, Mass.: Ginn, 1915.

Harris, Robert A., and Michael S. Lasky. *The Complete Films of Alfred Hitchcock*. Rev. ed. New York: Citadel Press, 2002.

Hazen, Robert M., and Margaret Hindle Hazen. *Keepers of the Flame: The Role of Fire in American Culture, 1775–1925*. Princeton, N.J.: Princeton University Press, 1992.

Heinlein, Robert. *Time for the Stars*. New York: Tor Books, 2010.

Henkin, David M. *City Reading: Written Words and Public Spaces in Antebellum New York*. New York: Columbia University Press, 1998.

Hitchcock, Alfred. "After-Dinner Speech at the Screen Producers Guild Dinner." In Gottlieb, *Hitchcock on Hitchcock: Selected Writings and Interviews* 54–58.

———. "Close Your Eyes and Visualize!" In Gottlieb, *Hitchcock on Hitchcock*, 246–49.

———. "Film Production." In Gottlieb, *Hitchcock on Hitchcock*, 210–26.

———. "If I Were the Head of a Production Company." In Gottlieb, *Hitchcock on Hitchcock*, 172–75.

———. "The Murder of Monty Woolley." *Look*, June 15 1943.

———. Papers. Margaret Herrick Library, Academy of Motion Picture Arts and Sciences, Beverly Hills, California.

Hogle, Jerrold E. "Introduction: The Gothic in Western Culture." In *The Cambridge Companion to Gothic Fiction*, edited by Jerrold E. Hogle, 1–20. Cambridge, Mass.: Cambridge University Press, 2002.

Howitt, Mary. *Birds and Flowers, and Other Country Things*. London: Weeks, Jordan, 1839.

Hunt, Frederick Knight. *The Fourth Estate: Contributions towards a History of Newspapers, and of the Liberties of the Press*. Vol. 1. London: David Bogue, 1850.

Hustvedt, Asti. *Medical Muses: Hysteria in Nineteenth-Century Paris*. New York: W. W. Norton, 2011.

Jacobowitz, Florence. "Hitchcock and Feminist Criticism: From *Rebecca* to *Marnie*." In Deutelbaum and Poague, *A Hitchcock Reader*, 452–73.

Jones, Ernest. *The Life and Work of Sigmund Freud*. Vol. 3. New York: Basic Books, 1953.

Jones, Kent, dir. *Hitchcock/Truffaut*. 2015; Universal City, Calif: Universal Pictures Home Entertainment, 2016. DVD.

Kenner, Hugh. *The Mechanic Muse*. New York: Oxford University Press, 1987.

Kracauer, Siegfried. *Theory of Film: The Redemption of Physical Reality*. New York: Oxford University Press, 1960.

Lant, Antonia. "The Film Crowd." In *Moving Pictures: American Art and Early Film*, edited by Nancy Mowll Matthews, Charles Musser, and Marta Braun, 159–64. Manchester, Vt.: Hudson Hills Press, 2005.

Latour, Bruno. "Foreword: The Flat Earthers of Social Theory." In *Accounting and Science: Natural Inquiry and Commercial Reason*, edited by Michael Power, xi–xvii. New York: Cambridge University Press, 1994.

———. *The Pasteurization of France*. Translated by Alan Sheridan and John Law. Cambridge, Mass.: Harvard University Press, 1988.

———. *Politics of Nature: How to Bring the Sciences into Democracy*. Trans. Catherine Porter. Cambridge, Mass.: Harvard University Press, 2004.

———. *Reassembling the Social: An Introduction to Actor-Network-Theory*. New York: Oxford University Press, 2005.

———. *We Have Never Been Modern*. Translated by Catherine Porter. Cambridge, Mass.: Harvard University Press, 1993.

———. *What Is the Style of Matters of Concern? Two Lectures on Empirical Philosophy*. Assen, Netherlands: Van Gorkum, 2005.

Lawrence, Amy. "American Shame: *Rope*, James Stewart, and the Postwar Crisis in American Masculinity." In Freedman and Millington, *Hitchcock's America*, 55–76.

———. "Constructing a Priest, Silencing a Saint: The PCA and *I Confess*," *Film History* 19 (2007): 58–72.

Le Bon, Gustave. *The Crowd: A Study of the Popular Mind*. 2nd ed. New York: Macmillan, 1897.

Lee, Gerald Stanley. *Crowds: A Moving-Picture of Democracy*. New York: Doubleday, Page, 1913.

Leitch, Thomas. "The Outer Circle: Hitchcock on Television." In Allen and Ishii Gonzalès, *Alfred Hitchcock: Centenary Essays*, 59–71.

Leitch, Thomas, and Leland Poague, eds. *A Companion to Alfred Hitchcock*. Malden, Mass.: Wiley-Blackwell, 2011.

Luckhurst, Roger. *The Invention of Telepathy*. New York: Oxford University Press, 2002.

Luddington, Charles. *The Politics of Wine in Britain: A New Cultural History*. New York: Palgrave Macmillan, 2013.

Luhr, William, and Peter Lehman, "*Experiment in Terror*: Dystopian Modernism, the Police Procedural, and the Space of Anxiety." In *Cinema and Modernity*, edited by Murray Pomerance, 175–93. New Brunswick, N.J.: Rutgers University Press, 2006.

MacDonald, Austin. *Montreal and Quebec for Dummies*. 2nd ed. Hoboken, N.J.: Wiley, 2006.

McGilligan, Patrick. *Alfred Hitchcock: A Life in Darkness and Light*. New York: ReganBooks, 2003.

McKittrick, Casey. *Hitchcock's Appetites: The Corpulent Plots of Desire and Dread*. New York: Bloomsbury, 2016.

McLaughlin, James. "All in the Family: Alfred Hitchcock's *Shadow of a Doubt*." In Deutelbaum and Poague, *A Hitchcock Reader*, 145–55.

Miller, D. A. "Anal *Rope*." *Representations* 32 (Autumn 1990): 114–33.

———. *Hidden Hitchcock*. Chicago: University of Chicago Press, 2016.

———. "Hitchcock's Understyle: A Too-Close View of *Rope*." *Representations* 121, no. 1 (Winter 2013): 1–30.

Miller, J. Hillis. "Hardy." In *The J. Hillis Miller Reader*, edited by Julian Wolfreys, 140–55. Stanford, Calif.: Stanford University Press, 2005.

Michie, Elsie B. "Unveiling Maternal Desires: Hitchcock and American Domesticity." In Freedman and Millington, *Hitchcock's America*, 29–54.

Modleski, Tania. "Suspicion: Collusion and Resistance in the Work of Hitchcock's Female Collaborators." In Leitch and Poague, *A Companion to Alfred Hitchcock*, 162–80.

———. *The Women Who Knew Too Much: Hitchcock and Feminist Theory*. 3rd ed. New York: Routledge, 2015.

Mulvey, Laura. *Death 24x a Second: Stillness and the Moving Image*. London: Reaktion Books, 2006.

Munro, Ian. *The Figure of the Crowd in Early Modern London: The City and Its Double*. New York: Palgrave, 2005.

Murdock, Catherine Gilbert. *Domesticating Drink: Women, Men, and Alcohol in America, 1870–1940*. Baltimore, Md.: Johns Hopkins University Press, 2001.

Naremore, James. "Hitchcock and Humor." In *Hitchcock: Past and Future*, edited by Richard Allen and Sam Ishii Gonzalès, 22–36. New York: Routledge, 2004.

———. "Hitchcock at the Margins of Noir." In Allen and Ishii Gonzales, *Alfred Hitchcock*, 263–77.

Ngai, Sianne. *Ugly Feelings*. Cambridge, Mass: Harvard University Press, 2005.

O'Donnell, Patrick. "James's Birdcage/Hitchcock's Birds." In *The Men Who Knew Too Much: Henry James and Alfred Hitchcock*, edited by Susan M. Griffin and Alan Nadel, 85–96. New York: Oxford University Press, 2011.

Oliver, Kelly. "Alfred Hitchcock: Fowl Play and the Domestication of Horror." In *Cinematic Thinking: Philosophical Approaches to the New Cinema*, edited by James Phillips. Stanford, Calif: Stanford University Press, 2008.

Olsson, Jan. *Hitchcock à la Carte*. Durham, N.C.: Duke University Press, 2015.

Orr, John. *Hitchcock and Twentieth Century Cinema*. New York: Wallflower Press, 2005.

Palmer, R. Burton, and David Boyd, eds. *Hitchcock at the Source: The Auteur as Adapter*. Albany: State University of New York Press, 2011.

Parsons, Deborah L. *Streetwalking the Metropolis: Women, the City and Modernity*. New York: Oxford University Press, 2000.

Perkins, V. F. "*I Confess*: Photographs of People Speaking." *CineAction* 52 (July 2000): 28–39.

Pettey, Homer B. "Hitchcock, Class, and Noir." In Freedman, *The Cambridge Companion to Alfred Hitchcock*, 76–91.

Peucker, Brigitte. "Blood, Paint, or Red? The Color Bleed in Hitchcock." In Freedman, *The Cambridge Companion to Alfred Hitchcock*, 194–206.

Phillips, Gene D. *Alfred Hitchcock*. Woodbridge, Conn.: Twayne, 1984.

Piso, Michele. "Mark's Marnie." In Deutelbaum and Poague, *A Hitchcock Reader*, 280–94.

Plotz, John. *The Crowd: British Literature and Public Politics*. Berkeley: University of California Press, 2000.

Poague, Leland. "'Tell Me the Story So Far': Hitchcock and His Writers." In Leitch and Poague, *A Companion to Alfred Hitchcock*, 141–61.

Poe, Edgar Allan. "William Wilson." In *Thirty-two Stories*, edited by Stuart Levine and Susan F. Levine. Indianapolis, Ind.: Hackett Publishing, 2000.

Pomerance, Murray. *Alfred Hitchcock's America*. Malden, Mass.: Polity, 2013.

———. *An Eye for Hitchcock*. New Brunswick, N.J.: Rutgers University Press, 2004.

———. *Marnie*. New York: Palgrave, 2014.

———. "Some Hitchcockian Shots." In Leitch and Poague, *A Companion to Alfred Hitchcock*, 237–52.

———. "Thirteen Ways of Looking at *The Birds*." In Palmer and Boyd, *Hitchcock at the Source*, 267–93.

Raubicheck, Walter, and Walter Srebnick. *Scripting Hitchcock*: Psycho, The Birds, *and* Marnie. Urbana: University of Illinois Press, 2011.

Reps, John William. *The Making of Urban America: A History of City Planning in the United States*. Princeton, N.J.: Princeton University Press, 1969.

Richards, Rashna Wadia. *Cinematic Flashes: Cinephilia and Classical Hollywood*. Bloomington: Indiana University Press, 2013.

Riddell, Charlotte Eliza L. *Daisies and Buttercups: A Novel of the Upper Thames*. London: Sampson Low, Marston, Searle & Rivington, 1883.

Rose, Flemming. *The Tyranny of Silence*. Washington, D.C.: Cato Institute, 2011.

Rosenbaum, Jonathan. "Trailer for Godard's Histoire(s) du Cinema." *Trafic* 21 (1997).

Rothman, William. *Hitchcock: The Murderous Gaze*. 2nd ed. Albany: State University of New York Press, 2012.

———. "The Universal Hitchcock." In Leitch and Poague, *A Companion to Alfred Hitchcock*, 347–64.

Royle, Nicholas. *Telepathy and Literature: Essays on the Reading Mind*. Cambridge, Mass.: Blackwell, 1991.

Ryall, Tom. *Alfred Hitchcock and British Cinema*. London: Athlone Press, 1996.

Salzberg, Ana. "VistaVision and the Cinematic Landscape of *Vertigo*." In Cunningham, *The San Francisco of Alfred Hitchcock's* Vertigo, 63–80.

Schantz, Ned. *Gossip, Letters, Phones: The Scandal of Female Networks in Film and Literature*. New York: Oxford University Press, 2008.

———. "Hospitality and the Unsettled Viewer: Hitchcock's Shadow Scenes." *Camera Obscura* 25, no. 1 (2010): 1–27.

Schnapp, Jeffrey T., and Matthew Tiews, eds. *Crowds*. Stanford, Calif.: Stanford University Press, 2006.

———. "Introduction: A Book of Crowds." In Schnapp and Tiews, *Crowds*, ix–xvi.

Sedgwick, Eve Kosofsky. *Epistemology of the Closet*. Berkeley: University of California Press, 1990.

Showalter, Elaine. "Hysteria, Feminism, and Gender." In *Hysteria beyond Freud*, edited by Sander L. Gilman, Helen King, Roy Porter, G. S. Rousseau, and Elaine Showalter, 286–344. Berkeley: University of California Press, 1993

Silet, Charles L. P. "An Interview with Evan Hunter." In Gottlieb and Brookhouse, *Framing Hitchcock: Selected Essays from the Hitchcock Annual*, 199–205.

Simmel, Georg. "The Metropolis and Mental Life." In *The Blackwell City Reader*, edited by Gary Bridge and Sophie Watson. Malden, Mass.: Blackwell, 2002.

Smith, Murray. *Trainspotting*. London: BFI, 2002.

Sobchack, Vivian. *Carnal Thoughts: Embodiment and Moving Image Culture.* Berkeley: University of California Press, 2004.

Solnit, Rebecca. *A Paradise Built in Hell: The Extraordinary Communities That Arise in Disaster*. New York: Viking Penguin, 2009.

Sprengler, Christine. *Hitchcock and Contemporary Art.* New York: Palgrave Macmillan, 2014.

Stefano, Joseph. *Psycho*. Screenplay, December 1, 1959. https://the.hitchcock.zone/files/scripts/Psycho.pdf.

Stevens, Brad. "Troubled Bodies: Notes on Hitchcock's Television Work." *Hitchcock Annual* 19 (2014): 82–130

Stoker, Bram. *Dracula*. New York: Oxford University Press, 2011.

Straumann, Barbara. *Figurations of Exile in Hitchcock and Nabokov*. Edinburgh: Edinburgh University Press, 2008.

Strauss, Mark Raymond. *Hitchcock's Objects as Subjects: The Significance of Things on Screen*. Jefferson, N.C.: McFarland, 2016.

Street, Sarah. "Hitchcock's Haberdashery." In Gottlieb and Brookhouse, *Framing Hitchcock*, 147–58.

Tamange, Florence. *A History of Homosexuality In Europe*. Vols. 1–2, *Berlin, London, Paris 1919–1939*. New York: Algora Publishing, 2006.

Toles, George. "Hitchcock's Female Gaze." In *A House Made of Light: Essays on the Art of Film*. Detroit, Mich.: Wayne State University Press, 2001.

———. "'If Thine Eye Offend Thee . . .': *Psycho* and the Art of Infection." In *A House Made of Light: Essays on the Art of Film*, 137–58. Detroit, Mich.: Wayne State University Press, 2001.

———. "Mother Calls the Shots: The Female Gaze." In *A House Made of Light: Essays on the Art of Film*, 188–232. Detroit, Mich.: Wayne State University Press, 2001.

———. "Occasions of Sin: The Forgotten Cigarette Lighter and Other Moral Accidents in Hitchcock." In Leitch and Poague, *A Companion to Alfred Hitchcock*, 529–52.

Totton, Nicholas. *Psychoanalysis and the Paranormal*. New York: Karnac Books, 2003.

Truffaut, François. *Hitchcock*. New York: Simon and Schuster, 1983.

Uroskie, Andrew. "Far above the Madding Crowd: The Spatial Rhetoric of Mass Representation." In Schnapp and Tiews, *Crowds*, 307–27.

Walker, Michael. *Hitchcock's Motifs*. Amsterdam: Amsterdam University Press, 2005.

Warf, Barney, and Santa Arias. "Introduction: The Reinsertion of Space into the Social Sciences and Humanities." In *The Spatial Turn: Interdisciplinary Perspectives*, edited by Barney Warf and Santa Arias. New York: Routledge, 2008.

Weir, Justin. *Leo Tolstoy and the Alibi of Narrative*. New Haven, Conn: Yale University Press, 2001.

Welsh, Alexander. *George Eliot and Blackmail*. Cambridge, Mass.: Harvard University Press, 1985.

Wiener, Norbert. *Cybernetics, or Control and Communication in Animals and Machines*. Cambridge, Mass.: MIT Press, 1961.

Williams, Byron. "Holding the Line." *Telephony: the American Telephone Journal* 60, no. 21 (1911): 645.

Williams, Linda. "Discipline and Fun: *Psycho* and Postmodern Cinema." In *Alfred Hitchcock's* Psycho*: A Casebook*, edited by Robert Kolker, 164–204. New York: Oxford University Press, 2004.

Wojcik, Pamela Robertson. *The Apartment Plot: Urban Living in American Film and Popular Culture, 1945 to 1975*. Raleigh, N.C.: Duke University Press, 2010.

Wollen, Peter. "An Alphabet of Cinema." In *Paris Hollywood: Writings on Film*, 1–24. New York: Verso, 2002.

Wood, Michael. "Fearful Cemetery." In Freedman and Millington, *Hitchcock's America*, 173–180.

Wood, Robin. *Hitchcock's Films Revisited*. Rev. ed. New York: Columbia University Press, 2002.

Yacowar, Maurice. *Hitchcock's British Films*. Hamden, Conn.: Archon, 1977.

Žižek, Slavoj. "Hitchcockian *Sinthoms*." In *Everything You Always Wanted to Know about Hitchcock, but Were Afraid to Ask Lacan*, edited by Slavoj Žižek, 125–28. New York Verso, 1992.

Zunshine, Lisa. *Getting inside Your Head: What Cognitive Science Can Tell Us about Popular Culture*. Baltimore, Md.: Johns Hopkins University Press, 2012.

INDEX